Voting for a Scottish government

MANCHESTER
1824

Manchester University Press

DEVOLUTION series

series editor **Charlie Jeffery**

Devolution has established new political institutions in Scotland, Wales, Northern Ireland, London and the other English regions since 1997. These devolution reforms have far-reaching implications for the politics, policy and society of the UK. Radical institutional change, combined with a fuller capacity to express the UK's distinctive territorial identities, is reshaping the way the UK is governed and opening up new directions of public policy. These are the biggest changes to UK politics for at least 150 years.

The *Devolution* series brings together the best research in the UK on devolution and its implications. It draws together the best analysis from the Economic and Social Research Council's research programme on Devolution and Constitutional Change. The series has three central themes, all of which are vital components in understanding the changes devolution has set in train.

1 **Delivering public policy after devolution: diverging from Westminster**: Does devolution result in the provision of different standards of public service in health or education, or in widening economic disparities from one part of the UK to another? If so, does it matter?

2 **The political institutions of devolution**: How well do the new devolved institutions work? How effectively are devolved and UK-level matters coordinated? How have political organisations which have traditionally operated UK-wide – political parties, interest groups – responded to multi-level politics?

3 **Public attitudes, devolution and national identity**: How do people in different parts of the UK assess the performance of the new devolved institutions? Do people identify themselves differently as a result of devolution? Does a common sense of Britishness still unite people from different parts of the UK?

Voting for a Scottish government

The Scottish Parliament election of 2007

Robert Johns, David Denver,
James Mitchell and Charles Pattie

Manchester University Press

Manchester and New York

distributed in the United States exclusively by Palgrave Macmillan

Published by Manchester University Press
Oxford Road, Manchester M13 9NR, UK
and Room 400, 175 Fifth Avenue, New York, NY 10010, USA
www.manchesteruniversitypress.co.uk

Distributed in the United States exclusively by
Palgrave Macmillan, 175 Fifth Avenue, New York,
NY 10010, USA

Distributed in Canada exclusively by
UBC Press, University of British Columbia, 2029 West Mall,
Vancouver, BC, Canada V6T 1Z2

British Library Cataloguing-in-Publication Data
A catalogue record for this book is available from the British Library

Library of Congress Cataloging-in-Publication Data applied for

ISBN 978 0 7190 8108 8   *hardback*

First published 2010

Typeset by R. J. Footring Ltd, Derby

Printed and bound in Great Britain by
CPI Antony Rowe Ltd, Chippenham, Wiltshire

Contents

Figures

Tables

Preface

The study on which this book is based – the 2007 Scottish Election Study – was financed by the UK Economic and Social Research Council (award ref. 000-22-2256) and the authors are very grateful for that support. We would also like to thank Joe Twyman, Special Projects Director at YouGov, for his considerable help throughout the fieldwork. Much of the research reported here has been presented in draft form at a range of conferences: the Elections, Public Opinion and Parties annual meeting, Bristol, September 2007; a special half-day seminar at the University of Strathclyde, Glasgow, September 2007; a ScotCen event on 'The 2007 election: earthquake, misfortune and revolution?', Edinburgh, October 2007; an ESRC seminar on 'Democracy after the nation state', Edinburgh, January 2008; a University of Glasgow/Electoral Reform Society conference on 'The impact of electoral reform on democratic engagement in Scotland', Glasgow, February 2008. In each case we thank participants for their useful comments and criticisms. We are also particularly indebted to Dr Christopher Carman, of the Department of Government at the University of Strathclyde, who worked with the authors in designing the third wave of the survey and has also provided valuable advice on many of the topics covered in this book.

1
The road to 'a historic moment'

As the results of the Scottish Parliament election of 3 May 2007 became clear, Alex Salmond, leader of the Scottish National Party (SNP) and soon-to-be First Minister, declared that they represented 'a historic moment' (*Herald*, 5 May 2007). In some ways at least, the description is apt. The outcome was a major new departure in Scottish politics, with the SNP emerging as the most popular party for the first time and going on to form the government of Scotland. Arguably, 2007 was the election at which devolution came of age. By producing not only a change of government but also a government of a different complexion to that in London, it emphasised that, under devolution, government in Scotland could have its own distinct flavour, different from that of government in the UK as a whole.

The aim of this book is to explain that notable result by examining the choices made by Scottish voters in 2007. It is worth remembering, however, that voters do not choose between outcomes, historic or otherwise (a point easily obscured by media commonplaces such as 'the electorate decided it was time for a change'), but simply choose a party. Hence, in a book concerned with understanding electoral behaviour, our focus is on explaining why the SNP proved an attractive option to many voters – especially as compared with the 2003 election – and, in particular, on identifying why voters preferred the party to Labour.

This is not to say that our analysis sheds no light on the question of just how historic the 2007 outcome was. However, given the focus on individual party choices, this question needs to be approached in a different way. The most striking feature of the 2007 election results was the sharp upturn in SNP support, and by identifying the key reasons for this we can assess how likely the party is to retain – perhaps even extend – that support. One possibility is that 2007 was a 'critical election', defined as one in which there is fundamental change – in public opinion on a key issue, or in the parties' ideological stances, or in the social and regional underpinnings of voting behaviour – which proves to be long-lasting and sets the pattern for future contests (Key, 1955).

Alternatively, the SNP's success may have been due to more short-term factors: a popular leader, an image of competence and an effective campaign. Generally it requires a few more elections to establish whether the apparently new features thrown up by a particular contest really do set long-term precedents or reflect short-term shifts in party popularity. Nonetheless, by investigating the bases for party choice in 2007, we can provide evidence throwing light on these possibilities.

No effort to explain this (or any) election can succeed without setting it in context, indeed contexts. In this chapter we focus on two aspects of context – the electoral system and what might be called the 'Scottish dimension' – that have been of enduring significance in Scottish elections and proved just as important in 2007. We then provide a brief account of the short campaign leading up to the election, and close the chapter by outlining the contents of the book and describing the survey data on which our analyses are based.

The electoral system

The first important aspect of the context of Scottish Parliament elections is the electoral system. A proportional system, known as the additional member system (AMS) or as a mixed member proportional (MMP) system, is used.[1] Under AMS, electors have two votes: one to elect a constituency representative, as under first-past-the-post (FPTP), and another to elect regional list representatives. As explained in further detail in Chapter 2, the list representatives provide some proportionality. Seventy-three constituency representatives are returned (based on the pre-2005 Westminster constituencies, plus Orkney and Shetland are each given a Member) and 56 representatives are elected for the eight regions. Changes introduced in time for the 2005 UK general election reduced the number of Westminster constituencies in Scotland so that in 2007 Scottish Parliament and Westminster constituencies were no longer co-terminous. The Scottish Parliament is elected for a four-year fixed term. The electoral system was imposed under the Scotland Act 1998, which implemented devolution after the 1997 referendum, and was adopted by the Labour government in preference to FPTP, as used in UK general elections, in order to make the Parliament more representative of Scottish opinion than would be possible under FPTP (especially given that there are four 'major' parties) and, therefore, more widely acceptable. In the previous devolution referendum, in 1979, 'No' campaigners had made much of the fact that a devolved Scottish assembly would be permanently dominated by one party (Labour) on the basis of the support of a relatively small minority of voters. This was not simply an act of political altruism on Labour's part, however, or a consequence of Liberal Democrat pressure. Labour had additional motives for imposing a proportional electoral system. The SNP was perceived to be a potential threat by the Labour Party and AMS would minimise the chances that the Nationalists could gain a majority of seats in the Parliament and from that position press strongly for independence.

Whatever the motives behind the introduction of AMS, the consequences of its adoption have been highly significant. It has ensured not only that no party has come to dominate the Scottish Parliament but also that the Parliament includes a variety of parties and independents. Although it is impossible to know how the SNP would have fared in a devolved Parliament elected by FPTP, it seems more than probable that it would have struggled to gain the credibility and base of parliamentary support that eventually allowed it to challenge Labour successfully in 2007. The significance of the implementation of AMS is emphasised if we consider briefly Scottish electoral politics before devolution.

Labour dominance and the electoral system pre-devolution

Scottish politics was dominated by Labour for about 40 years before devolution and this was largely due to the operation of the electoral system. From the 1960s, the simple plurality system produced results that were heavily disproportional, to Labour's advantage, and it was during this period that the myth of Labour's popular dominance emerged. Disproportionality was made more acute by the rise of third parties – the Liberals (and successor parties) and the SNP – after the 1964 general election. That election now appears to mark the beginning of the end of the two-party system in Scotland but, although Labour's vote share varied over the period from 49.9 per cent in 1966 to 35.1 per cent in 1983, its share of Scottish seats never fell below 50 per cent. From the 1979 election, the difference between Labour's share of seats and share of votes in Scotland was never less than 20 percentage points. The simple plurality system greatly magnified Labour's advantage in elections.

The experience of the Conservatives was a mirror image of that of Labour. From 1964, the electoral system worked to their advantage only once – in 1983, when 28.4 per cent of the Scottish vote translated into 29.2 per cent of seats. On the other hand, in 1997 the Conservatives won no seats at all, despite having 17.5 per cent of the votes. The party that suffered most consistently under FPTP, however, was the SNP, which never won as many seats as its vote share merited (on a proportional assumption). The difference between the SNP's share of votes and seats was almost always (except for 1983 and 1987) in double figures. Unlike in the UK as a whole, the Liberal Democrats (and their predecessors) were never major losers under simple plurality and occasionally they benefited from the system. In the two elections preceding devolution, their share of seats was broadly in line with their share of the vote.

By the 1997 election, the effects of FPTP in Scotland were clear – it worked considerably to Labour's advantage, was reasonably neutral for the Liberal Democrats but penalised both the Conservatives and the SNP. The consequences for party fortunes of changing to a more proportional system were thus apparent and the first elections for the Scottish Parliament confirmed expectations.

The first Scottish Parliament election, 1999

Writing about the effects of electoral systems in his classic text, Duverger (1954: 224–6) distinguished between mechanical and psychological factors working together to affect the representative outcome of elections. The mechanical factor is the straightforward 'under-representation' of third parties in simple plurality systems, but there is also a psychological factor because 'electors soon realize that their votes are wasted if they continue to give them to the third party' (Duverger, 1954: 226). This psychological factor might equally apply to an understanding of the effect of contesting elections in different arenas. Given that UK general elections would be expected to be less fruitful arenas for the SNP, with the media and public focus being predominantly on the main parties represented in the Commons, voters may have regarded supporting the SNP in these elections as wasting their votes. This 'arena effect' may explain at least part of the SNP's increased share of the vote in Scottish elections.

The first elections to the new Scottish Parliament were held in May 1999. The outcome reflected not only the new electoral system but also an 'arena effect' – that is, the fact that the election was a specifically Scottish affair. The key figures in the election were not the main parties and leaders in the House of Commons but the main parties and their leaders in Scotland. On the other hand, while the Scottish Parliament has a limited set of responsibilities, largely inherited from the Scottish Office, debate ranged more widely. Westminster politics and politicians continued to dominate the UK news media. The Scottish Parliament election saw an enhanced Scottish dimension rather than the end of British politics.

The results of the constituency element of AMS (see Table 1.1) showed little change from the 1997 UK general election, when constituencies were co-terminous with Scottish Parliament constituencies. Labour won 53 seats compared with 56 two years before; the Liberals won 12, one fewer; the SNP won an additional seat; and the Conservatives still won no seats. These figures masked a significant shift in voting support, however. While the Liberal Democrats and Conservatives were slightly down on their 1997 performance,

Table 1.1 *Results of Scottish Parliament elections, 1999 and 2003*

	Constituencies		*Regional lists*		*Total*	
	Vote (%)	*Seats*	*Vote (%)*	*Seats*	*No. of seats*	*% of seats*
1999						
Conservative	15.6	0	15.4	18	18	13.9
Labour	38.8	53	33.8	3	56	43.4
Lib Dem	14.2	12	12.5	5	17	13.2
SNP	28.7	7	27.0	28	35	27.1
Others	2.7	1	11.2	2	3	2.3
2003						
Conservative	16.6	3	15.6	15	18	13.9
Labour	34.6	46	29.4	4	50	38.8
Lib Dem	15.3	13	11.8	4	17	13.2
SNP	23.8	9	20.9	18	27	20.9
Others	9.7	2	22.3	15	17	13.2

Labour's share of the constituency vote fell from 45.5 per cent in 1997 to 38.8 per cent in 1999 and the SNP's rose from 22.1 per cent to 28.7 per cent. The vote shares in the list contests indicated even greater changes, notably a larger drop in Labour support.

More SNP parliamentarians were elected in 1999 than in all elections put together in the party's entire previous history. While the SNP and the Conservatives both lost out in the constituency contests, they made up ground on the basis of list votes. As Table 1.1 shows, the pattern whereby Labour and Liberal Democrat representation was largely based on the constituencies, while the SNP and Conservatives mainly relied on 'top ups' from the lists, was repeated in 2003.[2]

The fraying of the party system

A notable feature of Scottish Parliament elections has been the success of the 'others' (minor parties and independent candidates). It is not just that the two-party system has crumbled but that even the four-party system has been fraying. Again, this has a good deal to do with the electoral system. One case is that of Dennis Canavan, a Labour MP from 1974, who was prevented from standing as his party's constituency candidate for the Scottish Parliament in 1999: he put himself forward as an Independent and was returned (with the largest majority of all constituency MSPs) for the Falkirk West seat he had represented in the Commons. It was list voting that offered the greatest opportunities to 'others', however. The Scottish Green Party had no constituency candidates in 1999 but won 3.6 per cent of the list vote across Scotland and polled well enough in Lothians for Robin Harper to take a seat. The Scottish Socialist Party (SSP) had candidates in 18 constituencies and won a seat on the Glasgow list, where its leader, Tommy Sheridan, was elected.

This small crack in the four-party parliamentary system was widened significantly in 2003, when a total of 17 'others' were elected. The Greens added a further six MSPs and the SSP a further five to their parliamentary presence. Margo MacDonald, who had resigned as an SNP member after failing to win a high place on the party's Lothians list of candidates, stood successfully as an Independent list candidate and the Scottish Senior Citizens Party won a seat on the Central Scotland list. In the constituency contests, Dennis Canavan was returned again and Jean Turner, a doctor campaigning as an Independent against cuts in NHS provision, took Strathkelvin and Bearsden from Labour.

As will be seen in Chapter 2, however, the 'others' did less well in 2007. Dennis Canavan retired from politics and his seat was won by the SNP. The campaigning doctor lost her seat to a spin doctor standing for Labour. The Senior Citizens Party lost its only seat, the Greens lost five of their seven seats and the SSP lost all six of its seats. That left two Greens and Margo MacDonald as the only 'others'. The collapse in SSP representation followed an acrimonious internal feud which resulted in a split. After allegations about his personal life were made in a tabloid newspaper, Sheridan retained the support of just one of his SSP colleagues in the Scottish Parliament. In August 2006, he and Rosemary Byrne MSP split from the SSP and formed a new party, Solidarity. In the subsequent election, the two groups split the hard-left vote and won no seats. Although Solidarity won the internal battle, outpolling the SSP by 1.5 per cent to 0.6 per cent in the lists, even their combined votes were far fewer than in 2003.

The SNP was the main loser in the rise of the 'others' in 2003. As later analysis will show, however, it was the main beneficiary of their decline in 2007. To that extent, the electoral system also contributed to the SNP's success in 2007. The durability of that success depends in part on whether the shift from the minor parties to the SNP represented the transitory choices of anti-Labour protest voters or a more lasting transfer of loyalties to the Nationalists.

The 'Scottish dimension'

The new electoral system transformed the party system but does not itself explain the rise of the SNP from Scotland's third to first party between 1997 and 2007. A second contextual feature of Scottish Parliament elections is that devolved government itself ensured an emphasis on the Scottish dimension of politics. This provided the SNP with a more level playing field. This is not to equate a Scottish dimension with support either for the SNP or for further constitutional change. Labour, or any other party for that matter, might successfully take advantage of that context, especially given that the Scottish dimension operates alongside a British dimension. Making sense of the Scottish dimension has always been important in understanding electoral politics in Scotland but it has become still more important after devolution.

Reference to a 'Scottish dimension' can only be useful shorthand, however. Scottish Parliament elections are no more exclusively concerned with devolved matters than Westminster elections in Scotland are exclusively concerned with retained matters. Additionally, the handling of devolved responsibilities cannot be seen in isolation from debates on the same matters at Westminster. Health and education, for example, are better understood as involving parallel debates on both sides of the border. The differences are sometimes difficult to discern and sometimes exaggerated, while at other times real differences exist that are barely acknowledged. The nature of devolution, especially its financing, means that the scope for radically different policies in Scotland and elsewhere is constrained but electoral politics and public policy can operate in almost parallel universes. This is where symbolism plays a part. What may count more in electoral politics than actual public policy is the perceived extent of difference and the perceived scope for diversity. The very establishment of a Scottish Parliament dramatically intensified the public's perception that Scottish politics differs from politics in England. In the early days of devolution, there was a perception that the devolved institutions were more powerful than Westminster but this gave way to a more realistic assessment of their relative power (Park and McCrone, 2006: 17–18).

These perceptions were encouraged by the Parliament's early tendency to initiate bold, innovative policies. Flagship policies from the first Parliament included land reform, free personal care for the elderly and reform of student tuition fees. Labour had been more cautious than its Liberal Democrat coalition partner in pursuing distinctly Scottish policies, partly because it was also in government in London and would face criticism at Westminster for failing to pursue policies there that it had enacted in Scotland. The coalition in the second Parliament, elected in 2003, was less ambitious. This may have contributed to the growing appreciation of the weakness of the Scottish Parliament compared with Westminster but may also have contributed to demands for more powers and increased support for the SNP.

Before devolution, the Scottish dimension in politics had been defined largely in terms of support for a Scottish Parliament but its scope widened afterwards. Crucial to this was the idea that the Scottish government should stand up for Scotland in its dealings with Westminster. While Labour in Scotland benefited in the early years from its association with a popular Westminster government and was keen to emphasise its partnership with Tony Blair's government, contrasting this with what it portrayed as a potentially difficult relationship between London and a putative SNP-controlled government in Edinburgh, this message lost some of its appeal in 2007, for two reasons. First, association with the UK government had worked to Labour's advantage in Scotland only so long as the Blair government was held in high regard. Second, Labour in Scotland was unable and appeared unwilling to distance itself from some of the more unpopular policies and positions of Labour at Westminster. Labour's early emphasis on partnership with Westminster had its mirror image in the SNP's later criticisms of 'London Labour'.

The enhanced Scottish dimension also enabled the SNP to broaden its profile. Prior to devolution, while its role in taking a lead in opposition to the poll tax was recognised and it was perceived as a left-of-centre party, the SNP's profile was based largely on its support for independence. However, everyday activity in the Scottish Parliament showed the party concerning itself with bread-and-butter issues. Not only that, over the period leading up to 2007, the independence policy was refined and appeared to be relegated in importance. In 1999, independence was tenth on a list of 10 objectives drawn up by the party, provoking internal critics of the leadership to complain that the policy was being sidelined. In 2003, the party emphasised that its commitment to independence was conditional on support in a referendum, and this again stirred internal dissent, with a dissident MSP in 2004 accusing the leadership of watering down its commitment to independence and replacing this with support for a 'culture of independence' (*Herald*, 16 August 2006). By 2007, the commitment was to hold a referendum within the lifetime of the Parliament. The party appeared more or less united behind this policy, although it was criticised by other nationalist parties such as the SSP and Solidarity, both of which called for an immediate referendum. An interesting question concerns how the referendum policy was interpreted by voters. Did they see it as a dilution of the party's commitment to independence, or simply as the SNP's only practical route to achieving its ultimate goal? Either way, the referendum policy seems likely to have boosted SNP support among those opposed to independence but considering voting for the party on other grounds.

Foreign and defence policy rarely have a direct impact on the outcome of British elections (and are not devolved to the Scottish Parliament) but may have contributed to Labour's problems in Scotland. The Scottish Labour leadership acquiesced in the UK government's plans to build a replacement for the Trident nuclear weapon system, triggering the resignation of cabinet minister Malcolm Chisholm, and First Minister Jack McConnell's refusal to criticise the Blair government on Iraq aligned him and Scottish Labour with a policy unpopular with many Labour sympathisers. Although analysis in later chapters shows that Trident and Iraq had relatively little direct influence on voters' choices, the issues may have contributed to a general image of Labour in Scotland as being under London's control. The tendency for policy announcements on a range of matters to parallel those emanating from Westminster was in part a consequence of the nature of the devolved system of government. Even so, there was less effort to be *seen* to be different than there might have been. An alternative approach was pursued in Wales, where Rhodri Morgan, Labour's Welsh First Minister, emphasised the 'clear red water' between his administration and that in London. This too was unsuccessful, however, perhaps because it had less substance than the rhetoric suggested. Nonetheless, comparative evidence makes clear that parties and politicians need to distance themselves from unpopular associates elsewhere in the political system. It is almost axiomatic that American Congressional candidates and those seeking election within states distance themselves from unpopular Presidents of the same party but seek to win on the coattails of popular Presidents (Flemming, 1995). This pattern is long familiar to students of local elections and devolution has brought it to the fore in Scottish politics.

Three First Ministers and a funeral

In retrospect, there seem to be discernible differences in the approach to the Scottish dimension adopted by successive First Ministers. Donald Dewar's brief tenure as First Minister (1999–2000) was marked by stressing partnership with London. The most notable policy innovation, on student tuition fees, was a consequence (and a cost) of the coalition with the Liberal Democrats. On the other hand, under Dewar, it was decided that Scotland would not alter UK policy on care for the elderly. This 'partnership' approach made sense during a period when Tony Blair was still enjoying a lengthy honeymoon with the electorate.

Following Dewar's sudden death, which was followed by an impressive funeral service at Glasgow Cathedral, he was succeeded by Henry McLeish (2000–1), under whom a bolder approach was adopted. This brought him into collision with his Labour colleagues at Westminster. As well as reversing policy on care for the elderly, which resulted in serious intergovernmental disputes, McLeish set out to adopt a more distinctly Scottish approach in his efforts to rebrand the Scottish Executive as the Scottish government. This resulted in his being publicly attacked by Westminster colleagues and forced to withdraw the proposed rebranding. Adopting a more Scottish approach might have worked in distancing Labour in Scotland from an unpopular government in Westminster but was likely to backfire when the UK government was popular and asserted itself successfully, as it did in this instance. That rebranding did take place after the SNP took power and was accepted across the Parliament with little dissent. McLeish stood down after the disclosure of minor infractions of rules concerning his Westminster constituency office.

Jack McConnell's aim on becoming First Minister (2001–7) was to restore stability to the Scottish Executive. His frequently quoted objective was to 'do less, better'. Within two years, he had re-established stability and won a second term for Labour in coalition with the Liberal Democrats, albeit with a drop in Labour's vote share. McConnell's approach after 2003 remained one of maintaining stability in relationships with Labour at Westminster and he was generally successful in this. He was criticised, however, for failing to do much else. Indeed, one of his own campaign team in 2007 and a former Scottish Executive special adviser had written a withering critique of McConnell's leadership in a contribution to a book published during the election campaign: John McLaren (2007) argued that 'doing less, better' was 'never going to lead to great deeds' and that 'Initiatives like the ban on smoking and Fresh Talent stand alone rather than as part of a coherent narrative on health or on economic development'. Fresh Talent was an initiative that allowed overseas students to remain in Scotland for two years after graduating as part of a package of measures designed to tackle Scotland's population decline. The ban on smoking in public places had, in fact, originated as an opposition proposal, and was initially opposed by McConnell's Executive. McConnell had failed to cut out a distinct public policy profile. Stability and partnership with London had worked in 2003 but was not enough in 2007.

The SNP, meanwhile, had been weakened by serious internal battles in the lead-up to the 2003 elections as its MSPs, predominantly elected via regional lists, fought among themselves for top places on the lists. Immediately after the election, the party's leader, John Swinney, announced that its constitution would be reformed to ensure that there would be no repeat of the rancorous internal elections that dissipated energies. In April 2004, a special SNP conference introduced one member one vote for the election of the SNP leader, deputy leader and rankings of list candidates. Swinney himself was not to be the beneficiary. He resigned less than a week after a poor performance in the 2004 European elections. Alex Salmond, who had led the party from 1990 to 2000, was pressed to stand but initially ruled this out, misquoting William Sherman, the US Civil War general: 'If nominated I'll decline. If drafted I'll defer. And if elected, I'll resign.' A month later, he changed his mind and announced his candidacy, and ultimately triumphed with a substantial majority among SNP members in a three-way contest against Roseanna Cunningham and former party chief executive Mike Russell. Salmond had given up his seat in the Scottish Parliament in 2001 after standing down as SNP leader, and so new deputy leader Nicola Sturgeon stood in as leader in the Scottish Parliament until Salmond was returned as constituency MSP for Gordon in 2007.

Alex Salmond was a very familiar face in Scottish politics but his combative approach was thought to limit his appeal. Hence, during the period between his returning to the leadership and the 2007 elections, Salmond underwent training to help him present a more statesmanlike image. The party's research also suggested that negative campaigning was counter-productive and that the SNP needed a more positive approach. Influenced in part by the work of Martin Seligman, an American psychologist who had argued that elections were won by parties and politicians projecting positive messages (Seligman, 1998: 185–98), the SNP developed a new approach for the 2007 election. This campaigning style and a restored sense of purpose were crucial changes in the party between the two elections.

Labour, on the other hand, adopted its tried and tested approach of attacking the SNP for wanting to break up the Union, with its media backers repeating the apocalyptic predictions that always seemed to work in the past. Rarely in Scottish politics have the two main parties presented diametrically opposed messages, one positive and the other negative: hope versus fear. As shown in Chapter 7, this did not escape the attention of the electorate, which concluded that it preferred the SNP's positive approach. The party had learned lessons from earlier defeats. Labour, perhaps understandably, assumed that its approach needed little more than refinement.

The short campaign

In September 2005, Alex Salmond had given his party the target of winning an additional 20 seats in the 2007 election. At the time, most commentators dismissed this as an improbable goal and their scepticism looked warranted when Labour comfortably held Livingston and Glasgow Cathcart in by-elections (for Westminster and Hollyrood, respectively) later that same month. During 2006, however, the SNP drew level with and then overtook Labour in Scottish opinion polls and, unlike previous occasions when this had happened, remained clearly ahead in the first three months of election year.[3] The SNP, therefore, entered the short campaign in the lead and with Labour on the back foot. Three aspects of the short campaign are notable: the role played by the constitutional issue; the role of party leaders; and the nature of public policy debate.

As already indicated, the SNP stood by its commitment to independence but in proposing a referendum attempted to decouple the constitutional question from the election. The referendum itself became an issue, with each of the other main parties arguing against it. Labour supported the status quo and ruled out more powers for the Scottish Parliament. The Liberal Democrats argued for more powers, while the Conservatives acknowledged that there might be a case for more powers.

The usual negative campaigning against the SNP was less effective than normal. The *Daily Record* headline 'If Salmond wins next week I'll pack my bras and leave' was designed to catch attention and referred to the threat of the lingerie entrepreneur Michelle Mone to 'quit Scotland' if Alex Salmond won power. In the event, Mone and her bras remained in Scotland. In the past, such threats seemed to prove damaging to the SNP but in this election the party had its own business supporters and was able to publish a list of 100 such backers. Labour had to scramble together its own list in response. The central contest was thus between two left-of-centre parties competing for business support and addressing many more special meetings for the business community than in previous elections (*Scotsman*, 24 April 2007). A poll of business leaders conducted by the Forum of Private Business found no support for the proposition that Labour looked after their interests (*Scotsman*, 18 April 2007).

Not only did Labour fail to attract the level of support from business to which it had grown accustomed over the previous decade, but it could not even rely on the traditional solid support of the trade unions. At its annual meeting during the campaign, the Scottish Trades Union Congress passed by only one vote a motion calling on members to vote Labour. Unison, the largest union in Scotland, opposed the motion. Individual SNP candidates won backing from trade unions in the form of donations, while a number of unions also broke with Labour by calling for more powers for the Scottish Parliament. The days of monolithic corporate support for parties in Scotland appear to have ended in 2007, reflecting changes in the party system.

Labour's main campaign message was that an SNP government would bring turmoil and conflict in the lead-up to a referendum on independence. This message was repeated (and in a more focused and forceful manner than Labour itself achieved) by the *Daily Record*, Scotland's biggest-selling daily paper. It attacked the SNP as a one-man band, suggesting that Salmond had 'turned a once-democratic organisation into a cult' (*Daily Record*, 3 May 2007), and made every effort to raise the profile of Gordon Brown, reminding readers that he would soon succeed Tony Blair as Prime Minister (although Blair did not formally announce until 10 May his intention to resign in June 2007, he had said in the autumn of 2006 that he would step down within a year). The *Record*'s campaign coverage implied that the contest was between Brown and Salmond. Labour attempted to adapt its successful slogan from the 1997 general election in which it warned that there were only days left in which to save the NHS, but the message in 2007, '30 days to save devolution', proved less potent. 'Saving the Union' would have sounded too similar to John Major's campaign messages in 1992 and 1997, yet 'saving devolution' had little resonance among voters who hoped to see devolution extended and saw the SNP not as a threat to it but as one of the main vehicles for its achievement in the first place. The *Record* urged voters to vote tactically against the SNP, even encouraging those in some seats to vote Tory. This was reciprocated when Michael Forsyth, the Thatcherite last Conservative Secretary of State for Scotland, urged his party to support Gordon Brown's efforts to defeat the SNP. These unclear messages were not conducive to a successful Labour campaign.

A key feature of the SNP's campaign was the conscious effort to present a positive message. This was especially evident in the approach of the party leader, with Salmond abandoning his normally belligerent approach – at least for the duration of the campaign. When debating in previous elections, Salmond had shown little more than contempt for his opponents. In 2007, he showed uncharacteristic restraint. Having been a polarising figure in the past, his demeanour suggested an attempt to reach beyond his core supporters. Jack McConnell's problem was captured well when Patricia Hewitt, UK Health Minister, twice referred to him as Jack MacDonnell in a television interview. A stream of senior Labour politicians, notably Brown and Blair, came to Scotland throughout the short campaign. Designed to emphasise the partnership with London, this may simply have reinforced the notion that 'London Labour', as the SNP dubbed its opponent, was in charge.

There has long been policy convergence between the SNP and Labour in Scotland (excepting constitutional differences), although each has attempted to emphasise differences that were little more than shadings. One issue on which there was a real difference in 2007, however, was local government finance. While the Scottish Parliament's tax-varying powers are minimal, it has the power to address the vexed problem of local government taxation. The council tax, introduced to replace the poll tax, may not have acquired quite the status of its predecessor but the Scottish Executive struggled with an issue that came to be seen as important by voters during the 2007 election. The tried and tested approach of establishing an enquiry was to prove unsuccessful: the proposals of the Independent Review of Local Taxation (Burt, 2006) were strikingly conservative, given the widespread public view of the council tax as unfair. The overwhelming majority of voters preferred the more radical alternative of a local income tax, the policy advocated by both the SNP and the Liberal Democrats. Labour appeared unprepared for the emergence of the issue, perhaps hoping that the Burt review had pushed it off the agenda, and the minimal changes to the council tax that the party proposed during the campaign were not even mentioned in its manifesto. Labour was left exposed as the defender of an unpopular tax, without any clearly worked out reforms that could address public opposition.

A Scottish election is not an entirely Scottish affair and events elsewhere intruded, to Labour's discomfort. The 'cash for honours' saga which dogged Prime Minister Blair's last months in power continued to attract media attention during the election campaign. The Liberal Democrats, especially UK leader Menzies Campbell, continued to raise the question of the Iraq war, which also tended to undermine Labour. These points notwithstanding, one noticeable difference between the 2003 and 2007 campaigns was that the Scottish arena was more prominent in the latter (due perhaps to Iraq having fallen down the agenda rather, but also simply because the 2007 race was closer and, therefore, more newsworthy).

The press in Scotland is distinctive and has traditionally been hostile to the SNP. A major change occurred in 2007, when a number of newspapers supported the SNP. On the Sunday before polling day, *Scotland on Sunday*, the *Sunday Times*, *Sunday Herald* and *Sunday Express* all gave support to the SNP and the *Scotsman* also backed the party later that week. The support of all five papers was conditional, however, in that they all opposed independence. Moreover, in at least one case the conversion to the SNP was suspiciously last-minute – *Scotland on Sunday* had printed a negative profile of Salmond the week before it decided he should become First Minister. Arguably, the papers supporting the SNP were following opinion, and rather half-heartedly if not reluctantly, rather than leading it. In contrast, the support that Labour received from the (larger-circulation) tabloids, including the *Daily Record*, *Sun* and *Daily Mail*, was unequivocal. As one commentator described it, these papers 'waged a brutal campaign against the SNP' (Vass, 2007).

Conclusion

There is no simple explanation of how the SNP became Scotland's largest party in 2007 but this discussion suggests that its roots lie in the electoral system and devolution itself. AMS provided the SNP with more parliamentarians and a secure position as Scotland's second party in 1999, which was confirmed even following its poor performance in 2003. This new relevance increased the SNP's credibility. At the same time, the electoral system made it highly unlikely that the party would ever win an overall majority. Electoral politics in devolved Scotland is the politics of minority parties and none is likely to achieve the dominance once enjoyed by Labour. The fact that this limits Scottish governments' room for manoeuvre in itself may have helped the SNP, by easing fears that once in power the party would be able simply to rip up the constitution.

This is not to slip into a crude determinism in which institutional factors are seen as leading ineluctably to the SNP becoming the largest party. As ever, the records, tactics and images of parties and leaders were crucial factors in 2007. Labour had been in coalition with the Liberal Democrats since 1999 and in power in Westminster since 1997. On the adage that oppositions do not win elections but governments lose them, there was always the prospect that the costs of ruling would prove unsustainable for Labour. The SNP successfully positioned and presented itself as a plausible alternative, while Labour's tried and tested strategies proved less effective in 2007 than before.

Our task in this book is to investigate how and why voters in 2007 reacted to these various factors, and thus to explain the results of the election. In Chapter 2 we scrutinise those results themselves, chart the parties' fortunes over time and investigate regional variations in voting behaviour. Those variations are, of course, due in large part to socioeconomic differences across regions and that leads to consideration of the demographic and social sources of support for the various parties. Throughout the chapter a major concern is the question with which we began here, namely whether the results and the patterns of party support represent a decisive break with such patterns in previous Scottish elections.

Election outcomes generally reflect voters' assessments of the competing political parties and of their leaders and in Chapter 3 we take up the story of how partisanship and evaluations of parties and leaders affected voting in 2007. In part, it is a story of evolving trends in Scottish voters' long-term loyalties to particular parties. For instance, fewer voters identified with Labour in 2007 than in previous elections, even in its heartland areas, and the party found it harder than did its rivals to hold on to the votes even of those who said they still identified with it. In addition, we analyse the impact of the party and leader images held by voters. In respect of the latter, perhaps the key questions are whether Alex Salmond really was a significant electoral asset for the SNP and whether Tony Blair was a drag on Labour.

Elections offer an opportunity for citizens to pass judgement on the incumbent administration. In this respect, most British voters are normally concerned with the provision of key public services such as health and education and with the delivery of prosperity. Evaluations of government performance on these 'valence' issues loom large in electoral choice. The extent to which this holds true in Scotland in 2007 is explored in Chapter 4. In this case, voters could record their evaluation of the performance of the Labour–Liberal Democrat Scottish Executive and of how well they thought an SNP-led Executive might do instead.

Inevitably in Scotland, however, national identity and constitutional preferences play a significant part in elections and this subject is taken up in Chapter 5. National identity influences – though does not determine –

constitutional preference, and both relate to vote choice in predictable ways. The relationships between these three variables are complex, however, and the Scottish dimension involves a further crucial factor: the extent to which parties are believed to stand up for Scottish interests. In Chapter 5 we consider whether the SNP victory was an endorsement of its stance on independence or rather of its perceived readiness to govern in Scotland's interests under the current constitutional arrangements.

Election outcomes reflect whatever is on voters' minds when polling day arrives, and these considerations need not be confined to what is strictly at stake in those elections. Hence a recurring theme in studies of Scottish Parliament elections has been the extent to which they are influenced by the events and personalities of Westminster politics. In 2007, the key question was whether the election would become a referendum on an increasingly unpopular UK Labour government rather than a contest turning on the government of Scotland. The extent to which 2007 was truly a 'Scottish election' is assessed in Chapter 6.

In modern elections, many voters are still undecided about whom to vote for when the official campaign begins. Parties run intensive and extensive campaigns both nationally and in local constituencies to try to win over the undecided and to ensure that supporters actually turn out. The effects of the campaign efforts of the parties in 2007 are explored in Chapter 7. Among other things, we consider voter evaluations of the various parties' campaigns and the impact of campaign contacts on voters' choices.

In addition to persuading undecided voters, another purpose of campaigning is to reinforce and mobilise supporters, to encourage as many as possible to turn out and vote. Abstention was widespread in the 2007 election, with only just over half (53.9 per cent) of the Scottish electorate voting. In Chapter 8 we explore trends and patterns in turnout. We argue that the modest improvement in turnout compared with 2003 was due to the close contest between the two leading parties and more generally highlight the considerable similarity between Scottish and UK elections in the backgrounds and motivations of people who do turn out.

Chapter 9 is concerned with the administrative problems that beset the 2007 election, most notably the problem of rejected ballots. Having explored voters' perceptions of the scale and causes of the problem, the chapter goes on to consider whether the well publicised difficulties had any impact on voters' views of the Scottish political process. Did the episode create lasting worries about the fairness of elections in Scotland, or did it prove to be a storm in an electoral teacup?

In the final chapter, we draw together the results of our various analyses and return to the central question: why did the SNP win the 2007 election?

As outlined in the chapter, 2007 marked both the end of a long period of Labour hegemony in Scottish politics and also a remarkable turn-around in the SNP's fortunes. Whether or not it saw the kind of enduring shifts associated with a critical election as discussed above, 2007 certainly saw the end of 'business as usual' in Scottish politics. In concluding the book, we show how that came about.

Coda: the 2007 Scottish Election Study

In each of the following chapters we draw extensively on the results of specially commissioned surveys of the Scottish electorate, carried out under the auspices of the 2007 Scottish Election Study (SES). Specific technical information about these surveys – sampling methods, response rates, fieldwork dates and so on – is reported in Appendix 1, but it is worth noting here three features of the surveys that are important in understanding their use throughout the book.

First, the SES comprises not only multiple surveys but also a panel design, meaning that the same respondents are approached at each stage of data collection. The panel involved three waves – about a fortnight before polling day (1,872 respondents), immediately after polling day (1,552 respondents) and a follow-up survey in December 2007 (1,166 respondents). The last of these was specifically designed to explore public perceptions of the unforeseen administrative problems that afflicted the elections. The use of a pre–post panel, in which the same group of voters is interviewed just before and just after the election, has become standard practice in national election studies (see Clarke *et al.*, 2004). One major advantage is that it allows analysis of shifts in opinion over the course of the campaign (see Chapter 7). Another is that we can analyse party choice using information gathered before votes are cast. This alleviates a problem known as 'endogeneity bias', which is endemic in post-election surveys and means that respondents' answers to a range of questions are affected by their voting decision (Wlezien *et al.*, 1997). For example, if asked which party they regard as having the best policies on health, respondents who have already reported a Labour vote will be reluctant to answer anything but 'Labour'. The danger is that researchers will conclude that a preference for Labour's health policy led to a Labour vote when in fact the causality runs in the opposite direction. It is preferable, therefore, to ask the health policy question before the election. This does not eliminate endogeneity bias, because some people's pre-election responses will be biased by a voting decision that they have made already, but a pre–post panel is the best way to minimise such bias.

The second key feature of the surveys is that they were administered via the internet (by YouGov, Britain's leading internet survey company).

Using the internet offers considerable advantages of both cost and speed compared with the conventional face-to-face interview methods used in previous Scottish electoral research. It is the time factor that is crucial here. In each of the SES surveys, at least 80 per cent of respondents had completed the questionnaire within three days of receiving it (see Appendix 1). This means that all the pre-election respondents were surveyed at more or less the same stage of the campaign and that post-election respondents were surveyed at most a few days after polling day. This second point is important, given the ample evidence that voters' recall of what they did at an election becomes unreliable – and subject to a range of biases – within just a few weeks of polling day (Atkeson, 1999; Belli *et al.*, 1999). Yet major face-to-face surveys may take many weeks or even months to complete. This not only overstretches many voters' memories but also means that responses to key variables can be affected by changes in the political landscape which have little or nothing to do with the election being studied.

A final issue with our data concerns comparability with previous Scottish surveys. At various points in this book, we draw on Scottish Social Attitudes (SSA) data collected around the time of previous Scottish Parliament elections (see Paterson *et al.*, 2001; Bromley *et al.*, 2006), which are derived from face-to-face interviews. Neither the internet SES nor the face-to-face SSA surveys achieve anything close to a 100 per cent response rate, and the profile of respondents and non-respondents is likely to differ substantially between the two methods (Sanders *et al.*, 2007). These differences can be narrowed by using weights when analysing each survey – that is, by adjusting the data so that they reflect the demographic profile of the target sample rather than just those who responded. Unless otherwise stated, in analysing the data we have used YouGov's standard weight, which makes the SES sample representative of the Scottish electorate in terms of variables like age, gender, social class and newspaper readership. In relevant analyses, in addition, we use – and make clear that we are using – extra weighting variables which adjust the data so that they reflect the actual election outcome in terms of turnout and party vote shares. However, even with weighting, we should still be wary when comparing data from the internet and interview modes. Evidence about the effects of different modes of data collection is both limited and somewhat contradictory (Malhotra and Krosnick, 2007; Sanders *et al.*, 2007). Nonetheless, it is worth quoting the conclusion drawn by Sanders *et al.* (2007: 279) on the basis of a British Election Study comparison of internet and in-person surveys: 'by using high quality internet surveys, students of British voting behaviour are unlikely to be misled about the effects of different variables on turnout and party choice'. Since the questions of who voted, for whom and why are at the core of this book, that conclusion is reassuring.

Notes

1 It has been strenuously argued that the latter (MMP) is the preferable term, since AMS implies that those who are 'additional' are somehow less valuable or important than the 'real' members elected from constituencies (Lundberg, 2007). While acknowledging this argument, we will use AMS, since that is the term more familiar and more widely used in the Scottish context.

2 For commentaries on the results of the 1999 and 2003 elections see Denver and MacAllister (1999) and Denver (2003).

3 Voting intentions from Scottish opinion polls in the inter-election period and during the campaign are detailed in Appendix 2.

2

Results and the sources of party support

We begin our exploration of voting in the 2007 Scottish Parliament elections in this chapter by examining the election system and the results themselves and then providing a brief account of the demographic and socioeconomic underpinnings of party choice. In both cases, we consider the nature of the change in Scottish electoral politics represented by the 2007 results. The steep increase in SNP support clearly constitutes an important break with previous voting patterns but there remains the question of the origins of that increase. Did the party make gains by extending its reach into different regions of the country or by winning over new social groups, in the kind of fundamental realignment of support associated with critical elections (see Chapter 1)? Or did it win support across the board through a more straightforwardly political appeal to voters in general? Those questions recur throughout our exploration of the results. First, however, it is necessary to describe briefly the operation of the AMS electoral system used for Scottish Parliament elections.

The electoral system

As outlined in Chapter 1, under AMS each elector has two votes. One of these is cast in a single-member constituency to elect an MSP on the basis of a simple plurality. Seventy-three of the 129 MSPs in the Scottish Parliament are elected in this way. The elector's other vote is cast for a party list (or, occasionally, an unattached individual) and in this case the contest is at regional level. For the purposes of the list vote, Scotland is split into eight regions, each returning seven list MSPs. The procedure by which regional list seats are allocated is cumbersome to describe but not difficult to grasp. Each party's list vote total in the region concerned is first divided by the number of constituency seats that it has won in the region plus one. The party which has most votes after this calculation is awarded the first regional seat, the candidate in highest place on the list who has not already been elected being awarded the seat.

That party's original list total is then divided by the new number of seats won plus one and the next regional seat is awarded to the party which now has the largest number of regional votes. This procedure continues until all seven regional seats are allocated. The effect is that the total number of all MSPs that a party has in a region will be roughly proportional to its share of the regional list vote. All MSPs winning constituency contests are automatically elected, of course, but if a party has fewer MSPs elected via the constituencies than is warranted by its regional vote share, then it will normally gain some regional list members.

Under AMS, minor parties commonly concentrate on the regional lists (where they might gain one or two MSPs) rather than contesting constituencies (where they stand little chance of winning). In consequence, voters have fewer choices in constituency contests than at regional level. Thus, in 2007, 334 candidates stood in the 73 constituency contests (an average of 4.6 per constituency), with the vast majority (292) representing one of the 'big four' parties – Labour, the SNP, the Conservatives and the Liberal Democrats. Significant minor parties, such as the SSP and the Scottish Green Party, each had only one constituency candidate. In the regional lists, however, the number of options on the ballot ranged from 15 to 23. In addition to the 'big four', 10 parties had candidates in all eight regions. Nonetheless, small parties still face an uphill struggle. Although there is no formal threshold which a party must achieve in order to obtain representation (as in the German version of AMS, for example), in practice a party needs about 6 per cent of the votes in a given region in order to win one of the list seats.

The election results

The 2007 election was tightly fought. While the SNP emerged as the largest party in terms both of seats and votes (both regional and constituency), the margin of victory over Labour was narrow (Table 2.1). In the list voting, the SNP was just 1.8 percentage points ahead and the constituency vote was even closer, with the SNP just 0.7 points ahead. Thus, Scotland's two largest political parties were almost tied, with just under a third of the vote each, while the Conservatives and Liberal Democrats lagged some way behind, with 14 per cent and 11 per cent respectively of the regional list vote. As would be expected, the four major parties all did better in the constituency contests, where they faced few minor-party challengers, than in the list voting. The SNP had the smallest decrease from constituency to regional ballot – just 1.9 percentage points. The Liberal Democrats (a decrease of 4.9 points) and Labour (3.0 points) were the main losers in the list voting. The principal

Table 2.1 *Results of the 2007 Scottish Parliament election*

	Constituencies		Regional list		Total	
	Votes (%)	Seats	Votes (%)	Seats	No. of seats	% of seats
Conservative	16.6	4	13.9	13	17	13.2
Labour	32.2	37	29.2	9	46	35.7
Lib Dem	16.2	11	11.3	5	16	12.4
SNP	32.9	21	31.0	26	47	36.4
Green	0.1	0	4.0	2	2	1.6
Left	0.0	0	2.8	0	0	0.0
Others	2.0	0	7.8	1	1	0.8

Note: In this and subsequent tables, 'Left' refers to the combined vote of Solidarity, the SSP and Socialist Labour.

beneficiaries, of course, were the minor parties, whose combined vote share in the list voting was seven times greater than in the constituencies.

Given that the purpose of AMS is to produce representation in the Parliament which is broadly proportional to popular support, it is no surprise that the distribution of MSPs across the four major parties is roughly in line with their vote shares. There remains, however, a bonus in terms of seats for the largest parties, which is a feature of almost all electoral systems. Both Labour and the SNP are over-represented, although not to an enormous extent in either case. On the other hand, the minor parties lost out. Collectively they won almost 15 per cent of the regional list vote but this produced just three MSPs (slightly over 2 per cent of the total). Nonetheless, the outcome of the election was much more proportional than would have been achieved if it had been confined to FPTP in single-member constituencies. In that case, Labour would have emerged with an overall majority, despite coming second and taking less than a third of the popular vote. In fact, the SNP became the largest party in the new Parliament for the first time. However, with a total of 47 seats, just one more than Labour, the SNP was still well short of the 65 seats needed for an overall majority. Declaring that Labour had lost, the SNP announced that it would seek to form a government. After unsuccessful coalition negotiations with the Liberal Democrats – which foundered on the independence referendum issue – the SNP opted to form Scotland's first minority Executive.

To put the 2007 results into a longer-term perspective, Figures 2.1 and 2.2 chart levels of party support in elections in Scotland from 1997 to 2007. In terms of vote shares (Figure 2.1) the clearest trend is Labour's slide in popularity, from winning just over 45 per cent of the Scottish vote in the party's 1997 UK landslide to less than a third of the vote in 2007. Labour's general

Figure 2.1 *Constituency vote shares at general elections and Scottish Parliament elections, 1997–2007*

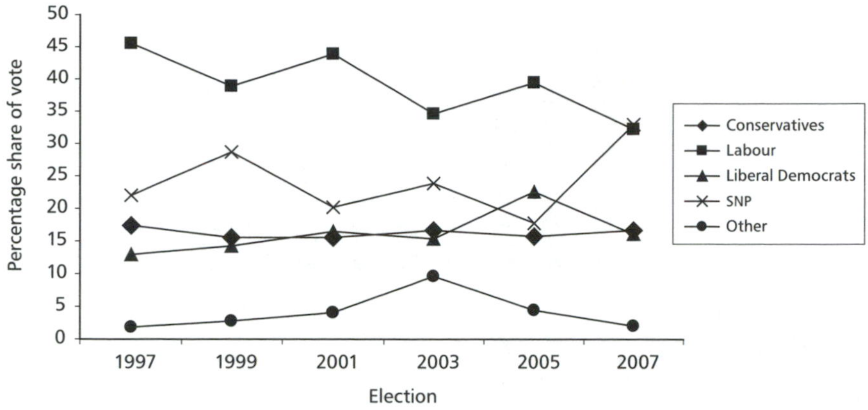

Note: Vote shares for the Scottish Parliament elections refer to the constituency contests.

election performances over the period were always better than its showing in the Scottish Parliament elections but the downward trend is plain. Labour, it seems safe to conclude, can no longer assume electoral hegemony in Scotland.

On the other hand, no one party was the clear beneficiary of Labour's gradual decline over the decade. Support for the Scottish Conservatives largely flat-lined throughout the period. In contrast, the Liberal Democrats made steady gains from 1997 – and a sharp advance in the 2005 general election – due partly to its ability to appeal to disgruntled Labour supporters throughout Britain (Fieldhouse and Cutts, 2005). In 2007, however, the Liberal Democrats lost much of the ground gained, falling back to roughly the same level of public support that they had enjoyed in Scotland in the early 2000s. The 'others' (i.e. minor parties and independent candidates) provide another case of surge and decline. In the 2003 Scottish Parliament election, just under 10 per cent of the constituency votes (and a still more impressive 22 per cent of list votes) went to candidates outwith the four main parties. In 2007, however, the minor parties' collective showing fell back to the same level as in the first Scottish Parliament election, in 1999. On the constituency side, this was due in part to their learning to play the AMS game and mostly opting not to field candidates in no-hope constituency battles. However, the minor parties also lost ground at regional level – together (which they conspicuously were not in 2007) their share of the list vote fell seven points, to 15 per cent.

The most striking change in party fortunes at the 2007 election, however, was the substantial jump in support for the SNP. This was not the continuation

Figure 2.2 *Number of MSPs (regional and constituency) elected for major parties, 1999–2007*

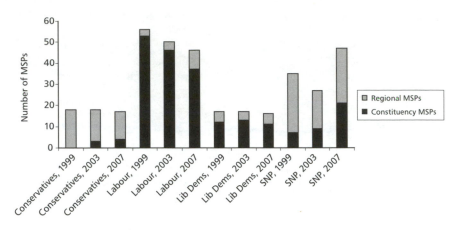

of a steady upward trend. As with Labour, support for the SNP fluctuated between UK and Scottish elections but in the opposite direction, with the SNP tending to do better in the latter. However, the party has been far from uniformly successful in Scottish elections. After a surge in the first post-devolution election, in 1999, the SNP performed poorly in 2003 (although still on a par with its pre-devolution showings in Westminster elections). In 2003, the party seemed to have suffered in particular from the rise of the 'others' and, on the face of it, looks like the principal beneficiary of their decline in 2007. The SNP's victory cannot be attributed simply to Labour's problems, since the major upturn in Nationalist support came after 2005, by which time Labour had already sustained its heaviest losses in vote share. Opinion poll data (see Appendix 2) suggest that the SNP surge was triggered by the change of leadership in 2004, when Alex Salmond replaced John Swinney. There were, of course, factors other than leadership at play in the election – as will become clear in subsequent chapters. For the moment, however, the key point is that if the previous election is taken as the point of comparison, then the main story of 2007 is one of SNP rise rather than of Labour decline.

Similar conclusions can be derived from the changing nature of party representation in the Scottish Parliament. The numbers of Conservative and Liberal Democrat MSPs elected have remained relatively constant (Figure 2.2). Labour's representation was at its peak in 1999 but declined in each subsequent election, while the number of SNP MSPs fell between 1999 and 2003 but then increased to a new high in 2007. For most parties, there have also been changes over time in the proportion of their MSPs elected in constituency contests, as opposed to via the lists. In 1999, all 18 Conservative MSPs were elected via regional lists and list MSPs have continued to dominate Tory ranks. Nonetheless, the party thereafter began to re-establish itself at constituency level and in 2007 won four constituency seats. Labour, on the other hand, has always obtained the bulk of its MSPs via the constituency route, due largely to its dominance in the central belt. Nonetheless, the number of Labour list MSPs increased from only three in 1999 to nine in 2007, as the total number of Labour MSPs declined from 56 to 46. In previous elections, almost all of Labour's list MSPs came from regions beyond the central belt but in 2007, while three were elected in the Highlands and two in North East Scotland, a further three came from Mid Scotland and Fife and one from Lothians. The SNP, meanwhile, travelled in the opposite direction. The proportion of its MSPs elected in constituencies increased considerably, from 20 per cent in 1999 to 33 per cent in 2003 and 45 per cent in 2007. Furthermore, whereas in the first two Scottish Parliament elections the party took constituency seats in only four of the eight electoral regions, in 2007 the SNP won at least one constituency seat in every region except South of Scotland.

The geography of party support

The fact that the SNP not only won more constituency seats but won them in what, for it, had hitherto been barren regions calls for a more detailed consideration of the geography of party support in 2007. It also leads us back to the question posed at the outset of the previous chapter, concerning whether this election 'broke the mould' of voting behaviour in Scotland. The large increase in SNP support redrew the Scottish electoral map, but we are interested here in whether substantially new patterns in the geography of voting behaviour have been established. That is one indicator of a critical election (see Archer and Taylor, 1981). We begin by reporting the breakdown of the list vote by parliamentary region (Table 2.2). There is a clear regional geography of party support. Labour's best performances were in its traditional heartlands – Glasgow, West of Scotland and Central Scotland. The party did noticeably less well in more rural regions. In contrast, the Liberal Democrats polled weakly throughout the central belt but did better in the North East and, especially, its long-term stronghold of the Highlands and Islands. Conservative support was also weakest in the industrial central belt, with the party performing best in the agricultural South, where it won three of its four constituency seats. The SNP's support was more evenly spread and the party won more than a quarter of the vote in every region. Its weaker performances came in the South and West and in the two biggest cities but the SNP's best showing, 41 per cent in the North East, surpassed even Labour's performances in its erstwhile fortresses of Glasgow and Central Scotland.

Table 2.2 Percentage party shares of list votes by region, 2007

	Central Scotland	Glasgow	Highlands and Islands	Lothians	Mid Scotland and Fife	North East Scotland	South of Scotland	West of Scotland
Conservatives	8.5	6.7	12.6	13.1	16.2	14.5	22.6	15.2
Labour	39.6	38.1	17.7	26.3	26.3	20.0	28.8	34.2
Lib Dems	5.1	7.1	19.9	12.7	13.3	15.7	10.1	8.4
SNP	31.4	27.0	34.4	26.5	33.0	40.5	27.8	28.3
Green	2.5	5.2	4.6	7.0	3.8	3.1	3.3	3.0
Left	3.4	6.6	2.1	2.5	1.9	1.7	2.2	3.0
Others	9.5	9.3	8.7	11.9	5.5	4.5	5.2	7.9

Table 2.3 Percentage point changes in vote shares in party list voting, 2003–7

	Central Scotland	Glasgow	Highlands and islands	Lothians	Mid Scotland and Fife	North East Scotland	South of Scotland	West of Scotland	Total
Conservatives	-0.7	-0.8	-3.4	-2.0	-1.4	-2.9	-1.6	-0.5	-1.6
Labour	-0.8	+0.4	-4.6	+1.8	+1.0	-0.2	-1.2	-1.6	-0.1
Lib Dems	-0.8	-0.2	+1.1	+1.7	+1.3	-3.1	-0.2	-3.9	-0.5
SNP	+8.9	+9.9	+11.0	+10.3	+10.0	+13.2	+9.4	+8.7	+10.1
Green	-2.2	-1.9	-3.7	-5.0	-3.1	-2.1	-2.4	-2.7	-2.9
Left	-5.3	-10.1	-4.2	-3.7	-3.6	-3.5	-4.4	-5.4	-5.0
Others	+0.9	+3.5	+3.4	-3.0	-4.5	-2.0	-0.6	+5.4	0.0

There is little new about these geographical variations in party support. Similar patterns were apparent in 2003 as well as in 1999 and, indeed, in Westminster elections. Table 2.3 shows, for each party in each region, the change in its share of the list vote between the 2003 and 2007 elections and it is immediately apparent that the geography of Scottish voting changed little. Vote shares changed, of course, but these changes were strikingly uniform across Scotland. Thus, the SNP's share increased by about 10 points in all regions (with a slightly greater advance in the North East). The small decline in Conservative support was also fairly uniform across regions, as was the almost unchanged Labour share of the list vote (apart from a tighter squeeze on both parties in the Highlands and Islands). The trend in Liberal Democrat support varied more, with small increases in some regions and declines elsewhere. These fluctuations appear almost random, but there is a hint that the Liberal Democrats did better in regions where the minor parties lost most heavily and declined most where the minor party vote share held up best. Overall, the underlying geography of party support stayed fairly static between 2003 and 2007 and, for that matter, between 1999 and 2007. At all three elections Labour did best in the central belt and the major cities, the Liberal Democrats and Conservatives in rural areas, while the SNP vote share was fairly consistent across regions, save for an especially strong showing in the North East.

To a considerable extent, long-standing regional variations in party support reflect demographic and socioeconomic differences across Scotland, so that stability in electoral geography tends to suggest that the social underpinnings of party choice have also remained fairly stable. To test this suggestion more directly, Table 2.4 shows correlation coefficients measuring the association between party support (percentage share of list vote) at the constituency level for each of the three Scottish Parliament elections and four key socioeconomic variables (derived from the 2001 census).[1] The latter measure the class character of a constituency (the percentage of professionals and managers), housing tenure (the percentage of households renting from the council or from a housing association), whether rural or urban (the percentage employed in agriculture) and the general level of affluence or deprivation (the percentage of households without a car). The results show that the Conservatives do better the more middle class and agricultural a seat is; they do worse where there are more social renters and households without a car. The pattern for the Liberal Democrats is a paler version of that for the Conservatives. All the coefficients are in the same direction but are less strong. The distribution of Labour support is a mirror image of the Conservative picture – Labour does better where there are more social renters and households with no car, and worse in more middle-class and rural areas. In the case of the SNP, however, the coefficients are strikingly different from those for the other parties. Apart

Table 2.4 *Correlations between regional list vote shares and socioeconomic characteristics of constituencies*

	% professional/ managerial	% social renters	% in agriculture	% with no car
Conservative				
1999	0.378	−0.679	0.580	−0.589
2003	0.289	−0.660	0.658	−0.608
2007	0.276	−0.595	0.644	−0.566
Labour				
1999	−0.272	0.681	−0.654	0.603
2003	−0.408	0.741	−0.575	0.531
2007	−0.307	0.705	−0.620	0.570
Lib Dem				
1999	0.177	−0.515	0.485	−0.461
2003	0.259	−0.512	0.371	−0.461
2007	0.274	−0.522	0.381	−0.422
SNP				
1999	−0.351	0.194	0.114	−0.216
2003	−0.404	0.061	0.129	−0.169
2007	−0.343	0.018	−0.045	0.006

Note: $N = 73$ (constituencies); correlations significant at the $p < 0.05$ level are in bold.

from the class structure variable (the more middle class the seat, the less well the SNP does), none of the other coefficients is statistically significant. In other words, the level of SNP support across constituencies is not related to differences in housing tenure, the general level of affluence or the importance of agricultural employment. The absence of strong relationships between SNP support and social context has been observed over a lengthy period (Jaensch, 1976) and, indeed, none of these results is exactly news to observers of Scottish politics and elections. There are some minor fluctuations in the size of the coefficients from election to election (and it should be remembered that, as time passes, the 2001 census data become increasingly out of date) but what is striking is the consistency of the results. The relationships between the socioeconomic structure of constituencies and the level of party support in 2007 differed hardly at all from the relationships found for 1999 and 2003. There is no sign here, then, of a major remaking of the social geography of support for any of the major parties.

These are aggregate-level data, which tell us about how party support varies according to the overall social and economic make-up of different constituencies. They can do no more than hint at the relationships between the choices of individual voters and their sociodemographic characteristics. In order to address the question of 'who voted for whom?' more directly, we need data at the individual level. The same is true when we consider trends in vote shares between elections. The fact that, overall, the SNP was the big gainer and the 'others' were the big losers between 2003 and 2007 is not in itself proof that a large number of those who supported a minor party in the first election switched to the SNP in the second. To demonstrate that, we need to find out how individuals voted in the two elections. In the remainder of the chapter, therefore, we use SES data to scrutinise the relationships and trends observed so far and, in particular, to examine the sources of the SNP's gains.

Who voted for whom in 2003 and 2007?

The most direct way of comparing voting behaviour in 2003 and 2007 – and thus of judging whether the changes in vote shares represent fundamental or more ephemeral changes – is to find out how the same people voted in the two different elections. Ideally this would involve surveying the same respondents at successive elections but, since the SES is not an inter-election panel, we have to rely on our respondents' recall of their previous vote. There are obvious problems in asking people to recall a vote cast four years previously. Memory is tested especially sorely in the Scottish context, with two choices to remember (constituency and list vote) and one choice to try to forget, namely the vote cast in the intervening general election. Moreover, 2003 was a bumper year for 'others' and it is votes for such minor parties that are more easily forgotten (Himmelweit et al., 1978). Finally, survey respondents tend to wish to appear consistent and so vote in 2007 is likely to influence recall of 2003 vote.

These expected biases are visible in the 2007 data on 2003 vote recall. While 22 per cent of actual list votes in 2003 were cast for a party other than the 'big four', only 14 per cent of 2003 votes recalled in 2007 were for these 'others'. The SNP's shares of recalled constituency and regional votes were 27 and 26 per cent respectively, somewhat higher than the actual vote shares of 24 and 21 per cent. There were similar 'inflations' of the Labour and Liberal Democrat vote, whereas recalled Conservative support was weaker than the actual vote share. Apart from the under-reporting of minor-party voting, however, the biases are quite small. Table 2.5 shows the 'flows of the vote' for list and constituency contests between 2003 and 2007 on the basis of recalled 2003 vote.[2]

A first point to make about the data is that vote switching was very common. Aggregate stability in election results conceals a great deal of volatility

Table 2.5 *Vote in 2007 (regional and constituency) by recalled 2003 vote*

	Recalled 2003 vote (percentage of respondents)					
	Did not vote	*Conservative*	*Labour*	*Lib Dem*	*SNP*	*Other*
2007 regional vote						
Did not vote	**42**	14	9	9	9	12
Conservative	11	**65**	2	6	0	6
Labour	13	3	**69**	14	2	7
Lib Dem	9	1	6	**41**	2	6
SNP	13	9	9	16	**81**	24
Other	11	8	5	14	5	**46**
N	242	138	340	155	270	144
2007 constituency vote						
Did not vote	**42**	13	10	8	9	23
Conservative	13	**60**	4	6	2	2
Labour	16	7	**65**	13	2	15
Lib Dem	11	6	5	**51**	5	13
SNP	15	13	14	21	**82**	23
Other	3	2	3	1	1	**25**
N	248	141	402	186	296	63

Source: Post-election survey.[3]

in party choice at the individual level. Labour and the Conservatives retained the support of only around two-thirds of their 2003 voters and for the Liberal Democrats the proportion is even smaller. The significant exception is the SNP, which held on to more than four in five of its 2003 voters. This unusually high proportion was a cornerstone of the SNP's victory in 2007. To some extent, the Nationalists' success in terms of vote retention is a result of their relatively poor performance in the earlier election, in which the party was reduced to something closer to its core support. Yet in Labour's case, although 2003 was hardly a high point of support for the party, many who voted for it then were unwilling to do so again in 2007. In a tight election like 2007, this gap between Labour and the SNP in votes retained is enough to have made the difference.

Those who had supported one of the other parties in 2003 – whether the Conservatives, the Liberal Democrats or a minor party – were more likely to switch to the SNP than to Labour. The gap is especially pronounced among 2003 voters for an 'other' party, about a quarter of whom switched to the SNP. This raises the possibility of 'indirect' switching from Labour to the SNP. The 2003–7 data show that direct switching in that direction was not especially common (though more common than shifts in the other direction), which is perhaps not surprising given the long-standing rivalry between the two. However, SSA survey data from the 2003 election show that many voters who had supported Labour in 1999 voted for a minor party in 2003 (Bromley et al., 2006) and then, as we have seen, many 'others' switched to the SNP in 2007. It could be, therefore, that the 'others' served as a stepping stone between the two major parties.

A rather different kind of switching between parties is 'ticket-splitting': voting for different parties in the constituency and regional list ballots at the same election.[4] Again, survey data are essential for accurate measurement, as the extent or patterns of ticket-splitting cannot be identified from aggregate election results. The proportion of voters choosing different parties in the constituency and list contests, according to the relevant surveys, increased over the period: from 18 per cent in 1999 to 28 per cent in 2003 and then up to 30 per cent in 2007. This trend is driven largely by an increase in splitting between major and minor parties. In 2003, this was due to the impressive showing by the minor parties; in 2007, it had more to do with the fact that very few minor parties contested constituency seats. Almost all of those who supported a minor party (or an independent candidate) on the list were thus forced into either ticket-splitting or leaving the constituency vote blank (see Chapter 9). Among those who took the former course, the largest proportion (31 per cent) cast their constituency ballot for the SNP. A different perspective is given by calculating the proportion of constituency voters for the major parties who switched to a minor party in the list voting. The SNP lost least in this respect – only 14 per cent of its constituency voters cast a list vote for one of the 'others'. Finally, a far from trivial proportion (11 per cent) of the voters voted for two different major parties, and every possible permutation thereof was reported by at least some SES respondents in 2007. Splitting between Labour and the Liberal Democrats was the single most common combination, but there was also a good deal of splitting between parties supposed to be sworn enemies.

Whether we are concerned with switching between 2003 and 2007 or with ticket-splitting in 2007, it is clear that in the latter election the SNP picked up significant support from the full range of other parties. That suggests that its 2007 gains are likely also to have been made across the demographic and socioeconomic board. We can explore this by looking at how various groups split between the parties in 2007 and how this compares with 2003. The analysis is based on regional list voting. Since it involves comparison of the (internet) SES 2007 and the (face-to-face) SSA 2003 surveys, interpretation of the data requires the usual caveat about comparability[5] and another warning is necessary with respect to the size of some subgroups. For example, self-identified Catholics comprised only around 10 per cent of each survey sample and, once abstention is taken into account, only a small number of

Table 2.6 *List vote by demographic group in 2007 and change 2003–7 (row percentages)*

| | 2007 | | | | Change, 2003–7 | | | |
	Conser- vative	Labour	Lib Dem	SNP	Conser- vative	Labour	Lib Dem	SNP
Sex								
Male	14	29	10	35	−5	−1	+2	+14
Female	14	30	13	27	+1	+1	−2	+7
Age								
18–34	13	33	11	26	+3	+4	+1	+6
35–54	10	30	12	31	−3	+2	−3	+6
55+	19	25	10	35	−2	−6	+1	+17
Residence								
Urban	12	34	11	28	+1	+1	0	+7
Rural	19	19	13	37	−6	−2	−2	+16

Sources: Pre- and post-election surveys; SSA 2003.

cases (around 100) remain for analysis. This means that the 'plus or minus 3 per cent' margin of error commonly associated with survey samples widens considerably and so we should be wary of reading too much into minor differences across groups or across time.[6]

We begin with three basic demographic variables: sex, age and whether the respondent lives in an urban or a rural area.[7] All three are related to party choice and in each case there is evidence of change compared with 2003 (see Table 2.6). First, men were more likely than women to vote SNP in 2007. There was no such 'gender gap' in 2003 – it was the party's recent converts who were more likely to be men – and observers might be tempted to attribute the change to leadership effects, with Alex Salmond's charms being of a kind that might appeal more to a male constituency. Yet, on a longer view, it is 2003 rather than 2007 that looks unusual: for decades, the SNP has tended to win more of its votes from men (Miller, 1981: 147–8; Paterson, 2006).[8] Turning to age, here there is a more novel development. The SNP surge in the 1970s owed much to support from younger people (Kendrick, 1983) and the average SNP voter was much younger than the average for the electorate as a whole. The Labour vote, in contrast, was somewhat stronger in older age groups. However, this age gap in voting had more or less closed by the 1990s (Surridge, 2004; Paterson, 2006). The striking thing about the 2007 results is that the original pattern appears to have been reversed. The SNP made a huge (17-point) gain among the over-55s. The long-term trend can be at least partly explained by generational change, since the youthful Nationalists of the 1970s had moved into more senior age categories. But such slow generational shifts cannot account for the abrupt shifts between 2003 and 2007. Finally, and more predictably, the SNP polled especially well among voters living in rural areas. As expected, the Conservatives did so as well, but there is evidence of the party losing rural ground to the SNP. The geographical basis of the other parties' support changed little, with Labour still the leading party among urban voters.

Rural–urban differences are partly a reflection of other social influences on party choice and Table 2.7 reports on five of these. In the past, the traditional class basis of Labour and Conservative voting was well established, whereas a distinguishing feature of the SNP when it emerged in the 1960s and 1970s was its ability to win votes from all classes (Miller, 1981; McCrone, 1992: 164–6). Subsequently, the SNP and Labour moved in opposite directions, the Nationalists gaining among the working class while Labour's dominance in that group weakened as it won more middle-class support.[9] Indeed, the parties have converged so much in this respect that knowing a voter's social class is no longer much help in predicting whether he or she would vote Labour or SNP (see Paterson *et al.*, 2001: ch. 4; Surridge, 2004). There is some sign in the 2007 data that those longer-term trends are continuing. Indeed, the figures suggest that Labour outpolled the SNP among the middle class and was less popular than the Nationalists among working-class voters, although the differences are small. The data on housing tenure tell a similar story: the SNP gained among owners and renters alike, whereas Labour won increased support from owners but lost considerable ground among renters.

The results for highest educational qualification reinforce the impression that party choice did not vary greatly across different social strata. Both Labour and the SNP made large gains among voters with degrees, largely at the expense of the minor parties, for which graduates had voted in very large numbers in 2003. In Britain as a whole, the Liberal Democrats are particularly well supported by the best-educated voters, but in Scotland in 2007 they lost ground among this (growing) group. There is more evidence of a relationship between religious denomination and party choice and in this case little changed between 2003 and 2007. Catholic voters continue to support Labour in large numbers (no other group comes close to 50 per cent support for a party) but they were as likely as Protestants and the non-religious to switch to the SNP in 2007. There is further evidence of the secularisation of Scottish electoral politics in the six-point fall in the proportion of Church of Scotland adherents voting Conservative. Intriguingly, the data on newspaper readership and vote appear to run parallel to the account in Chapter 1 of the way the

Table 2.7 *List vote by social group in 2007 and change 2003–7 (row percentages)*

| | 2007 | | | | Change 2003–7 | | | |
	Conservative	Labour	Lib Dem	SNP	Conservative	Labour	Lib Dem	SNP
Social class								
A, B	18	28	12	26	−1	+8	−4	+12
C1	12	28	13	34	−8	−1	+4	+13
C2, D, E	9	34	7	37	−1	−5	0	+10
Housing tenure								
Own	16	30	11	30	−2	+3	−3	+10
Rent	10	29	13	34	+1	−8	+7	+9
Highest qualification								
Degree	16	26	14	25	−1	+15	−5	+16
'A' level or equivalent	13	25	13	33	−5	0	+1	+12
'O' level or equivalent	13	34	7	35	0	−3	−3	+5
None	12	36	8	31	0	−7	−1	+9
Religion								
None	13	27	13	32	+3	+1	+2	+9
Church of Scotland	15	28	10	35	−6	−1	−3	+13
Catholic	10	46	5	28	+3	−3	−4	+13
Newspaper								
None	8	26	17	29	−5	−1	+6	+6
Tabloid	12	38	8	31	−1	−2	−1	+7
Broadsheet	19	22	11	33	−2	+7	−7	+19

Sources: Pre- and post-election surveys; SSA 2003.

press lined up behind the parties in 2007. The SNP made particular headway among readers of the 'broadsheet' newspapers, several of which endorsed the party – although not independence – for the first time. Thus, the Nationalists opened up a clear lead over the other parties among this group, while Labour retained an advantage among tabloid readers.

The fact that broadsheet readers switched disproportionately to the SNP does not constitute proof that they were swayed by those newspapers. It may be that broadsheet readers have other social characteristics or attributes that inclined them towards the SNP in 2007 (and that those newspapers' endorsements were a case of following rather than influencing public opinion). This illustrates the fact that, in order to judge their separate independent effects, we need to consider all of the demographic and socioeconomic variables simultaneously. It is not only such background variables that matter, however. For instance, a gender gap in voting may reflect differences between men and women in their policy priorities, their identities, their evaluations of party leaders and so on. Our analyses need to take account of these attitudes and preferences too. In short, we need to include a wide range of potential influences on party choice in analyses in order to identify those that have an independent impact. We present such analyses in Chapter 10, where we include the demographic and socioeconomic variables considered here, and these enable us to conclude whether the patterns seen in Tables 2.6 and 2.7 involve genuine causal effects.

Conclusion

With Labour supplanted as Scotland's largest party and the SNP taking power for the first time in its history, the outcome of the 2007 election was certainly momentous. The closeness of the race between the two leading parties was also a novelty for elections in Scotland. Yet the analyses in this chapter reveal a great deal of stability in Scottish electoral behaviour. Vote shares for three of the major parties – the Conservatives, the Liberal Democrats and most notably Labour – shifted little between 2003 and 2007. The geography of party support remained largely the same, although the successful party reached beyond its traditional strongholds and the less successful tended to retreat into theirs. Nonetheless, those strongholds remained the same for each party. Moreover, the sociology of party support also changed little. None of these results points to a major shake-up of electoral politics in Scotland.

There was, of course, one major change – the sharp increase in support for the SNP. Given that Labour's support remained roughly at 2003 levels, it would be truer to say that the SNP won the 2007 election than that Labour lost it. Where, then, did these extra SNP votes come from? Consistently throughout this chapter, the answer has been: from across the board. The party's gains were almost uniform across the eight electoral regions and it attracted erstwhile supporters of all the other parties. Although the aggregate results suggest that the SNP's gains came largely at the expense of the 'others', individual-level analysis reveals a more complex picture, in which the SNP won over disproportionate numbers of minor-party voters but also made substantial

gains elsewhere (as well as retaining the large majority of its own 2003 voters).
Moreover, the party's success was not rooted in any particular social group:
its vote share increased by roughly the same amount among non-manual and
manual workers, home-owners and renters, Protestants and Catholics, and so
on. Interestingly, it was the demographic rather than the social variables that
showed some evidence of a change in the basis of SNP support (although the
party still made at least some gains in all categories). Comparing men and
women, there was not so much a realignment but rather the re-emergence
of an old alignment. On the other hand, the SNP's greater popularity among
older voters represents a new departure in Scottish elections. In all other
respects, however, the basic underpinnings of voting behaviour in 2007 were
largely unchanged from previous elections.

It makes little sense, therefore, to search for sociological explanations
of the 2007 election result or even to try to identify long-term social trends
of which the result might have been the inevitable culmination. This was
not, then, a critical election on a conventional reading of that term. The
foundations underlying voting behaviour in Scotland did not change between
2003 and 2007; the point is that the SNP was able to build a victory on those
foundations. Indeed, the very abruptness of the upturn in SNP support is
enough to implicate short-term political forces rather than glacial social or
demographic change. Our task in the following chapters is to explore these
political factors – leaders, policies, performance and image – and to build an
explanation for the popularity that enabled the SNP to become Scotland's
governing party.

Notes

1 To save space, we will not always report parallel analyses of both constituency and
   regional list voting. Sometimes the distinction is important but usually the two
   analyses convey the same substantive message. Where only one analysis is reported,
   it will be of the regional list vote unless otherwise stated and justified. It can be
   argued that the list vote is a clearer indication of voters' preferences, since they
   had the full array of parties to choose from.
2 The data here are weighted to reflect the actual 2007 vote shares. However, we
   do not apply a turnout weight, and so in this sample the proportions in the 'did
   not vote' category are substantially lower than would be the case in the electorate
   as a whole.
3 Unless otherwise stated, all of the sources for this and subsequent tables refer to
   the relevant waves of the 2007 SES.
4 See Carman and Johns (2007) for a more detailed analysis of ticket-splitting at
   the 2007 election.
5 Note, however, that differences in the sociodemographic profile of the samples
   matter less here. The fact that the internet survey attracts disproportionate

numbers of graduates, for example, is not a problem because the focus of analysis is not the size of that group but its voting behaviour in the two elections. For this analysis, the two samples are weighted to reflect the actual regional list vote shares in the corresponding election.

6 For this reason, we also omit the minor parties, for which too few people voted to allow reliable inferences about their social background. One consequence of this is that the vote percentages add up to less than 100. While most tables in this book report column percentages, here for reasons of space we report row percentages.

7 The urban/rural split is based on the standard Office for National Statistics (ONS) classification. Respondents are classified as 'urban' residents if they fall into one of the first two ONS categories: 'large urban area' or 'other urban area'.

8 The scale of this gender gap, both in 2007 and in some previous elections, is unusual by international standards (Studlar *et al.*, 1998) and it is worthy of further research.

9 This is a basic summary of more complex relationships and trends (see McCrone, 1992: ch. 6; Bennie *et al.*, 1997: ch. 7).

3
Voters, parties and leaders

Throughout the democratic world, political parties dominate elections and the results generally reflect voters' assessments of the competing parties. In Scotland, as elsewhere, numerous party attributes – such as ideological stances, reputations for competence and perceived commitment to the national interest – are important in elections and we address these in later chapters of this book. In this chapter, however, we consider voters' more general attitudes towards the parties competing in 2007. These attitudes take two broad forms. First, some voters – often referred to as 'party identifiers' – have long-standing attachments to political parties. They think of themselves as supporters of a party and their enduring attitudes towards the parties strongly influence such voters' political thinking and behaviour. Second, at any given election voters will typically form opinions about and impressions of the various parties. Although these are more transient than party identification, they can, nonetheless, have an important influence on choices at that particular election. Indeed, the previous chapter, in demonstrating that the SNP gained support across all demographic and social groups, suggested that the party in 2007 simply proved more appealing to voters in general than it had hitherto.

We also look in detail at voters' evaluations of the leaders of the main parties. Leaders are very prominent in modern election campaigning and political coverage more generally and 2007 was no exception, with media attention focused particularly on the two candidates most likely to become First Minister, Jack McConnell and Alex Salmond. Moreover, there was already compelling if circumstantial evidence that leadership mattered for party choice, because the SNP's poll upturn had followed quickly upon Salmond's return to the helm. Leadership is therefore a potential explanation for the SNP's triumph in 2007. This is in line with much recent research emphasising the importance of leaders in voting decisions and showing, in particular, that leaders are inextricably linked with parties in voters' minds (Clarke *et al.*, 2004; Butt, 2006). In short, many voters judge parties by their leaders and vice versa (see below). Hence the two are considered together in the following discussion.

Party identification

The traditional understanding of party identification in Britain is set out by Butler and Stokes (1969) and is a crucial element in their framework for explaining party choice. From this perspective, identification with political parties shares a good deal in common with religious affiliation or even support for a football team. It is an emotional connection that is forged early, often following a family tradition or perhaps influenced by peers in social settings like the workplace. Once developed, these attachments are thought to be stable and enduring, typically lasting a lifetime; hence they are sometimes referred to as 'party loyalties'. The strength of this approach is that it can explain why a large proportion of the electorate turns out and votes for the same party in election after election.

Evidence from Butler and Stokes's study and much subsequent research shows, hardly surprisingly, that those who identify with a party are highly likely to vote for it. Importantly, this is not simply because such voters are blindly loyal, voting more or less automatically for their party. Party identification also has an indirect influence on vote choice because of its capacity to influence other political opinions. Those who identify with a party are disproportionately likely to believe, for example, that the party is united, can run the economy competently and chooses superior candidates. They are also prone to accept policy positions and changes relatively uncritically. We will see evidence of such 'partisan bias' throughout this chapter and beyond. It is easy to see why it would reinforce partisan attachments and thus further increase the likelihood that identifiers will vote for their party.

Of course, not everyone is a party identifier and, indeed, there is clear evidence that the proportion of party identifiers in virtually all Western electorates has fallen sharply over the past 50 years or so (Dalton and Wattenberg, 2000). One key reason for this, very clearly applicable in the Scottish context, is that social change has left fewer people exposed to the kind of contexts in which the strongest partisan loyalties are formed. For instance, the decline of heavily unionised industries like mining, steelmaking and shipbuilding, and the loosening (due to greater geographical mobility and council house sales) of working-class communities have eroded class consciousness and in turn Labour Party loyalty (Särlvik and Crewe, 1983). Meanwhile, congregations have been steadily shrinking in the Church of Scotland, a significant source of Conservative partisanship (Seawright and Curtice, 1995). Others emphasise political (as opposed to social) causes of declining identification with the major parties, and point to those parties' economic failures, lurches to the ideological extremes and sluggish or misguided responses to the rise of new issues such as devolution (see, for example, Heath et al., 1991). These explanations highlight another point about party loyalties, namely that they can vary in strength over time as identifiers react to changing political circumstances. For instance, it is widely argued that 'New' Labour's shift to the centre weakened the commitment of its left-wing adherents – they still identify with the party but less wholeheartedly than before. This is important because the electoral behaviour of weaker identifiers cannot be so easily predicted as that of those whose attachment is very strong. In sum, whether we are talking about the number of partisans or the strength of their loyalty, the key message is the same: there are fewer and fewer voters on whose support parties can confidently rely at election after election.

Party identification in Scotland since 1974

Before examining party loyalties at the 2007 election, we begin by taking a longer view. The standard party identification survey question is worded as follows: 'Generally speaking, do you think of yourself as Conservative, Labour, Liberal Democrat, Scottish Nationalist, or what?' That question has been asked in a long series of surveys conducted at the time of Westminster elections. Taking 1974 as a starting-point (since the Scottish sample was rather small in surveys prior to that year), we can track the changing loyalties of voters over the next 30 years or so (Table 3.1).

Table 3.1 *Party identification (direction and strength) at general elections, 1974–2005 (percentage of respondents)*

	1974	*1979*	*1983*	*1987*	*1992*	*1997*	*2001*	*2005*
Conservatives	28	31	23	25	27	16	16	14
Labour	38	39	42	35	36	45	41	39
Lib Dems[a]	7	9	11	16	7	11	6	10
SNP	19	11	11	9	20	17	20	15
Others	1	0	0	1	1	1	2	5
None	7	9	13	15	10	11	16	17
N	*1,128*	*706*	*354*	*341*	*930*	*868*	*261*	*904*
Very strong	27	20	24	21	15	15	14	13
Fairly strong	52	49	50	46	50	47	45	45
Not very strong	21	32	26	34	35	38	41	42
N	*862*	*674*	*295*	*305*	*887*	*805*	*235*	*800*

Note: [a]Liberal in 1974 and 1979; Liberal/SDP/Alliance in 1983 and 1987.
Sources: British Election Studies 1974–2005.

Identification with each of the main parties has ebbed and flowed over time – generally following the same trends as electoral support – but some more persistent results show through. Throughout this period, roughly two in five voters have expressed identification with Labour. This consistency starkly contrasts with the halving of Conservative loyalty. The Liberal Democrats (and their forerunners) and the SNP, even at the peak of their fortunes, were unable to clear the 20 per cent hurdle. Of course, the big advantage for Labour over the SNP needs to be put in context, namely that these data were collected at Westminster elections. The big gainer over time in the table is 'None', confirming that party identification in Scotland, as elsewhere, is in decline.

We can see that decline even more clearly in the figures for strength of party attachments (lower panel of Table 3.1). In each survey, those reporting an identification were then asked whether it was 'very', 'fairly' or 'not very' strong. The trends over time are very clear. The proportion of attachments described as 'very strong', never particularly high, was down to around one in eight by 2005. Meanwhile, the group of what might be called 'party leaners', that is those only weakly identifying with a party, has expanded to over 40 per cent of all identifiers. Combining the two parts of the table, we can say that over half of the respondents in the 2005 survey were either non-partisan or only weak identifiers with a party.

Party identification at the 2007 election

Many researchers have criticised the standard survey question used to elicit party identification on the grounds that it tends to presume that respondents have an identification. The rather abrupt use of 'or what?' at the end, it is suggested, might dissuade people from admitting that they have no particular party attachment (Bartle, 2001; Sanders et al., 2002). For this reason, in the SES we used an alternative two-part question.[1] First, respondents were asked 'Generally speaking, do you think of yourself as a supporter of any one political party?' Those who say 'no' are then asked 'Do you think of yourself as a little closer to one political party than to the others?' Respondents answering 'yes' to either question are then asked to name the party. This leaves us with three groups of voters: party identifiers, 'leaners' and non-identifiers.

In 2007, these three groups formed quite neat fractions of the Scottish electorate (Table 3.2). Half of voters thought of themselves as supporters of a party. The remaining half was itself divided more or less 50:50 between those who reported themselves a little closer to a particular party and those who disclaimed any such leaning. It is particularly noteworthy that around a quarter of voters do not report any attachment to parties. Not only is that rather higher than the proportion of Scots answering 'none' to the traditional question (see

Table 3.2 *Party support (identification and leaning), 2007*

	% of respondents	*% of respondents*	*% of respondents*
Party identifier?			
Yes	50		
No	50		
N	1,774		
		Closer to party?	
		Yes 24	
		No 26	
		N 865	
	Identifiers	*Leaners*	*Overall*
Conservatives	16	17	12
Labour	40	30	27
Lib Dems	10	15	9
SNP	30	27	21
Left	2	3	2
Green	1	5	2
Others	2	3	1
None	–	–	26
N	884	414	1,774

Source: Pre-election survey.

Table 3.1) but it also suggests that a considerable proportion of votes in 2007 were available, as opposed to being predetermined by partisan loyalties.[2]

Turning to the split of supporters among the parties (lower panel of Table 3.2), we see results similar to those in Table 3.1. There is one important difference, however, in that here the SNP is clearly the challenger to Labour, claiming the support of 30 per cent of those who identify as party supporters. The Nationalists' challenge to Labour is still more obvious in the column of leaners, whose support is generally spread more evenly across the parties (including the minor parties – the Greens in particular seem to attract sympathisers rather than outright supporters). The right-most column of the table is based on the full sample and thus provides an indication of how partisan attachments – both identification and leaning – are distributed in the electorate as a whole. As we have seen, 26 per cent deny any particular sympathy. Around the same proportion (27 per cent) report an attachment to Labour and 21 per cent are SNP sympathisers. The other parties trail some distance behind. These results confirm the SNP's ascent from also-ran behind a dominant Labour Party (Table 3.1) to direct challenger (Table 3.2) in terms

Table 3.3 *Pre-election party identification and vote (regional and constituency), 2007 (percentage of respondents)*

	Pre-election party identification					
	None	*Conser-vatives*	*Labour*	*Lib Dems*	*SNP*	*Other*
Regional vote						
Did not vote	59	36	44	16	30	27
Conservative	4	51	2	0	1	3
Labour	7	3	40	2	0	7
Lib Dem	5	0	4	59	1	0
SNP	13	8	3	9	65	13
Other	11	3	7	16	4	50
N	*830*	*106*	*262*	*58*	*188*	*30*
Constituency vote						
Did not vote	59	36	44	15	30	28
Conservative	6	49	1	2	1	14
Labour	10	5	44	7	1	10
Lib Dem	8	2	5	66	2	7
SNP	15	7	4	7	66	31
Other	2	2	2	3	1	10
N	*831*	*105*	*264*	*59*	*187*	*29*

Sources: Pre- and post-election surveys (weighted by turnout).

of party identification. Doubtless part of the difference is due to our data being collected at a Scottish Parliament election. There was a sharp upturn in the SNP's fortunes between the 2005 general election and 2007 (see Figure 2.1), however, and this evidence suggests that the party did not gain just fleeting approval but also some longer-term attachments.

The case should not be overstated, however. The fact remains that Labour went into the 2007 campaign with a significant advantage over the SNP (and a huge lead over the other parties) in terms of enduring party loyalties. This, in effect, gave Labour a head-start in the election. The question that arises is whether Labour was able to capitalise on this advantage by getting its supporters out on polling day and the answer is a clear 'no' (Table 3.3). Of those who, prior to the election, had described themselves as Labour supporters, only 40 per cent cast a regional ballot for the party. A larger proportion – indeed almost half – stayed at home and 16 per cent voted for a different party. Quite a few of the latter opted for one of the minor parties, in line with the popular perception that the party's heartlands have become disaffected by

'New' Labour's eschewal of radical politics. In terms of converting support into regional votes, Labour lagged behind all of the other parties, but the contrast with the SNP is by far the starkest. Of pre-election SNP identifiers, 65 per cent voted for the party on the regional list and almost all of the rest did not vote. In the constituency voting, the pattern for the two parties was similar. Although the figures are slightly better for Labour, this is only because fewer votes were lost to minor parties, which, for the most part, did not stand in the constituency contests.

As well as maximising support from its own supporters, the SNP also proved the most successful of the major parties in attracting votes from those who identified with rival parties. Supporters of the Conservatives, Liberal Democrats and minor parties were all more likely to defect to the SNP than to any other party. Given the heated contest between the two leading parties, it is not surprising that Labour identifiers were not as ready as others to switch to the SNP. Nonetheless, at least a handful did so, whereas none of the pre-election SNP supporters in our sample went on to cast a regional vote for Labour. Finally, the SNP also proved appreciably more popular than Labour among non-identifiers. Given that this group comprises at least half the electorate, this last advantage is especially important.

To summarise this section, we have seen that around half of voters describe themselves as supporters of a particular party and a further quarter report at least some leaning towards a party. Moreover, most of those who identify with a party then go on to vote for it. These enduring loyalties thus serve as an important anchoring point for parties as well as for many voters. However, there remains considerable leeway for short-term forces to influence voters and elections. Not only is there a significant – and growing – proportion of the electorate that disclaims any partisan attachment, but also substantial numbers of identifiers were willing to disregard their longer-term sympathies when voting. Put simply, the potential 'floating vote' is large and getting larger. In 2007, many of these voters floated in the direction of the SNP, which suggests that the party was making a positive impression at the time. In the next section we test that conjecture by examining voters' evaluations of the parties.

Evaluations of the parties

Given that so many voters went into the 2007 election without a strong sense of loyalty to any particular party, it is essential to consider their reactions to each of the parties competing for their votes. A great deal of research has emphasised that attitudes to parties, unlike party identification as tradition-ally conceived, are not stable (see, for example, Fiorina, 1981; Clarke *et al.*,

2004). Instead, citizens react to changes in parties' perceived performance, leaders, issue priorities and ideological stances. Voters' attitudes are thus, in effect, 'running tallies' of their assessments, both positive and negative, of the parties over time. The detailed information underlying such evaluations may well be forgotten but the overall tally – the general impression of the party – remains. It should be noted, however, that voters in reaching their assessments probably pay more heed to recent events and impressions than those in the more distant past.

While Labour has long enjoyed an advantage in terms of enduring party loyalties, there are reasons to suppose that in 2007 these 'running tally' attitudes were more favourable to the SNP and less to Labour. As suggested in Chapter 1, Labour's problems at UK level rubbed off on Labour in Scotland. Having won the 2005 UK general election with a bit to spare, the government quickly ran into a period of unpopularity and trailed the Conservatives in UK general election opinion polls from April 2006 onwards. It was the SNP – now led by Alex Salmond – which overtook Labour in Scottish Parliament election opinion polls and throughout 2006 the party's ratings showed a steady upward trend. The suggestion that 'running tally' evaluations tended to favour the SNP in 2007 is given some indirect support from the data in the previous section which highlighted the SNP's popularity among non-identifiers. To address the issue more directly, we asked respondents to report their feelings about the competing parties on a scale from 0 ('strongly dislike') to 10 ('strongly like'). Calculating the mean ratings across respondents gives an idea of how each party was regarded by the Scottish electorate in 2007. We also calculated the standard deviation (s.d.) of ratings for each party. These are measures of the spread of scores and thus of the extent of disagreement about the parties among voters. Large standard deviations signify that a party was widely liked and widely disliked; smaller figures mean that most voters shared a similar view of the party.

Looking first at the ratings of all voters (left-hand panel of Table 3.4), we can see that none of the parties proved especially popular. None of the average ratings is higher than 5, the middle point of the scale, and the average rating overall was 4.1. This makes sense in the Scottish context, in which no party commands anything like majority support. From that perspective, each party has more opponents than supporters. On the other hand, the overall average was clearly dragged down by two parties which were particularly disliked in 2007 – the Conservatives and Scottish Socialists. The former evidently remained in the doldrums as far as Scottish public opinion was concerned. The low score for the latter is predictable given that their ideological position lies some distance away from that of the average voter. The other parties have similar mean ratings, although, as suggested earlier, the SNP enjoyed a narrow

Table 3.4 *Ratings of parties on an 11-point like–dislike scale by all respondents and by non-identifiers*

| | All respondents | | | Non-identifiers | | |
	Mean	s.d.	N	Mean	s.d.	N
Conservatives	3.2	3.0	1,760	3.4	2.8	879
Labour	4.4	3.2	1,767	4.0	2.8	884
Lib Dems	4.7	2.6	1,743	4.7	2.4	867
SNP	4.8	3.5	1,754	4.7	3.1	879
Green	4.5	2.7	1,713	4.5	2.7	851
SSP	2.8	2.7	1,690	2.8	2.6	838
All parties	4.1	2.9		4.0	2.7	

Source: Pre-election survey.

advantage over Labour. It is also noticeable that SNP ratings show the highest standard deviation, indicating that the party was especially popular with some voters but also repelled plenty of others. This is probably due both to its stance on independence for Scotland, an issue which excites strong views, and to its leader, Alex Salmond, who, as we shall see shortly, also tended to polarise opinion in 2007. In contrast, the standard deviation of Liberal Democrat ratings is relatively small, reflecting that party's moderate politics and generally inoffensive public image.

Fairly obviously, voters who identify with a party are predisposed to like it more (and usually to like the other parties much less). It is useful, therefore, to look at ratings net of the influence of partisanship. One way of doing this is to exclude party identifiers from the calculations (as in the right-hand panel of Table 3.4). For the most part, this makes little difference but it does result in a noticeable drop in the average Labour rating (from 4.4 to 4.0). This shift is predictable given that, having the most identifiers, Labour benefits most from partisan bias. The upshot is that the SNP's popularity lead over Labour was wider among non-identifiers. As we saw in Table 3.3, this translated into an advantage on polling day.

Another way of taking account of partisan predispositions is simply to look at the like–dislike ratings from identifiers with each party in turn (Table 3.5); we combine both identifiers and leaners in these analyses. The first point to note is that SNP identifiers were the keenest on their own party, with a mean rating of 9.0. Labour identifiers were noticeably less enthused, on average rating the party at only 7.9 on the like–dislike scale. Affections between supporters of the erstwhile coalition partners went largely unrequited. For Labour supporters, the Liberal Democrats were clearly second favourites but

Table 3.5 *Ratings of parties on an 11-point like–dislike scale by pre-election party identification*

| | Party identification/leaning | | | |
	Conservatives	Labour	Lib Dems	SNP
Conservatives	8.0	1.8	3.3	2.1
Labour	1.8	7.9	3.6	2.7
Lib Dems	3.5	4.8	8.3	4.1
SNP	2.4	3.4	3.8	9.0
Green	2.9	4.5	5.6	5.0
SSP	0.8	2.9	2.4	3.4
N (minimum)	204	447	141	357

Source: Pre-election survey.

Liberal Democrat identifiers were markedly less impressed by Labour and were, indeed, slightly more positive about the SNP. There was a similar asymmetry among the leading parties: Labour supporters rated the SNP higher than vice versa. Even Conservative supporters, traditionally the most strongly opposed to independence, tended on balance to prefer the SNP to Labour. Tory identifiers were also by some distance the least impressed by both the Greens and the SSP.

The evidence in this section confirms that, on the whole, Scottish voters evaluated the SNP more positively than Labour in 2007. This helps to explain why non-identifiers (and those who identified with other parties but 'defected') voted disproportionately for the Nationalists. The very tight race between the two leading parties can thus be seen as the cancelling out of two gaps: Labour's head-start in terms of long-term loyalties and the more favourable short-term evaluations of the SNP in 2007. In turn, then, explaining the SNP's narrow victory means accounting for the positive impression that it had acquired among voters. In the remainder of this chapter, we examine one plausible explanation: the party leaders.

Evaluations of the party leaders

The notion of 'presidentialisation' is often invoked in discussions of modern British electoral politics (Foley, 2000; Mughan, 2000). Television, increasingly the dominant medium of political coverage, lends itself to a personalised treatment of party politics. Moreover, parties' campaigns nowadays are usually strongly focused on their leaders, who, therefore, figure prominently not only in media coverage but also in party literature. With party leaders thus paraded before the electorate almost all the time, it is not surprising that attitudes to leaders have a significant effect on voters' decisions. Tony Blair, for example, proved a considerable asset to Labour in the 2001 general election but four years – and the Iraq war – later he had become something of a liability, costing the party votes and seats (Evans and Andersen, 2005).

Broadly speaking, there are two main ways in which party leaders influence party choice at elections (King, 2002: ch. 1). The first is a direct effect: a voter simply chooses the party whose leader he or she would most like to see as Prime Minister (or First Minister in the Scottish context). This can be described as direct because it bypasses party, which plays no role in the decision. An indirect effect, the second possibility, occurs when voters make judgements about a party based on its leader and these judgements in turn influence party choice. Returning to the example of Tony Blair, some of the key characteristics – notably moderateness and competence – that underpinned 'New' Labour's appeal in 1997 were derived from Blair himself (Denver and Fisher, 2009). This projection of leader characteristics on to parties makes a lot of sense. As the case of Labour under Blair showed, powerful leaders can indeed shape parties in their own image. Moreover, whereas parties are complex and perhaps quite nebulous entities, leaders are more tangible – we see and hear them on our television screens day after day – and thus easier to evaluate. Especially for those less interested in and knowledgeable about politics, a choice between leaders rather than between parties may be the more straightforward option. It should be acknowledged, however, that the inference is not all in one direction. Some voters will project the strengths and weaknesses of a party on to its leader and, of course, those who strongly like (or dislike) a party are prone to adopt the same attitude towards whoever is in charge. Disentangling the complex interrelationship between party and leader evaluations is probably impossible but the key point for present purposes is that leaders are an important ingredient in the impressions of parties formed by voters and thus have the potential to shape voting decisions.

Since the popularity of each party depends in part on its leader, we need to consider voters' attitudes to all of the Scottish leaders in 2007 but we will pay particular attention to opinions about the Labour First Minister, Jack McConnell, and the SNP leader, Alex Salmond. Although there is no constitutional requirement that the First Minister be the leader of the largest party, the media nonetheless tended to present these two as the only realistic contenders for the post. Hence they were particularly prominent in coverage of the campaign and had most to win or lose from direct leadership effects on voting. Polling evidence in the run-up to the election suggested that Salmond enjoyed a clear popularity lead over McConnell (and indeed the other party leaders), an advantage that the SNP sought to cash in on by replacing their party name with the slogan 'Alex Salmond for First Minister' as the label for the SNP list on regional ballot papers. This was an obvious attempt to boost the impact of leadership on party choice.

Our analysis is not confined to the major Scottish contenders, however. There are good reasons to suppose that the Westminster leaders could also have influenced voters in 2007. For one thing, they, too, were quite prominent in the campaign. Prime Minister Tony Blair, his imminent replacement Gordon Brown and Conservative leader David Cameron all made well publicised visits to Scotland in the run-up to polling day, thus blurring further the distinction (probably already very unclear in most voters' minds) between the Scottish parties and their British counterparts. More generally, however, the Scottish electorate is not immune to Britain-wide trends in political opinion. Despite devolution, what happens at Westminster affects everyone and the reactions of Scottish voters to national UK politics are bound to colour their approach to elections within Scotland. When Scottish voters were deciding whether to support Labour in 2007, for example, they are likely to have been influenced by the party's leadership – and, indeed, its record and policies – at UK level as well as within Scotland. Hence there was much speculation that Scottish Labour would suffer in 2007 because of Tony Blair's post-Iraq unpopularity and, in particular, that the Prime Minister's visits to Scotland during the campaign could do Labour more harm than good.

Leader evaluations in 2007

We first examine how the various leaders were evaluated by voters, using the same 0–10 like–dislike scale used to measure feelings about parties. Considering first the Scottish leaders, it is clear that Alex Salmond was indeed the most popular (left-hand panel of Table 3.6) and that he had a clear advantage over Jack McConnell. At the same time, his mean rating – at 4.8, the same as that of his party – is still below the middle point on the scale, indicating that plenty of voters were less keen on the SNP leader. This point is reinforced by the relatively large standard deviation of ratings of Salmond – he was a more polarising figure than any of the other Scottish leaders. Annabel Goldie, leader of the Scottish Conservatives, proved more popular than her party, with a mean rating of 4.1 (slightly higher than McConnell). Comfortably the least popular of the leaders was Tommy Sheridan of Solidarity, although he was evaluated more positively than the SSP, from which he had recently split amid considerable acrimony (see Chapter 1). Our earlier suggestion that the election was commonly framed as 'McConnell versus Salmond' receives at least indirect support from the varying

Table 3.6 *Ratings of party leaders on an 11-point like–dislike scale by all respondents and non-identifiers*

	All respondents				Non-identifiers			
	Mean	*s.d.*	*% 'don't know'*	*N*	*Mean*	*s.d.*	*% 'don't know'*	*N*
Jack McConnell	4.0	2.9	8	*1,722*	3.7	2.7	11	*864*
Alex Salmond	4.8	3.3	8	*1,715*	4.5	2.9	11	*860*
Nicol Stephen	4.3	2.6	26	*1,386*	4.2	2.5	31	*662*
Annabel Goldie	4.1	2.7	21	*1,473*	4.1	2.6	27	*701*
Tommy Sheridan	3.3	3.1	10	*1,693*	3.2	3.0	12	*850*
Tony Blair	3.8	3.3	5	*1,776*	3.4	3.0	7	*902*
Gordon Brown	4.4	3.1	6	*1,764*	4.2	2.9	8	*890*
David Cameron	3.8	2.6	8	*1,726*	3.9	2.5	11	*866*
All leaders	4.0	3.0			3.9	2.8		

Source: Pre-election survey.

proportions of respondents answering 'don't know' to these questions. While only 8 per cent were unable to report an attitude towards the front-runners for First Minister, the proportions for Goldie and Nicol Stephen, leader of the Scottish Liberal Democrats, were much higher. For a variety of (political and non-political) reasons, Tommy Sheridan was a rather more familiar figure than these. However, the lowest proportions of 'don't know' responses were for the Westminster leaders. It is especially noteworthy that as many people offered opinions on relative newcomer David Cameron, Conservative leader since December 2005, as did on McConnell, First Minister since 2001, or on Salmond, prominent on the Scottish political scene for longer still. The fact that Scottish voters express opinions on British leaders does not constitute proof that these opinions influenced votes in 2007 but it is suggestive in that direction. If there was such influence, then the implications for Labour depend considerably on whether voters were looking back at Tony Blair or forward to Gordon Brown, since the two were respectively the second-most unpopular and the second-most popular of the politicians included in the survey. Meanwhile, David Cameron's ratings indicate that, at the time, he was no great asset to the Conservatives in Scotland.

We need to take account of the partisan predispositions that are likely to colour these leader evaluations. As before, a first stage is to examine the mean ratings of leaders among non-identifiers (right-hand panel of Table 3.6). These

Table 3.7 *Ratings of party leaders on an 11-point like–dislike scale by pre-election party identification*

	Party identification/leaning			
	Conservatives	*Labour*	*Lib Dems*	*SNP*
Jack McConnell	2.5	6.0	4.0	3.0
Alex Salmond	3.1	3.6	4.0	8.2
Nicol Stephen	3.4	4.1	6.1	4.7
Annabel Goldie	6.5	3.4	4.2	3.7
Tommy Sheridan	1.6	3.3	2.9	4.1
Tony Blair	2.0	6.7	2.8	2.5
Gordon Brown	2.0	6.9	3.7	3.4
David Cameron	6.7	3.1	4.5	3.0
N (minimum)	*165*	*354*	*127*	*325*

Source: Pre-election survey.

potential floating voters report a pattern of attitudes very similar to that of the overall sample and, in particular, their ratings show the same advantage for Salmond over McConnell (and indeed over all the other leaders). The other noteworthy feature of the results among non-identifiers is that the proportions of 'don't know' responses are even larger than for all respondents. Just a fortnight before polling day, almost one-third of voters with no party identification could not offer any opinion on the leader of the Scottish Liberal Democrats. As before, it is also instructive to break down the ratings by the party identification (or leaning) reported by voters (Table 3.7). There are some parallels with the party evaluations in Table 3.5. SNP supporters were by far the most enthusiastic about their own leader, with a mean rating of 8.2. This contrasts sharply with the lukewarm endorsements of Jack McConnell and Nicol Stephen by their parties' supporters (average ratings of 6.0 and 6.1, respectively). Labour supporters were noticeably more positive about both Blair and Brown than about the First Minister but supporters of all three other main parties delivered a fairly damning verdict on Tony Blair.

In the next section, we address the relationship between these leadership evaluations and party choice in 2007. Before that, a useful preliminary step is to look at how closely leaders and their parties were associated in voters' minds. One way of doing this is to calculate the correlation between voters' ratings of a leader and their ratings of that leader's party (Figure 3.1). The larger the correlation coefficient, the tighter is the connection between leader and party. In 2007, the closest such association was between Alex Salmond and the SNP, with ratings strongly correlated, at 0.80. One reason for this is probably that, in the absence of a separate British party, Salmond was the undisputed leader of the SNP. In parties with both Scottish and British leaders, it seems that the latter were the more readily associated with the party in voters' minds: the coefficients involving Blair and Cameron comfortably exceed those for McConnell and Goldie. The analysis implies that the British party leaders were at the forefront of voters' minds as they considered the parties competing for votes in the Scottish Parliament election, even though these leaders were not candidates and were not as heavily involved in campaigning as their Scottish counterparts.

Of course, correlation is not the same as causation. In this context, strong statistical associations between the variables are ambiguous: they could mean that voters judge parties by their leaders or leaders by their parties. If the latter is true – voters look favourably on a leader only because of a prior preference for his or her party – then a vote for that party cannot reasonably be attributed to the influence of the leader. However, the evidence in this section gives reason to doubt that leadership evaluations are driven by party preferences.

Figure 3.1 *Pearson correlations between like–dislike ratings of leaders and their parties*

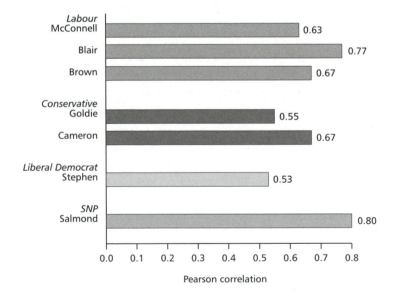

Source: Pre-election survey.

Nicol Stephen and Annabel Goldie were the leaders least familiar to voters yet theirs are also the two weakest correlations in Figure 3.1. This is not what we would expect if, confronted with less well known leaders, voters simply applied their party preferences when evaluating those politicians. The fact that the strongest correlations are for Salmond and Blair suggests that evaluations of the SNP and Labour were driven – at least to some extent – by opinions about their prominent leaders, thus opening up the possibility of a leader effect on voting in 2007. We explore that possibility in the next section, assessing the benefits accruing to the SNP from Alex Salmond's popularity advantage and the costs imposed on Labour by the unpopularity of its First Minister and its outgoing leader at Westminster.

Leadership evaluations and party choice

We begin by focusing on the rival candidates for First Minister. Using the like–dislike ratings, the Scottish electorate can be divided into three groups: those preferring Salmond, those preferring McConnell and those neutral between the two (i.e. giving them the same rating on the 0–10 scale). Comparing the voting behaviour of these groups gives an indication of the impact of leader evaluations. It is essential to control for partisan predispositions, however. Labour sympathisers are likely both to have preferred Jack McConnell and to have voted Labour and if we do not take account of this we will drastically overestimate the effect of leaders on vote choice. Hence we look at party choice by leadership preference among four types of voter – SNP supporters (identifiers and leaners), Labour supporters, other party supporters (combined) and those who disclaimed any partisan attachment or leaning.

Table 3.8 shows that the vast majority of SNP supporters rated Salmond higher than McConnell (and most of the rest voted for the party anyway). In stark contrast, substantial minorities of Labour supporters were either undecided between the two leaders or actually preferred Salmond and more than half of these voters deserted Labour on polling day, plenty of them voting for the SNP. Salmond also looks to have won over supporters of other parties. Not only did they tend to prefer him to McConnell but those who did voted SNP in significant numbers (24 per cent). There is a similar pattern among non-identifiers, with Salmond the more popular leader and also better able to translate that advantage into votes. Among the (smaller) group of non-identifiers who preferred McConnell, only 38 per cent voted Labour. The corresponding proportion for Salmond and the SNP was 47 per cent.

These results point to two problems for Labour. First, Jack McConnell was simply less popular than Alex Salmond. Second, even those who preferred McConnell could not be relied upon to support his party. The latter point

Table 3.8 *Preferred leader and party choice by pre-election party identification (percentage of respondents)*

		Preferred leader		
Party identification	*Regional vote*	*Salmond*	*Neutral*	*McConnell*
SNP	SNP	92	79	75
	Other	8	7	0
	Labour	0	14	25
	N	*238*	*14*	*8*
Labour	SNP	28	15	0
	Other	32	40	22
	Labour	40	44	78
	N	*57*	*52*	*188*
Other	SNP	24	10	6
	Other	76	83	85
	Labour	0	7	9
	N	*130*	*83*	*101*
None	SNP	47	29	11
	Other	47	55	51
	Labour	7	16	38
	N	*129*	*76*	*79*

Sources: Pre- and post-election surveys (weighted by turnout).

could be attributed to a lack of enthusiasm for the Scottish Labour leader but there are plenty of other possibilities. One is that positive attitudes towards McConnell were swept away on the tide of negative opinions of Tony Blair. That suggestion relates to the major question – addressed in detail in Chapter 6 – about whether voters were choosing on the basis of Scottish matters or passing comment on events and personalities at Westminster. Here we report on an analysis designed to clarify the relative importance of Blair and McConnell in voters' decision-making in 2007. Evaluations of Gordon Brown are included too, on the grounds that his imminent succession might have limited whatever losses Labour might have sustained from anti-Blair sentiment. The analysis is based on logistic regression, a statistical technique that is used several times in this book and which is explained in Appendix 3, which also contains the full results from this analysis (Table A3.1) and subsequent regression analyses.

Figure 3.2 *Evaluations of Labour leaders and predicted probability of voting Labour: (a) regional list vote; (b) constituency vote*

(a) Regional list vote

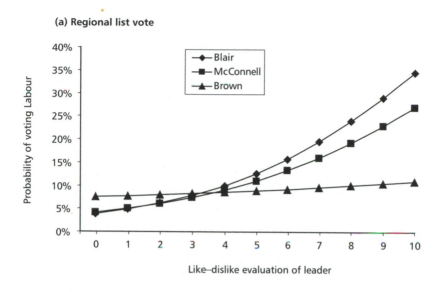

Like–dislike evaluation of leader

(b) Constituency vote

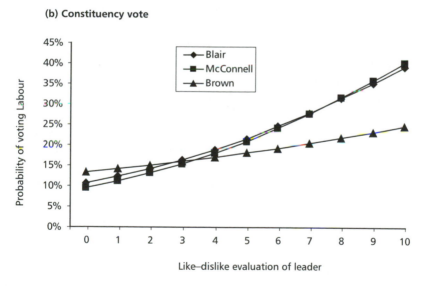

Like–dislike evaluation of leader

Sources: Pre- and post-election surveys.

This technique can show how, as voters' evaluations of each leader change, so does the probability of their voting Labour. The technique allows for such calculations while holding other important factors – in this case voters' party identification and their opinions of the other leaders – constant.[3]

The simplest way to illustrate regression results is with a graph. Naturally, we would expect the graph to show upward slopes in this case: the more that voters like each Labour politician, the more likely they are to vote for the party. The key point is the steepness of the slope for each leader. A gentle slope means that the likelihood of voting Labour is not very responsive to evaluations of that leader; put another way, those evaluations are not a particularly important influence on party choice. That turns out to be the case for Gordon Brown in the regional list voting (Figure 3.2a). Holding constant party identification and attitudes to Blair and McConnell, those who 'strongly liked' Brown were not much more likely to vote Labour than those who 'strongly disliked' him. The other slopes are markedly steeper, however. Among voters who strongly disliked Blair or McConnell, there was only a 4 per cent chance of a Labour regional vote, but at the 'strongly like' end of the scale those probabilities climbed to 35 per cent for Blair and 27 per cent for McConnell. The steeper slope for Blair indicates that evaluations of him were somewhat more important than those of McConnell. However, the difference is relatively small and disappears altogether when we look at constituency voting (Figure 3.2b). Here again there is little evidence that the impending replacement of Blair with Brown did much to sway vote choices but there is clear evidence that, in this case, the First Minister was no less prominent in voters' minds than the outgoing Prime Minister. The problem for Labour, however, was that he was also not much more popular.

Echoing a point made at the end of Chapter 2, we need to acknowledge an important caveat to the discussion and data in this section. Party identification is not the only factor that might influence both leadership evaluations and vote choice. For example, some voters may evaluate Tony Blair positively because they associate him with a period of economic stability and prosperity. Others may like Alex Salmond because he leads a party that is committed to Scottish interests. In these cases, the real drivers of vote choice would not be attitudes to the leaders but Labour's record on the economy and the SNP's image as a party fighting for Scotland. If we do not control for these other matters, we may overestimate the influence of leaders on voters' decisions. In Chapter 10, we report more comprehensive analyses in which leader evaluations are included along with a variety of other possible factors influencing party choice. Those results give a more precise estimation of the impact of Messrs Salmond, McConnell, Blair and the others on voting behaviour in 2007.

Conclusion

The results of any election reflect both enduring partisan attachments and the popularity of the parties at that point in time. Anyone doubting the importance of long-term loyalties need only compare the Conservatives and Liberal Democrats in 2007: the latter party was clearly more popular among voters as a whole but the Conservatives could count on a solid (if dwindling) base of party identifiers. Similarly, Labour's advantage over the SNP in terms of party attachments constituted an electoral head-start. Yet that head-start was quite narrow and was further eroded by Labour's struggle even to get its supporters to the polls. Moreover, there is a large and growing number of voters who simply do not feel an attachment to any particular party. These are potential floating voters and, in practice, they – plus those willing to defect from their 'usual' party – could be said to be the most important voters, since they determine election outcomes by switching to and from parties.

That point was vividly illustrated in 2007. The SNP owed its narrow victory over Labour to its popularity advantage at the time of the election. Crucially, this advantage was especially wide among voters lacking any particular partisan leaning – that is, those voters who tend to determine election outcomes. The pervasiveness of the SNP's popularity advantage is also noteworthy. It extended to supporters of the Conservatives, despite their traditional antipathy to the Nationalist cause, and to supporters of the Liberal Democrats, Labour's erstwhile coalition partners. This support from across the political spectrum suggests that the SNP's popularity had little to do with its ideological or issue positions – including its pro-independence stance – since these would be expected to repel some groups while attracting others. Likelier sources of SNP advantage are those broader political characteristics that have potential appeal for all voters.

Among such characteristics, one obvious possibility is the party's leader. As we have seen, Alex Salmond and the SNP were very closely associated in voters' minds. Salmond was noticeably more popular than his rival Jack McConnell (a difference that again extended more or less throughout the electorate) and the evidence suggests that this was converted into electoral support. However, there are reasons for caution before crediting the success of the SNP in 2007 entirely to Alex Salmond. First, the particularly wide variation in ratings of Salmond point to his being a polarising figure – while many voters clearly wanted 'Alex Salmond for First Minister', there were also many who did not. Second, the relative strength of Salmond's ratings was no more striking than the relative weakness of Jack McConnell's. Insofar as leadership mattered in 2007, it was not just about Salmond's popularity but also McConnell's lack of appeal. Third, the fact that Labour could not even command the support of those who clearly preferred Jack McConnell shows that voting decisions were about more than who would become First Minister. The most fundamental point, however, is that we need to consider the important distinction between direct and indirect leadership effects. Did voters like the SNP because of Alex Salmond, or because of what Alex Salmond had done for the party? We will be better able to answer that question once we have looked in more detail at voters' impressions and expectations of the parties in 2007.

Notes

1 This question is drawn from the long-running British/Scottish Social Attitudes series.
2 In reality that proportion is almost certainly somewhat larger. Party identification and political interest obviously go hand in hand and our sample is very likely to be skewed towards the politically involved. One way of reducing this bias is to weight the data by turnout, such that non-voters are no longer under-represented. With that weight applied, the proportions of supporters, leaners and non-identifiers are 43 per cent, 24 per cent and 33 per cent, respectively.
3 None of the SNP identifiers in the SES pre-election survey cast a regional vote for Labour, which makes it impossible to estimate the impact of that variable on Labour support. Hence in this and subsequent analyses of regional list voting we use the post-election measure of SNP identification instead. A long series of tests has shown that this switch causes no noteworthy shifts in the other results or their statistical significance.

4
Issues, policies and performance

Despite the importance of party leaders and party images in elections, issues remain the currency of much political debate. In respect of issues, competing parties generally have two concurrent aims at election time. First, each seeks to persuade voters that it is best equipped to deal with the most important issues. Second, however, the parties also attempt to ensure that the issues on which they are the favoured party are seen as the most important. Campaigns thus involve attempts at both persuasion and agenda-setting. Hence, in analysing the impact of issues in elections, we need to consider both policy preferences and competence evaluations on the one hand and importance, or 'salience', on the other. In other words, in 2007 we needed to ask voters about which issues mattered to them as well as about which party they thought best placed to handle those issues. It is worth noting at the outset that issue salience, like the campaign agenda, is no respecter of constitutional boundaries. For example, while defence is an issue reserved for Westminster and it was the House of Commons that voted in March 2003 to send troops into Iraq, this did not prevent that war from being a highly salient issue two months later in the Scottish Parliament election.

For politicians, issues and policies go hand in hand. For voters, however, the importance of the latter is easily overstated. Few have any detailed knowledge – or even a rough grasp – of party policies. As Philip Converse famously put it, 'a large proportion of the electorate simply does not have meaningful beliefs, even on issues that have formed the basis for intense controversy among elites for substantial periods of time' (Converse, 1964: 245). This is not to say that policies are irrelevant. Rather, they tend to matter only in a broad-brush way that reflects the typical voter's lack of knowledge of – or interest in – policy detail. For example, voters may know little about the specifics of Conservative and SNP proposals on health but they can recognise the former as being generally more sympathetic to private sector involvement. Or, returning to the example of Iraq, voters could be forgiven for losing track of the various parties' plans for troop withdrawals but they are much more likely to remember that Labour supported the war and the Liberal Democrats opposed it. To this extent, 'policy voting' is largely confined to a few major issues on which voters choose a party whose stance broadly matches their own.

On some issues, however, neither voters nor parties adopt different stances. As elsewhere, more or less everyone in Scotland is in favour of less crime and better schools and hospitals. Not many voters are opposed to peace and prosperity. These are examples of *valence* issues (Stokes, 1963) – those on which almost all voters share the same goal. In these cases, the 'issue' for the voter is about which of the parties is most likely to achieve the relevant goal. The contrast is with *position* issues, which refers to those on which voters adopt different positions (for or against, for example), such as the Iraq war or the introduction of identity cards. Evidence from recent British elections strongly suggests that valence issues have more influence on voting decisions than position issues (Clarke *et al.*, 2004, 2009). One reason for this is the ideological convergence of the main parties. This not only guillotined debate on major position issues – like the privatisation of major industries or the rights of trade unions – but also reduced policy differences on education and health, thus rendering these policy areas more like valence issues. In Scotland, it could be suggested that 'New' Labour's shift to the political centre was particularly important, not only because it reduced the gap between the party and the Conservatives but also because it virtually eliminated any left–right ideological difference with the party's main rival, the SNP (Bennie *et al.*, 1997; Paterson, 2006). Labour and the SNP, it could be argued, remain clearly distinct only on the constitutional question relating to Scotland's position in the United Kingdom.[1]

In this context, electoral competition is not primarily about policy or ideology but about performance and delivery. Voters judge governing parties primarily by their record in office. With opposition parties, the estimation of likely performance is more difficult (Butt, 2006) and so voters rely on general impressions: has the party appeared competent and united in opposition and are its promises credible? Such impressions are often strongly influenced by leader evaluations (Clarke *et al.*, 2004). This means that voters' expectations of a party's performance are unlikely to vary much across issues. Perceptions of competence on any given issue are apt to be inferred from broad impressions of party image (Trilling, 1975). Hence in this chapter we look at general assessments of competence as well as perceived performance on specific issues.

Parties and the issue agenda

We begin by examining the issues that were uppermost in voters' minds in 2007. This helps not only to map out the campaign battleground but also to explain party choice. As Särlvik and Crewe (1983: 222) put it, 'one would expect a stronger relationship between issue opinions and voting among those who consider a given issue important than among those who are less concerned'. In the pre-election survey, respondents were asked the following open-ended question: 'What will be the single most important issue for you when deciding how to vote in the Scottish Parliament election?' The question was repeated (suitably amended) in the post-election wave, thus enabling us to track changing issue salience over the campaign period. The advantage of using an open-ended question, in which answers were typed in rather than chosen from a list of options, is that we avoid prompting respondents simply to choose an issue that they recognise as having been prominent in the campaign rather than indicating one which actually mattered to them when voting. The disadvantage is that open-ended questions elicit a bewildering variety of answers and to make sense of the data we need to sort these answers into categories. Here, we present information on the nine issues mentioned most often and even that leaves around a third of answers to be subsumed into an 'other' category (Table 4.1).

The 'constitutional question' – a broad category encompassing references to independence for Scotland, maintaining the Union and the powers of the Scottish Parliament – was clearly the most salient issue in the 2007 election.[2] Moreover, its relative importance grew during the campaign. Indeed, the widening concern with that issue was the only really noteworthy (and the only statistically significant) shift in the agenda between the pre- and post-election surveys. Given the obvious significance of Scotland's constitutional status to

Table 4.1 *Distribution of 'most important issue' responses, pre- and post-election (percentage of respondents)*

	Pre	*Post*	*Change, pre–post*
Constitutional question	19	26	+7
Health	9	7	–2
Council tax	9	9	0
Law and order	8	7	–1
Education	6	6	0
Economy/tax	6	6	0
Environment	3	3	0
Iraq	1	3	2
Trident	2	2	0
Other	37	31	–6
N	*1,152*	*916*	

Note: Respondents answering 'don't know' or 'no important issues' are excluded.
Sources: Pre- and post-election surveys.

parties and voters alike, the role of this issue in the 2007 election is discussed in detail in the next chapter. At this stage, it is worth emphasising that, even in the post-election survey, only a quarter of those mentioning an issue cited the constitutional question in any of its aspects. The remainder were spread over a wide range of other issues, with small but far from trivial proportions of respondents mentioning each of the core valence issues – health, education, law and order, and the economy – that tend to dominate Westminster elections (Clarke *et al.*, 2004). The council tax is clearly a position issue – the question was whether or not it should be replaced by something else – and, other than the constitution, was the only such issue cited reasonably often. Strikingly, two position issues widely believed to drive opposition to Labour at Westminster – the Iraq war and the replacement of Trident missiles – were seldom mentioned. This tends to suggest that, in some respects at least, 2007 was a genuinely 'Scottish' election.

The overall figures for issue salience conceal important differences within the electorate. Some issues tend to be the preoccupation of one party's supporters, while others are of more general concern. It is of particular interest to examine the priorities of voters lacking a prior party identification, however, since it is perhaps more likely that their choice of party would be influenced by their issue opinions than would be the case with loyal party supporters. Breaking down respondents by party identification and focusing on the pre-election report of the 'most important issue', we find some predictable results. The constitutional question was mentioned most frequently by SNP

Table 4.2 *Pre-election 'most important issue' responses by party identification (percentage of respondents)*

	Pre-election party identification				
	None	*Conser-vatives*	*Labour*	*Lib Dems*	*SNP*
Constitutional question	12	26	13	8	45
Health	12	4	11	12	3
Council tax	8	9	6	8	9
Law and order	8	6	11	3	8
Education	7	3	11	5	2
Economy/tax	6	6	9	8	4
Other	47	44	39	58	30
N	*502*	*95*	*210*	*66*	*196*

Note: Respondents answering 'don't know' or 'no important issues' are excluded.
Source: Pre-election survey.

supporters and – doubtless for very different reasons – was also a prominent concern among Conservatives (Table 4.2). For the rest of the electorate, however, the constitutional issue does not stand out as being markedly more prominent than the other areas shown in the table. Labour identifiers were disproportionately concerned with the core valence issues like health, law and order, the economy and, especially, education. Non-identifiers had a similar pattern of responses while generally showing quite a diverse range of concerns – the six particular issues identified account for only just over half of their responses. Hence no party seeking to win over uncommitted voters, as well as to get out its own supporters, could afford to focus too closely on any one single issue – whether the constitutional question or any other.

Having mapped out the campaign battleground, our next step is to assess which parties were thought best equipped to deal with the issues identified as important. After reporting their 'most important issue', respondents were asked which party they thought best able to handle that issue. We focus on the results from the post-election survey since these reflect the success or otherwise of the parties in persuading the electorate of their priorities and capacities. The results are generally consistent with those we have just considered. Thus, since almost half of SNP identifiers gave constitutional concerns as the issue most important to them, it is not surprising that half of those nominating this issue regarded the SNP as the best party to handle it (Table 4.3). The other big Nationalist advantage was on the other position issue in the table, local taxation. While the SNP also enjoyed a small advantage over Labour on law

Table 4.3 *Party best able to handle each 'most important issue'* (*percentage of respondents*)

| | *'Most important issue'* | | | | | |
	Consti-tution	*Council tax*	*Health*	*Law and order*	*Educa-tion*	*Economy*
Conservative	14	5	14	33	2	22
Labour	26	7	36	13	48	47
Lib Dem	3	13	14	8	15	11
SNP	50	59	21	23	23	5
Other	3	10	7	2	6	2
Don't know	3	6	9	20	6	13
Labour–SNP gap	**−24**	**−52**	**+15**	**−10**	**+25**	**+42**
N	*242*	*86*	*58*	*60*	*52*	*55*

Source: Post-election survey.

and order, it was the Conservatives who were most widely trusted to combat crime. Labour enjoyed its biggest leads, especially over the SNP, on key valence issues: education, health and, especially, the economy. The advantage accruing to Labour on this last issue, however, is limited because – as we shall see in Chapter 6 – this was the one major issue that respondents plainly saw as the responsibility of the UK government at Westminster rather than the Scottish Executive at Holyrood. Moreover, since all three of those issues were especially important to Labour identifiers, it could be that the party's leads are the result of partisan bias: those who already support Labour are prone not only to regard health and education as more important but also to deem their party as best equipped to handle those issues. We return to this point below when looking at issue performance evaluations among the electorate as a whole.

The fact that an issue was important to voters in 2007 does not necessarily imply that it swung many votes in the election. Salience is a necessary but not a sufficient condition for an issue to influence electoral behaviour. Voters must also perceive differences between the parties on the issue. We provided an overview of those differences above but did not explore why voters regarded some parties as well (or not so well) equipped to handle the various salient issues. Broadly, there are two types of reasons, corresponding to the distinction between position and valence issues drawn above. Voters might prefer party A to party B on an issue because their own policy positions tend to fall closer to those of party A. Alternatively, they may prefer B to A on a valence issue because they regard B as generally more competent to deliver the shared goals in that area. In the next section we investigate the first possibility, and assess the extent to which the electorate recognised policy differences between the major parties and, where there are such differences, gauge the impact on the vote in 2007.

Position issues and policies

Our post-election survey included the following question: 'Considering every-thing that the SNP and the Labour Party stand for, how much difference would you say there is between them?' On the whole, the responses to this question suggest that voters saw plenty of clear water between the two leading contenders. Two-thirds of respondents saw either 'a great deal' or 'quite a lot' of difference, and only around one in 10 perceived 'not very much' or no difference at all (Table 4.4). The picture is somewhat different when we look at the breakdown by party identification. Unsurprisingly, supporters of Labour and especially the SNP were the most likely to see the two parties as standing a long way apart. Non-identifiers tended to see a rather narrower

Table 4.4 *Perceived degree of difference between SNP and Labour, overall and by party identification (percentage of respondents)*

	All respondents	*By pre-election party identification*			
		Labour	*SNP*	*Other*	*None*
A great deal	26	29	47	24	17
Quite a lot	42	46	27	41	38
Some	21	18	12	20	29
Not very much	9	7	3	14	12
None at all	2	0	0	1	5
N	*1,411*	*264*	*215*	*293*	*639*

Sources: Pre- and post-election surveys.

gap, although even among this group more than half of respondents fell into one of the top two categories.

We can be more specific about the policy areas in which respondents saw these clear differences between Labour and the SNP by looking at perceptions of the parties' broad policy stances. Respondents were asked to place their own and their impression of the parties' positions on three (11-point) scales representing key issue dimensions (taxing and spending, dealing with crime and the constitutional issue). The extreme points on these scales were labelled thus:

0 = government should cut taxes a lot and spend much less on health and social services; 10 = government should raise taxes a lot and spend much more on health and social services;

0 = tough on criminals; 10 = tough on the causes of crime;

0 = abolishing the Scottish Parliament and returning to pre-devolution arrangements; 10 = independence for Scotland.

There has long been political debate about the appropriate balance between keeping taxes down and spending enough to maintain and improve public services. The data suggest that this is a matter of consensus rather than controversy in Scottish politics (Figure 4.1). Overall, on the basis of mean scores, respondents placed Labour, the SNP, the Liberal Democrats and themselves at almost exactly the same point on the scale, denoting a slight preference for increasing taxes and spending. Even the Conservatives were placed, on average, only just to the 'cut taxes' side of the scale's mid-point. On dealing with crime there was rather less perceived agreement. The Conservative Party was clearly seen as tougher on criminals than were the other parties and the average voter was also inclined in that direction. This helps to explain why

Figure 4.1 *Mean self placements and party placements on tax/spending, crime and constitution policy dimensions*

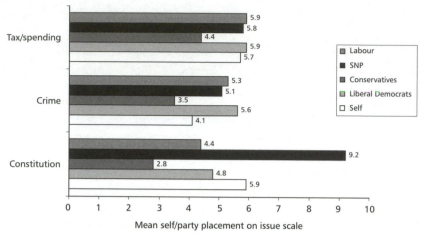

Mean self/party placement on issue scale

Source: Pre-election survey.

the Conservatives were most commonly seen as best able to handle the crime issue (see Table 4.3). Again, however, the positions of the other three main parties – especially Labour and the SNP – were barely distinguished by the average voter. In the next chapter we look in detail at the placement of all the major parties on the constitution dimension. Here we simply note that, insofar as voters saw 'a great deal' or 'quite a lot' of difference between Labour and the SNP, it must have been on the constitutional question rather than on either of the other two dimensions. By extension, since neither party was appreciably closer to the average voter on tax and spending or crime, neither will have derived any significant electoral advantage (at least, not over their chief rival) from its positions on those dimensions.

These results vindicate our description of health, education and crime as valence issues. In theory, parties can adopt markedly different policy positions on all three issues but in practice that was not the case with the major contenders in 2007. Necessarily, then, competition on those issues was more about how capable each party was to deliver the outcomes that were generally supported. We explore that facet of party competition in the next section. First, however, there was one position issue (in addition to the constitutional question) that was very conspicuous in the 2007 campaign, namely the council tax and its possible replacement by a local income tax.[3] As we have seen, this issue was reported as important by almost 10 per cent of SES respondents in both survey waves. Such 'flash' issues – those which do not recur in election after election – on devolved matters are unusual in Scottish elections: nothing comparable arose in 2003 and in 1999 perhaps only student tuition fees received a similar level of attention (Paterson *et al.*, 2001: 36). The crucial point about council tax in 2007 is that opinion about it was heavily skewed – it was overwhelmingly unpopular. Both before and after the election, survey respondents were asked 'Which of these do you think is the better way of raising the money needed by local councils in Scotland: i) to tax people according to the value of the house or flat in which they live? or ii) to tax people according to how much income they have?' Among those expressing an opinion (around one in 10 respondents in each wave had no view), huge majorities (89 per cent in the pre-election survey, 87 per cent in the post-election survey) chose the latter option. The scale of this backing for local income tax is such that it was clearly not confined to supporters of the parties advocating the policy (SNP and the Liberal Democrats). Indeed, pre-election support for local income tax was at 82 per cent among Labour and 79 per cent among Conservative identifiers, despite both parties campaigning actively against it.

Clearly, Labour stood to gain very little from steadfastly defending the council tax. Equally clearly, the overall election results show that plenty of people must have voted Labour despite favouring a local income tax. The key question, especially pressing given the closeness of the election, is whether Labour's support for the council tax cost the party votes. Initial evidence suggests that it did. As in a similar analysis in the previous chapter, we break down the sample of voters into four groups: SNP supporters (identifiers and leaners), Labour supporters, other party supporters (combined) and those lacking any partisan attachment or leaning. Within each group there are perceptible differences in party choice at the election between those on each side of the local taxation issue (Table 4.5). The expected pattern obtains in each case: Labour polled less strongly and the SNP more strongly among those preferring local income tax. The problem for Labour, of course, is that this group represents the vast majority of the electorate. Even among its own sympathisers, Labour could call on only 72 per cent support from those who preferred local income tax (compared with 84 per cent among those favouring council tax). Moreover, the pattern is especially noticeable among the key group of voters without a partisan leaning. Among the large group of unaligned voters who opposed the council tax, the SNP enjoyed an eight-point lead over Labour.

We noted above that relatively few respondents mentioned either the Iraq war or the replacement of Trident missiles as their most important issue when deciding how to vote in 2007. This implies that these issues had a limited impact on party choice but it is worth probing this question a little further, for two reasons. First, while few in number, the voters concerned about these

Table 4.5 *Regional vote by preferred local taxation and prior party support*

Party identification/ leaning	Regional vote	Preferred local tax (percentage of respondents)	
		Council	Local income
SNP	SNP	83	90
	Other	6	9
	Labour	11	1
	N	18	206
Labour	SNP	0	8
	Other	16	21
	Labour	84	72
	N	49	266
Other	SNP	3	16
	Other	76	80
	Labour	21	4
	N	34	245
None	SNP	8	30
	Other	50	49
	Labour	42	22
	N	24	200

Sources: Pre- and post-election surveys.

issues could have been important – they might, for example, have been Labour identifiers who defected from the party in 2007 in protest at the Westminster party's policies in these cases. Second, Iraq and Trident could have mattered to many more voters, including crucial 'swing' voters, even if those issues were not their top priorities. Certainly, both issues could have contributed to respondents' perceptions of differences between Labour and the SNP, since the Nationalists had been vocal in opposition both to the Iraq war and to the replacement of Trident. In the 2003 election, voters who opposed the war were significantly less likely to vote either Labour or Conservative (Curtice, 2006: 105). Although these parties may have benefited from the declining salience of the war, they stood to lose from the trend in public opinion about it. In 2003, the electorate was fairly evenly divided on the issue but by 2007 it was split more or less 4:1 against the war (Table 4.6).[4] There was a more even split on Trident but again, on balance, the UK government's policy was unpopular, with 51 per cent opposed to replacing the missiles compared with 34 per cent in favour. On each issue, Labour sympathisers (identifiers

Table 4.6 *Regional vote by attitudes towards the Iraq war and Trident and prior party support*

Party identification/ leaning	Regional vote	Iraq war (percentage of respondents)		Replacing Trident (percentage of respondents)	
		Anti	Pro	Anti	Pro
Labour	SNP	8	7	11	5
	Other	24	20	25	22
	Labour	68	73	64	73
	N	168	101	140	130
None	SNP	31	24	35	22
	Other	52	42	47	53
	Labour	17	34	18	25
	N	186	38	114	72

Sources: Pre- and post-election surveys.

and leaners combined) were generally less hostile than the electorate overall. Nonetheless, significant proportions were opposed, often strongly, to their party's policies. Moreover, on Iraq, non-partisan voters were very hostile to the UK government's policy, giving them a reason for antagonism towards Labour in 2007.

In order to avoid a deluge of data we concentrate on those two groups – Labour supporters and non-partisans – in addressing the potential impact of the Iraq and Trident issues on party choice in 2007. To simplify things further, we exclude those choosing the neutral option on the relevant attitude questions. There is evidence that opposition to Iraq and (especially) Trident deterred Labour sympathisers from voting for the party (on the regional list, at least) in 2007. Among these respondents, there was a nine-point difference in support for Labour depending on whether the voter favoured or opposed the replacement of Trident (Table 4.6). The same is true of non-partisan voters but in that case there is a definite asymmetry, with Iraq having a noticeably bigger influence on support for Labour. Significantly, however, these losses were not necessarily the SNP's gain. The Nationalists benefited much more from opposition to Trident replacement than from opposition to Iraq. This may be due to the party's long-standing association with unilateralism.

The entwining of the Trident issue with national identity and consti-tutional preferences and, indeed, of the Iraq issue with attitudes to Tony Blair reinforces the need for comprehensive analyses that include all of these disparate but linked factors simultaneously. Such analyses can provide a more precise estimate of the impact of issues. For the moment, however, it seems possible that these one-off issues – whether devolved, like the council tax, or reserved to Westminster, like Iraq and Trident – are more likely to influence voters' choices than the kind of broader policy differences that were characteristic of more ideologically polarised times. In the case of recurring important issues such as health, education and crime, only the Conservatives seem to have carved out a remotely distinctive policy niche. On these sorts of issues it seems likely that performance trumps policy and it is to performance evaluations that we now turn.

Valence issues and performance

One of the features of a valence interpretation of voting behaviour is that it focuses attention squarely on the contenders for government. Voters who choose on the basis of ideology might support a party of any size but valence voting is about assessing past and future performance in office. Inevitably, therefore, it mainly concerns the larger parties. The picture is complicated somewhat in Scottish Parliament elections by the proportional electoral system, which makes single-party majority government extremely unlikely. A diligent valence voter would thus face the difficult job of assessing the likely make-up of the next government as well as the likely performance of various permutations. Voters seek to simplify such complex decisions, of course, and to do so they focus mainly on the larger parties, which will inevitably lead the possible coalitions. As we saw in Chapter 2, it is not only voters who simplify matters in this way. The media also presented the 2007 election basically as a contest between Labour and the SNP to form the next government, such that a less attentive voter could easily have forgotten that neither party stood any realistic chance of winning an outright majority.

In the SES, then, when addressing performance on various issues, we asked respondents for two evaluations: first, of the performance of the Scottish Executive (as it was then usually called) over the previous four years and, second, of the likely performance of an SNP-led Executive had it been in power over the same period. These questions were asked about six specific areas, all of which can be described as valence issues (at least in this context, given the limited policy distance between Labour and the SNP). Health, education, and law and order were covered in the pre-election survey; the remaining issues (the economy, transport and the environment) were asked about in the post-election wave. Performance was rated on a five-point scale – from 'very badly' to 'very well' – which has been collapsed into three categories to simplify the presentation (with 'don't know' responses excluded). We also

Table 4.7 *Evaluations of performance on key issues by the Scottish Executive and a hypothetical SNP-led Executive (percentage of respondents)*

	Executive 2003–7	SNP-led Executive	Executive 2003–7	SNP-led Executive	Executive 2003–7	SNP-led Executive
Pre-election survey issues	Health		Education		Law and order	
Well	33	36	36	36	24	35
Neither	27	32	32	33	36	33
Badly	39	32	32	31	40	32
Odds ratio		1.32		1.01		1.79
N	1,694	1,427	1,643	1,391	1,692	1,440
Post-election survey issues	Economy		Transport		Environment	
Well	32	37	26	37	31	37
Neither	40	22	35	31	41	34
Badly	29	41	39	32	28	29
Odds ratio		0.81		1.72		1.23
N	1,332	1,208	1,317	1,155	1,276	1,129

Sources: Pre- and post-election surveys.

report (Table 4.7) odds ratios summarising the differences between the two parties in the balance of positive and negative evaluations,[5] with ratios over 1 indicating an advantage for the SNP.

The results are rather mixed. There was considerable uncertainty in evaluating performance, especially the likely performance of an SNP-led Executive (the smaller Ns in those rows indicating much larger numbers of 'don't know' responses). There was also little agreement among the electorate as a whole about these evaluations – few entries in the table deviate far from the 33 per cent that would represent an exactly even split among the categories. On balance, however, the data in the table suggest a valence playing-field that sloped against Labour. As indicated by the odds ratios, there is a noticeable advantage for the SNP on four of the six issues, especially on law and order, which was a prominent concern among voters according to campaign polls as well as our own 'most important issue' data. The only good news for Labour was its lead on the economy, which derived partly from positive evaluations of the party's record but mainly from that being the one issue on which well over one-third of respondents thought that the SNP would have performed badly. The results suggest crime as fertile campaigning territory for the SNP, with the economy being safer ground for Labour. That said, public estimation of the economic risks posed by an SNP government will have been limited by the general perception of the economy as largely Westminster's province. Ironically, then, the Nationalists had at least one reason in 2007 to be grateful for the limits on Holyrood's financial powers.

So far the findings are in line with the previous results on 'party best to handle most important issue' (see Table 4.3). In other important respects, however, these data tell a rather different story from the earlier analysis. On health and education, Labour enjoyed moderate leads over the SNP among voters for whom these were the top priority issues. Yet among the electorate as a whole, the party's performance ratings were no better (education) or actually worse (health) than the SNP's. One interpretation is that those citing health and education as most important were already Labour partisans. If so, the apparent advantage for Labour (or at least the possibility of winning votes from the SNP) on these issues was illusory. Since the analysis in this section is based on all voters, it is the SNP's claim to a lead on health and education that looks stronger.

In addition to influencing 'most important issue' responses, partisan predispositions are also an obvious reason for the mixed picture in Table 4.7. Labour identifiers were markedly more likely to rate the Executive perform-ance favourably and to have expected little of an SNP-led Executive, while the reverse was true of SNP partisans. We do not report those results in full here since they are hardly startling and the key question – where and how do evaluations vary independent of partisan predispositions? – can be answered by comparing across issues in Table 4.7. For example, the SNP's relative strength on law and order and relative weakness on the economy cannot both be accounted for by the balance of partisan sentiment in the electorate. These reflect real differences in parties' strengths and weaknesses as perceived by Scottish voters. Moreover, because issue performance evaluations are thus at least partly independent of partisanship, they have the potential to exert a separate influence over overall impressions of the parties and, ultimately, over voting behaviour.

We now turn to those broader impressions of the performance and competence of the parties. In the pre-election survey, using a similar five-point rating scale, we asked respondents 'How good or bad a job of running Scotland do you think Labour ministers in the Scottish Executive have done in recent years?'[6] Parallel questions were then asked about Liberal Democrat ministers in the Scottish Executive and about how the UK Labour government had run Britain. The overall report for Labour in government, whether in Edinburgh or London, is not particularly favourable (Table 4.8). The standard way of calculating satisfaction ratings is to subtract negative from positive evaluations and this would give Labour ratings of −14 and −15 respectively

Table 4.8 *Evaluations of overall performance by Scottish Labour and Liberal Democrat ministers and Labour at Westminster (percentage of respondents)*

	Labour in Executive	Lib Dems in Executive	UK Labour government
Very good	3	2	5
Good	27	26	29
Neither	27	42	17
Bad	24	17	26
Very bad	20	13	23
Good–bad	−14	−2	−15
N	1,738	1,597	1,797

Source: Pre-election survey.

at these two levels. The performance of Liberal Democrat ministers in the Executive was rated somewhat more highly, with roughly equal numbers of positive and negative evaluations. These results should be accompanied by a warning – many voters in Scotland were only dimly aware that there was a coalition government at all, and the Liberal Democrats' presence in government was frequently overlooked (Johns and Carman, 2008). The markedly smaller *N* confirms that more respondents answered 'don't know' when asked about the Liberal Democrats, and the relatively large proportion opting for 'neither good nor bad' may also signal uncertainty more than ambivalence.

We should not overstate the bleakness of the picture for Labour that is painted by these data. In the first place, plenty of respondents gave the party a reasonably favourable report.[7] Second, many of the negative evaluations are likely to have been reported by supporters of the other parties and they have partisan motives for focusing on the party's failures rather than its successes in office. The converse is of course true of Labour partisans but they are clearly outnumbered by supporters of the other parties together. To substantiate these speculations, we report evaluations of Labour's performance at Holyrood and at Westminster among supporters (identifiers and leaners combined) of each of the main parties in turn, and also among non-partisans. The evaluations of this latter group really do make depressing reading for Labour (Table 4.9). Whether it was Holyrood or Westminster performance that was in question, non-partisan respondents were particularly harsh judges of Labour, with overall ratings (−32 and −34) markedly worse than those among the electorate as a whole. In this context it is easy to see why Labour struggled to win support from floating voters in 2007. Two other points are worth noting about the breakdown by party identification. First, there does seem to be a

Table 4.9 Evaluations of overall performance by Labour in Scotland and at UK level by party support (percentage of respondents)

| | Pre-election party identification | | | | | | | | | |
| | None | | Conservatives | | Labour | | Lib Dems | | SNP | |
	Scotland	UK	Scotland	UK	Scotland	UK	Scotland	UK	Scotland	UK
Very good	1	0	2	1	8	18	0	0	0	1
Good	16	21	8	10	59	62	27	23	12	13
Neither	34	24	18	8	24	11	34	24	24	17
Bad	29	31	31	32	6	7	27	36	34	38
Very bad	20	24	40	49	3	2	13	17	30	32
Good–bad	**-32**	**-34**	**-61**	**-70**	**+58**	**+71**	**-13**	**-30**	**-52**	**-56**
N	372	405	204	206	468	471	143	149	370	374

Source: Pre-election survey.

slight 'coalition bonus' for Labour, with Liberal Democrat supporters disproportionately positive about their ally's performance at Holyrood. Second, Labour owes its high overall ratings almost entirely to the 'good' rather than the 'very good' category. Remarkably few respondents, even among its own supporters, were able to deliver a resoundingly positive verdict on the party's performance, especially at Holyrood. Such lukewarm endorsement helps to explain another side of Labour's problems in 2007, namely the tendency of its own supporters not to vote or to defect to other parties.

In line with arguments in previous chapters, it is important to consider how the various issues at play in the 2007 election operated in combination and to include control variables in the analysis. There are two key questions here. First, which issues were more and which were less important? Second, did the more important issues have an *independent* impact on party choice, even controlling for the attitudes to parties and leaders analysed in the previous chapter? Logistic regression is the appropriate means of addressing both questions. In addition to party identification and leader evaluations, we include the following issue variables in the regression models: the 11-point policy position scales on taxes and spending and on crime; preferred local taxation; attitudes to the Iraq war and the replacement of Trident; and performance evaluations on the four most important valence issues – law and order, health, education and the economy. We ran two parallel analyses. In the first, as in the previous chapter, we analysed the probability of voting Labour (as opposed to any other party). In this case the performance evaluations included are retrospective evaluations of the Executive's performance. In the second analysis, we model the choice between the two leading contenders for office. The dependent variable is the probability of voting Labour as opposed to SNP (with other voters excluded) and in this case performance evaluations are measured by subtracting assessments of how well or badly the SNP would have done from evaluations of Executive performance. As before, full details of the analyses are given in Appendix 3 (Table A4.1) and we use a chart here to illustrate the key results. The issue variables are measured on different response scales and so, in order to enable more meaningful comparisons,[8] we measure the effect of a standard deviation change in each variable on the probability of a Labour vote (Figure 4.2).

Predictably, given the lack of difference between the parties, the policy scales are largely irrelevant in each case. Interestingly, the local tax effect is far stronger (and significant only) in the 'Labour versus all others' analysis, indicating that the SNP was not a particular beneficiary of antipathy to the council tax. In contrast, the effects of opinions on the Iraq and Trident issues were stronger in the 'Labour versus SNP' regression, which not only suggests that the latter profited from public opposition to Labour policies but also perhaps that those issues had a distinctively Scottish dimension. Turning to the

Figure 4.2 *Effect of issue opinions on the odds of a constituency vote for Labour versus all other parties and versus the SNP*

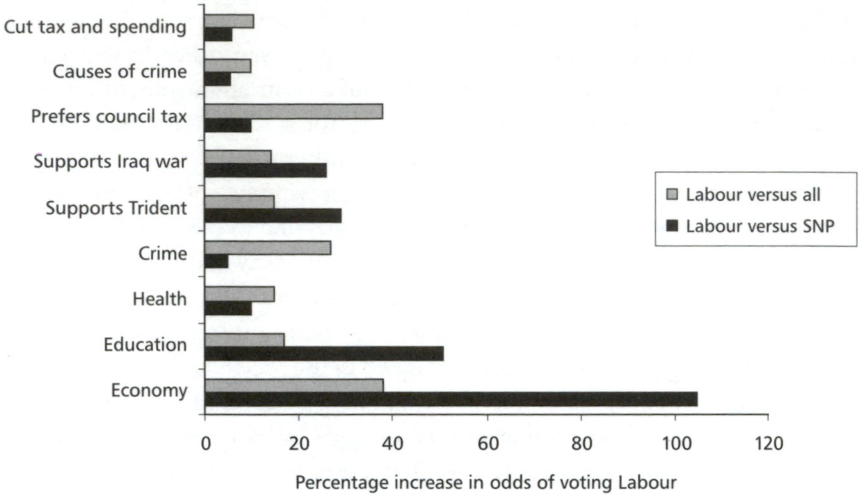

Percentage increase in odds of voting Labour

Sources: Pre- and post-election surveys.

valence issues, there is little evidence that the SNP gained from its lead over Labour on law and order, while health is perhaps surprisingly unimportant in both analyses. The really strong effects relate to education and the economy, with each of these issues proving to be a powerful influence on the choice between Labour and the SNP. The particularly striking result on the economy, coupled with the results in Table 4.7 showing Labour's lead on the issue, bolsters the suggestion that this would have been fertile campaigning territory for the party. More broadly, the analysis suggests that 2007 was largely an election about valence issues, with the council tax the most notable exception to the rule.

Conclusion

In Chapter 3 we saw that Labour held an advantage over the SNP in terms of long-term party attachments but struggled to convert these sympathies into turnout and support. In this chapter we have presented some evidence explaining why the party encountered these difficulties. Its commitment to the council tax was hugely unpopular and looks to have cost it votes. When compared directly with the SNP, Labour did not enjoy its traditional clear leads on the core public service issues of education and health, and its record on crime left voters distinctly unimpressed. The party's economic record was viewed more favourably but relatively few voters regarded this as a crucial issue. The only other bright spot for Scottish Labour was the limited collateral damage it sustained as a result of the Iraq war and the Westminster government's policy on Trident. However, given the balance of public opinion on these issues, there is little reason to suppose that they won Labour any extra votes.

Apart from local taxation (and of course the constitutional question) there were few policy differences and virtually no ideological distance between the main parties in 2007. This reinforces the importance of 'performance politics', as does the multiplicity of 'most important issues'. No campaign focused on one or two issues was going to win a broad coalition of support. A likelier route to success was to try to foster an image of general competence from which voters might then infer a party's ability to deliver on a range of issues. Here Labour might have been expected to have a clearer advantage, being an established party of government, in direct contrast to the inexperienced SNP. However, Labour's performance received at best a mixed report from voters as a whole and the key group of non-partisans was still less impressed. Crucially, their criticism was levelled as readily at the Scottish Executive as at the Westminster government. Meanwhile, the SNP's inexperience did not translate into widespread fears about its capacity to deliver on key issues. Only on the economy was mistrust the voters' typical reaction to the SNP. Labour attempted to capitalise on this in its campaigning but, as we see in the next chapter, the approach taken – to link the issue to the constitutional question and to highlight the economic risks of independence – had its risks.

Notes

1 Hence, in 1999, a voter's left–right position was not a significant predictor of either Labour versus SNP voting or of defection from a Labour vote in 1997 (Paterson *et al.*, 2001: chs 4, 8).

2 As this example indicates, our coding takes no account of the 'direction' of a respondent's opinion on an issue. The 'independence' category, therefore, includes both those keenly anticipating and those dreading that outcome.

3 This issue received intense media coverage, which may partly be explained by the understandable relief of journalists at finding an issue on which there were clear policy differences between the major parties.

4 This is based on a question asking respondents how much they agreed or disagreed with the statement 'Britain was wrong to go to war with Iraq'. Those who strongly disagreed are labelled as 'strongly in favour' of the war. With Trident, the question was 'The UK government has decided to replace Trident, Britain's nuclear weapon system, when it comes to the end of its current life. How much do you agree or disagree with this decision?'

5 For example, the ratio for health reported in Table 4.7 indicates that the odds of evaluating the SNP positively are 1.32 times the odds of evaluating Labour positively on that issue (i.e. $[35.9/32.3]/[33.3/39.4] = 1.32$).

6 Since the same Labour/Liberal Democrat coalition had been in power in both terms of the Scottish Parliament it seemed sensible to keep the wording vague. It would have been unreasonable to expect respondents to confine their verdict specifically to the 2003–7 period and unrealistic to expect only the more recent term to influence evaluations and party choice.

7 Moreover, experience has probably left voters expecting mediocrity in government performance. Hence respondents delivering a neutral or even a somewhat negative verdict on Labour's performance may not regard this as unusual and, by extension, they may also doubt that another party would have done better.

8 In order to maintain a clean comparison, we also include effects that were not statistically significant. Rigid application of, say, a $p < 0.05$ significance level would overstate the difference between two issues for which the coefficients fell just either side of that yardstick.

5
The Scottish dimension

At the institutional level, Scottish politics has always been different. Since 1885 there has been a Scottish (now Scotland) Office in Whitehall and special parliamentary procedures grew up alongside distinct governmental institutions for Scotland. The structure of local government is different. Additionally, the Scottish economy, housing market and religious and social structure have differed from those of the rest of the UK. These differences – and their attendant public policy implications – have given rise to distinctive patterns of political behaviour and have meant that many issues common to the different parts of the UK have long had a specifically Scottish aspect. Since every region of the UK is distinct in some way, this might have been unremarkable but for the fact that there is a strong and distinct Scottish national identity. More important for political behaviour than separate institutions has been the perception of difference. Integration and assimilation were often resisted, most voters instead demanding the protection of Scotland's distinctive status and interests. The extent to which the Scottish dimension assumed a positive valence status in Scottish politics is rarely remarked upon, yet it is one of the most enduring and pervasive aspects of UK politics. Over the course of the twentieth century, political parties came to understand that success in elections demanded paying heed to the 'Scottish dimension'.

As the inverted commas imply, this dimension is contextual and mutable. There has been one constant, however, in that opposition parties throughout the last century criticised the governing party for failing to take it into account, only to face the same criticism themselves when in office. In this respect the Scottish dimension more closely resembles a valence than a position issue (see Chapter 4), being ultimately a matter of whether parties can deliver agreed outcomes. No party departs from the consensus that Scottish interests should be protected and furthered. The question for voters in Scotland – whether at Scottish Parliament or UK general elections – is about which party is best placed to address those interests (Miller, 1981: 258–9; Bennie et al., 1997: ch. 10; Brown et al., 1999: 157–8; Paterson et al., 2001: 40–1). Any party perceived as acting against Scottish interests will suffer in electoral terms, as the Conservatives found from 1979 onwards. Of course, the question of how Scottish interests are best served is strongly linked to the constitutional question. The relationship between the key position issue of Scotland's constitutional status and the key valence issue of serving Scottish interests needs to be explored. The 2007 election reinforced two important features of this relationship. First, voters need not endorse a party's constitutional position in order to acknowledge its commitment to Scottish interests. Second, a party's discourse on the constitutional question may convey signals – positive or negative – to voters about that party's commitment to Scottish interests. Together, these two points go a long way to explaining how the SNP was able to defeat Labour in 2007.

National identity

Before considering Scotland's constitutional status, we have to acknowledge the prior existence of something distinctive about politics north of the border. It is worth stressing that this distinctiveness operates at the level of perceptions. The extent to which Scottish political institutions and public policies were actually different from those elsewhere is open to interpretation. Nevertheless, they contributed to a sense of separateness that provided the basis for a national political identity and in turn fed into demands for constitutional change. In other words, national identity preceded political nationalism in Scotland, rather than the other way around, as has been understood by many scholars of nationalism (Breuilly, 1993; Schulze, 1994). Demands for some level of autonomy and for distinct Scottish institutions are predicated on the existence of a sense of Scottish national identity (and in turn those institutions reinforce the sense of being Scottish). It follows that the strength of national identity is an important determinant of the potency of demands for autonomy.

There are, however, countervailing forces encouraging greater unity, even assimilation, within the UK as a whole. Caramani (2004: 1) has described in the European context the 'major long-term phenomenon over almost two centuries' of the 'nationalization processes' through which 'highly localized and territorialized politics that characterized the early phases of electoral alignments' result in the disappearance of 'peripheral and regional specificities'. Certain public policies and the welfare state were also thought to integrate the components of the UK. The shared experience of war was thought relevant, as was the existence of a British common market (Mitchell, 1996: 43–57). The evidence of Scottish institutions reinforcing Scottish national identity has to be set against the evidence of British and UK institutions reinforcing a British identity. Meanwhile, class politics was also thought to encourage integration, by leading voters to identify with fellow members of the same class elsewhere in the UK rather than with those of different classes within their nation.

This was true as long as class remained important and there was intra-class cohesion. However, the decline of class voting in Britain (Franklin, 1985) opened up opportunities for alternative types of politics, including those based on territory. Among others, Keating (1988) noted the continuing importance of the territorial dimension of politics and challenged the assumption that integration was inevitable. From the 1960s, the peripheries across many European states revolted against the centre, for a variety of reasons, including the incomplete nature of nation-building at state level, the development of distinct economic interests among key groups and an enduring sense of identity stimulated by cultural revivals. All three elements are relevant to understanding the politics of national identity in Scotland and the diverse bases of Scottish national identity meant that it could be mobilised either by existing British-wide parties or by nationalist parties.

The heterogeneous nature of national identity serves as a reminder that it does not operate in isolation but alongside other identities, which may undermine or reinforce it. Hence it does not follow that those groups in society that make Scotland most distinct are among the most Scottish, either in their national identity or in their constitutional preference. Presbyterianism, for example, remains a distinguishing feature of Scottish society and Presbyterians

Table 5.1 *National identity by religion, class and sex (percentage of respondents)*

	Religion			Subjective class		Sex	
	None	Church of Scotland	Catholic	Working	Middle	Male	Female
Scottish not British	29	24	29	30	20	26	28
More Scottish than British	32	37	35	32	33	30	33
Equally Scottish and British	26	34	23	26	30	28	28
More British than Scottish	5	4	6	4	8	7	5
British not Scottish	9	1	7	8	9	9	7
N	797	312	145	804	522	685	721

Source: Pre- and post-election surveys.

have a strong sense of being Scottish. They have not been the strongest advocates of home rule or independence, however, and have not supported the SNP to the extent that might be expected if there were a close association between nationalism and Scotland's established church (Miller, 1981: 146). As seen in Chapter 2, the relationship between religion and party choice has weakened considerably over time and religious differences in national identity are also slender. SES respondents were asked to place themselves on a spectrum ranging from 'Scottish not British' through to 'British not Scottish'. As Table 5.1 shows, Church of Scotland adherents were more likely to choose 'equally Scottish and British' than other groups but the overall leaning towards 'Scottishness' over 'Britishness' is equally clear in all three religious categories.[1]

Social class is also closely linked to national identity in Scotland. Here we focus on subjective class – the class people think they belong to – consistent with both the focus on identity and the fact that subjective class has proved a stronger influence on voting behaviour than objective class. For some time in Scotland, objectively middle-class people have been more likely than their counterparts in England to identify subjectively with the working class, which has disadvantaged parties with a more middle-class appeal (Bennie *et al.*, 1997: 101–4). This difference itself tied in with national identity and, in particular, with a growing alignment of Scottish and working-class identity during the 1980s, when the Conservatives were in power in London. However, the subsequent depolarising of left–right politics and the election of a Labour government at Westminster loosened the connection between class and national identity. The 2007 data show that working-class voters remained more likely to report an exclusively Scottish identity but the differences were narrower than in the past. Political changes have been reflected in the politics of Scottish national identity.

In Chapter 2 we noted that the SNP was especially popular among male voters in 2007, as in most previous elections. One conceivable explanation is that Scottish national identity has a greater appeal for men, not least because of its associations with sport (football and rugby, for example). The evidence here contradicts that possibility. If anything, men's identities are more British than are those of women (though the differences are small). The SNP's particular appeal to men – or problems in attracting support from women – must have some other basis. Overall, our figures replicate the general pattern – notably consistent across social groups – of a clear leaning towards Scottish identification, with few people reporting a predominantly British identity.[2] Nonetheless, only around a quarter of respondents disclaimed British identity altogether.

There was a clear association between national identity and party choice in 2007 (Table 5.2). Not surprisingly, the SNP did best at the Scottish end of the spectrum, while the Conservatives – and, in a more recent development, the Liberal Democrats – polled relatively well at the British end. At least in the

Table 5.2 *Party choice (regional list) by national identity (percentage of respondents)*

Party choice	Scottish not British	More Scottish than British	Equally Scottish and British	More British than Scottish	British not Scottish
Conservative	3	8	19	33	31
Labour	21	31	39	38	18
Lib Dem	5	10	14	11	23
SNP	60	34	16	6	8
Others	11	17	13	12	19
N	283	338	327	66	83

Source: Post-election survey.

case of the SNP and the Conservatives, these are long-established tendencies reflecting the nature of those parties' core support. However, most voters have both Scottish and British identities and it is this middle ground that is crucial in determining the outcome of Scottish elections. In 2007, the SNP polled slightly more strongly than Labour among those who described themselves as 'more Scottish than British' but was a long way back among the (almost as large) group of 'equally Scottish and British' voters. In an echo of the discussion in Chapter 2, the relationship between national identity and SNP support in 2007 was very similar to the pattern in previous elections (e.g. Bennie *et al.*, 1997: 105; Paterson, 2006). The distinctive feature is that the party's vote increased in all categories. Given that neither the extent of Scottish identity nor its relationship with party choice has changed much over recent years, national identity is another factor to which the steep increase in the SNP's vote cannot plausibly be attributed.

Constitutional preferences

In some cases the link between national identity and party choice may be simple and direct: those who feel Scottish vote for a more obviously Scottish party. Another plausible explanation, however, is that the link is indirect and runs via constitutional preferences. Those who feel Scottish are more likely to favour greater autonomy and vote for parties which share that preference; those who feel British favour the Union and, in turn, a unionist party. In this section we investigate both links in that chain: from national identity to constitutional preferences and from constitutional preferences to vote. For a measure of constitutional preferences, we rely mainly on a question asking respondents how they would vote in a hypothetical referendum offering three options: keep the Scottish Parliament with its existing powers ('status quo'); keep the Scottish Parliament but give it greater powers ('more powers'); make Scotland an independent state ('independence'). This question more closely reflects the reality of today's constitutional politics than the long-running five-option question that also includes abolition of the Scottish Parliament and independence outside the European Union (neither of which was proposed by any major party in 2007 – see Chapter 1). However, we do draw on the latter question for comparisons over time and in later analyses of party choice (since support for the Conservatives may still derive partly from the small group of voters favouring a return to pre-devolution arrangements).

Overall, a clear plurality of respondents wanted further devolution. Almost twice as many (45 per cent) chose this option as opted for independence (23 per cent), while 32 per cent endorsed the status quo.[3] This immediately belies any characterisation of the 2007 election as a straightforward vote for independence. The proportion of voters for whom independence is the consti- tutional first choice is not large enough to have carried the SNP to victory and, in any case, had not risen perceptibly since 2003, when the Nationalist vote was far smaller (see Park and McCrone, 2006). As we show below, the SNP's success was owed in large part to voters who did not support independence.

The breakdown by national identity shows a clear relationship in the expected direction (Table 5.3). Independence was preferred by 54 per cent of 'Scottish not British' respondents, but by just 3 per cent of those with a predominantly British identity. Likewise, support for the status quo was far stronger at the British end of the spectrum. It should be noted, however, that this is far from a deterministic relationship. Almost half of the purely Scottish identifiers chose an option other than independence and large minorities of

Table 5.3 *Constitutional preference by national identity (percentage of respondents)*

Preference	Scottish not British	More Scottish than British	Equally Scottish and British	More British than Scottish	British not Scottish
Status quo	10	21	48	63	59
More powers	36	54	45	34	38
Independence	54	25	7	3	3
N	321	408	347	68	103

Source: Post-election survey.

predominantly British identifiers would like to see further devolution from Westminster. Indeed, the 'more powers' option proved relatively popular in all categories, suggesting that its appeal had little to do with national identity.

A simple and plausible explanation for this is that voters simply regarded further devolution as likely to deliver desired policy outcomes. Thus, there is a valence flavour to constitutional preferences. They reflect not only national identity but also assessments of the constitutional arrangements under which Scotland can be most effectively governed. Hence many of those who voted for devolution in the 1997 referendum were not strong Scottish identifiers but nonetheless had positive expectations of the performance of the new Parliament (Brown *et al.*, 1999: ch. 6; Denver *et al.*, 2000: 159–68; Paterson *et al.*, 2001: 112–13). More recently, Surridge (2006) reported that attitudes to the Union and to independence remained strongly influenced by valence considerations, such as the current system's capacity to deliver economic benefits. As Brown *et al.* (1999: 162) put it, 'Scots do not distinguish fundamentally between judging the effectiveness of policy and assessing the adequacy of the constitutional framework through which policy is made'. This divergence of national identity and constitutional preference means that both could independently affect party choice – voters may choose the 'wrong' party in terms of their national identity if they approve of its policy on the constitutional issue.

There are two ways of looking at the relationship between constitutional preferences and party choice: first, assessing how voters supporting the different parties split in terms of constitutional preferences; second, assessing how respondents favouring the different constitutional options split between the parties. Both convey useful information about the 2007 election. Table 5.4 shows the preferences of those voting for the four main parties and reveals a definite tendency for voters to favour the option advocated by their chosen party. It remains, however, a 'tendency'. More than a third of SNP voters wanted more powers rather than independence and around half of Labour

Table 5.4 *Constitutional preference by party choice (regional list) (percentage of respondents)*

Preference	Conservative	Labour	Lib Dem	SNP
Status quo	73	47	37	5
More powers	24	49	59	37
Independence	3	4	4	59
N	149	308	120	345

Source: Post-election survey.

Table 5.5 *Party choice (regional list) by constitutional preference*
(percentage of respondents)

	Status quo	*More powers*	*Independence*
Conservatives	31	8	2
Labour	41	32	5
Lib Dems	12	15	2
SNP	5	27	83
Others	12	18	8
N	*356*	*470*	*244*

Source: Post-election survey.

voters preferred more powers rather than the status quo defended by the party in its 2007 campaign. The Liberal Democrats, who actually did propose more powers, carried only around three in five of their voters with them, while insofar as the Conservatives were at least countenancing further devolution they were going against the wishes of the large majority of their supporters.

These data suggest, then, that the relationship between constitutional preference and party choice is far from perfect. It is also apparently asymmetric, in that an option like 'more powers' draws support from voters of all parties, while independence was favoured almost exclusively by SNP voters in 2007. These arguments are reinforced by Table 5.5, which shows the vote choices of those with different constitutional preferences. The overwhelming majority of independence supporters voted for the SNP (and those who did not usually supported one of the smaller left parties). However, those preferring the other two constitutional options were much more heterogeneous in their voting behaviour. Labour was the plurality choice in both cases but did not approach the dominance of the SNP among independence supporters. Indeed, among those wanting 'more powers' – the largest group – Labour was only five points ahead of the SNP. The latter's victory, then, was based not only on its dominance among independence supporters but also on its ability to win substantial support from voters opposed to independence.

Comparing these data with those from previous elections gives a clear picture of what was different about 2007.[4] In Table 5.6 we focus on the two leading parties and support for independence, and again describe the relationship in the two ways discussed above. Until 2007, the proportions of Labour and SNP voters supporting independence tended to move together, reflecting more general fluctuations in the popularity of the policy. Before 2007, the low point in both parties was in 1979, following the failed referendum, but

Table 5.6 *Support for independence and voting for Labour and the SNP,*
1974–2007

	1974	1979	1992	1999	2003	2007
% supporting independence among:						
Labour voters	17	8	20	16	16	6
N	303	222	294	419	292	363
SNP voters	48	33	57	56	59	69
N	225	91	188	304	197	391
% of independence supporters voting:						
Labour	28	29	31	25	22	6
SNP	59	49	56	62	55	80
N	179	61	183	277	211	377

Sources: 1974, 1979 and 1992 SES surveys; 1999 and 2003 SSA surveys;
2007 post-election survey.

support for independence in both parties had increased by 1992, after 13 years
of Conservative government. In 2007, however, the two diverged markedly.
The hitherto substantial minority of Labour voters favouring independence
dwindled to just 6 per cent, whereas an unusually large proportion of SNP
voters did so. The contrast between 2007 and previous elections is even more
striking when we look in the lower panel of the table, which shows the vote
choices of independence supporters. Whereas Labour had typically received
support from around a quarter of this group, in 2007 the proportion plum-
meted to 6 per cent and the SNP was evidently the principal beneficiary. The
SNP's share of the 'independence vote', which had not previously surpassed
62 per cent, rose 25 points, to 80 per cent, between 2003 and 2007.

Taken out of context, that steep increase might easily be construed as
indicating that the SNP placed particular emphasis on independence in 2007
and was hence able to win particularly strong support among voters favouring
the policy. Yet, as discussed in the opening chapter, in its 2007 campaign the
SNP did not take an especially strong pro-independence line or give more
than usual prominence to the policy. The commitment to a later referendum
as opposed to immediate moves towards independence made it easier for
voters to support the SNP even if they were unconvinced about independence.
The data in this chapter confirm the point: as Tables 5.4 and 5.6 both show,
a substantial minority of those who voted SNP in 2007 did not support
independence. It is unlikely that these voters would have responded to an
appeal strongly focused on independence. Rather, they were won over by

other aspects of what the SNP was offering in 2007, notably its perceived competence to govern under the current constitutional arrangements. To some extent, this is unconnected to the Scottish dimension *per se*; on the basis of the general valence yardsticks of performance and delivery, on the whole, the SNP was judged favourably by voters. There is a more specifically Scottish aspect to the argument, however. The SNP persuaded enough voters not only that the party could be trusted to govern but that it would govern in Scotland's interests. We turn to that important point next.

Looking after 'Scottish interests'

As shown in Table 5.6, ever since its emergence as a serious contender in elections, the SNP has shown the potential to win votes well beyond its core constituency of independence supporters. The party's major breakthrough in the early 1970s was driven less by a sudden surge in nationalist spirit and more by a feeling that Westminster rule was failing to defend Scotland's material interests, in particular with regard to North Sea oil. Reporting on a 1974 survey, Miller found that the 'overwhelming majority of Scottish electors felt the SNP's existence and electoral successes had been "good for Scotland"' (Miller, 1981: 92). Three-quarters of Labour and Conservative voters agreed, highlighting the point that the Scottish dimension goes well beyond party identities. Since then, many studies have emphasised the electoral importance of parties being seen to support Scotland's interests (Bennie *et al.*, 1997: ch. 10; Brown *et al.*, 1999: 157–8; Paterson *et al.*, 2001: 40–1). Given the history and purpose of the SNP, we would expect it to score well on this criterion. Perhaps the more pertinent question concerns how the other parties are thought to cater for Scottish interests, not least because they are

Table 5.7 *Perceptions of how closely the major parties look after Scottish interests (percentage of respondents)*

	Conservatives	Labour	Lib Dems	SNP
Very closely	3	9	6	37
Fairly closely	21	41	49	37
Not very closely	38	31	33	15
Not at all closely	34	19	12	11
N	1,353	1,377	1,333	1,353

Source: Post-election survey.

Table 5.8 *Mean party ratings on Scottish interests by party identification and constitutional preference*

	Conservatives	Labour	Lib Dems	SNP	N (min.)
Party identification					
Conservatives	1.9	1.0	1.3	1.6	160
Labour	0.8	2.0	1.6	1.7	345
Lib Dems	0.8	1.5	2.2	2.0	123
SNP	0.8	1.0	1.4	2.7	293
None	1.0	1.3	1.4	2.0	601
Constitutional preference					
Status quo	1.3	1.6	1.5	1.5	384
More powers	0.9	1.6	1.6	2.1	503
Independence	0.7	0.9	1.2	2.6	333

Sources: Pre- and post-election surveys.

all branches of – or at least closely associated with – British parties. Specifying that we were asking about the parties in Scotland, we asked respondents 'How closely do you think each of these parties looks after the interests of Scottish people in general?' As anticipated, the SNP had a clear advantage in this respect (Table 5.7). More than a third of respondents described the party as looking after Scottish interests 'very closely', while the corresponding percentages for the other parties were all in single figures. Labour was well adrift of its main rival and, indeed, even a little behind the Liberal Democrats when 'very closely' and 'fairly closely' are combined. Half of SES respondents described Labour in Scotland as looking after Scottish interests either 'not very' or 'not at all' closely. This leaves Labour with a pattern of responses more resembling that of the Conservatives – a party criticised as anti-Scottish (Mitchell and Bennie, 1995) – than that of the SNP.

Of course, these ratings are likely to be biased by partisanship and also strongly influenced by constitutional preferences. For example, respondents who evaluated the SNP less favourably are likely to be those most firmly convinced that independence would not be in Scotland's interests. In Table 5.8, therefore, we relate the perceptions of the parties to party identification and constitutional preference. To simplify matters, we show the mean rating on looking after Scottish interests for each party, based on a scale from 0 ('not at all closely') to 3 ('very closely'). Predictably, each party's identifiers see their own party as looking after Scottish interests better than any other. More strikingly, identifiers with all three other major parties rated the SNP second behind their own party and in none of these cases was it a distant second.

In other words, the SNP's claims to look after Scottish interests are at least grudgingly acknowledged even by those with a partisan incentive to dispute them. Moreover, the party had a clear lead on this front among those not identifying with a party.

There is a pronounced asymmetry in the relationship between the ratings and constitutional preference which works to the SNP's advantage. Not surprisingly, the SNP was rated much more highly than the other parties by those who favoured independence. In contrast, Labour's lead (over all of the other parties, including the SNP) was only marginal among those against any further constitutional change. Among the largest group, those wanting more powers, the SNP was comfortably ahead of both Labour and the Liberal Democrats. Clearly, although these ratings are influenced by constitutional preferences, the SNP is generally perceived to be a party particularly concerned with Scottish interests.

It might reasonably be wondered how voters determine whether a party 'looks after Scottish interests', given that it is a broad and rather vague notion. Vagueness does not mean unimportance, however. As noted in earlier chapters, many voters are relatively uninterested in and uninformed about the detail of policy, relying instead on broad impressions of the parties when choosing at election time. A party's perceived general concern for Scotland's interests is precisely the kind of impression that could swing voters' decisions for or against it. Since it remains an abstract and general notion, however, voters will rely on more concrete and specific cues in order to estimate whether parties are willing and able to stand up for Scotland. One such cue might be the parties' constitutional stances.

It is widely agreed that the Conservatives' unpopularity in Scotland since the 1980s derived in part from their opposition to devolution, not just because the majority of voters disagreed but also because it made the Conservatives appear anti-Scottish (Mitchell, 1990; Brown *et al.*, 1999: 89–90). Along similar lines, Paterson *et al.* (2001: 41) argue that 'the principal reason for Labour's "under-performance" in the first Scottish [Parliament] election was that it was not thought sufficiently capable of standing up for Scotland's interests within the Union' (see also Brown *et al.*, 1999: 110). It is conceivable, therefore, that Labour's opposition – in 2007 at least – to further devolution might have led voters to doubt the party's commitment to Scottish interests. In effect, there may be a general tendency among Scottish voters to associate a party's desire for greater autonomy for Scotland with a concern for Scottish interests. To test that supposition, we calculated correlations between voters' ratings of parties on Scottish interests with their perceptions of the party's constitutional stance (on the 0–10 abolition to independence scale described in the previous chapter). A positive relationship supports our suggestion that

Table 5.9 *Correlations between parties' perceived constitutional stances and perceived commitment to Scottish interests*

	Conservatives	Labour	Lib Dems	SNP	N (min.)
All voters	**0.09**	**0.19**	**0.19**	**0.16**	*1,333*
By constitutional preference					
Status quo	−0.04	**0.08**	**0.17**	0.06	*384*
More powers	**0.13**	**0.23**	**0.18**	**0.18**	*533*
Independence	**0.18**	**0.19**	0.06	**0.12**	*303*

Note: Correlations significant at the $p<0.05$ level are in bold.
Sources: Pre- and post-election surveys.

a party's support for autonomy persuades voters of its commitment to Scottish interests. In Table 5.9, the coefficients are shown for the full sample and also for each category of constitutional preference.

All but one of the correlations is positive and most are statistically significant. On the whole, then, parties seen as reluctant to grant more powers to Scotland are also less likely to be seen as looking after Scottish interests. The fact that voters were prone to read a lukewarm commitment to Scottish interests from the party's 2007 constitutional stance will probably have been costly to Labour's image, especially among voters favouring more powers but not independence. This is not only the largest group but also probably contains many of those people for whom general impressions are more important than specific constitutional positions. The correlations are also positive in the SNP analyses – the closer voters placed it towards the independence pole, the more likely they were to credit it with looking after Scottish interests. For the most part, the SNP's reputation for standing up for Scotland is likely to have more to do with its broader history and purpose than with its specific constitutional stances at a given election. Nonetheless, there is at least some evidence here that a clear pro-independence position helps to win the party wider support by convincing voters of its commitment to the national interest.

It is counter-intuitive to suggest that voters who do not themselves support independence would reward a party for advocating precisely that option. On the other hand, as the recent history of Scottish politics attests, a strong SNP performance on a platform of independence seems the scenario most likely to produce further devolution short of independence – the most popular preference among voters. For many of these, it can make sense to vote SNP provided that they see a Nationalist victory as more likely to deliver extra devolved powers rather than independence itself. In this respect, the SNP's promise of a referendum was important. Not only would this have improved the party's reputation for moderation and hence reduced the perceived risk of an SNP vote but also there was the possibility of a 'more powers' option in the proposed referendum. Voters favouring further devolution could, therefore, have cast an instrumental vote for the SNP. Evidence for this interpretation comes from the fact that those favouring 'more powers' were found to split two to one in favour of a referendum on independence, as promised by the SNP and opposed by Labour.

Party choice and the Scottish dimension

Finally in this chapter, we provide a more detailed analysis of the impact on voting behaviour in 2007 of national identity, constitutional preference and the parties' perceived commitment to Scottish interests. Considered separately, each is quite closely related to party choice. Yet they are also related to one another. In order to identify the independent impact of these variables, therefore, we need to analyse them simultaneously and also to control for background factors – most notably party identification – that could also be involved in the complicated relationships discussed in this chapter. As before, the appropriate analytical technique is logistic regression and so we continue to build on the model discussed at the end of the previous chapter. That model contained party identification, leader evaluations and issue opinions as predictor variables, to which are now added national identity, constitutional preferences and the perceived commitment of each party to Scottish interests.

In Chapter 4, on policies and performance, our main concern was with the two leading contenders for government but here we need to broaden the analysis to all four major parties and so we report four logistic regressions, one for each party.[5] In each case, we are measuring how various factors influence the likelihood of a voter choosing one party as opposed to any of the others. Put another way, we are identifying the factors that distinguish each party's support. As usual, the full results are presented in Appendix 3 (Table A5.1), while the key points are highlighted here. In order to simplify the presentation, there are separate charts for national identity, constitutional preferences and the perceived commitment of the different parties to Scottish interests.[6] The scale used in each figure is the same, meaning that the impact of each type of variable can be compared across charts.

We begin with national identity.[7] The results defy simple summary and perhaps expectations too. Holding other variables constant, Labour was likelier to win support at the Scottish end of the spectrum (Figure 5.1). More predictably, the reverse was true for the Conservatives, except that they proved

Figure 5.1 *Effect of national identity on the odds of voting for each party*

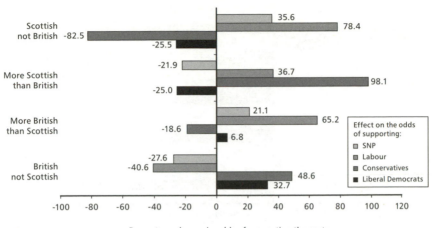

Percentage change in odds of supporting the party

Sources: Pre- and post-election surveys.

surprisingly popular with respondents describing themselves as 'more Scottish than British'. For the Liberal Democrats, national identity looks largely irrelevant: the party's support had a British tinge, but no more. Most strikingly of all, national identity exerted only a very weak independent effect on SNP voting: the odds of supporting the SNP differed little across the categories.

The key to understanding that counter-intuitive finding lies in the phrase 'holding other variables constant'. Scottish identity tends not to be a sufficient condition for SNP voting: insofar as Scottish identifiers vote for the SNP, this is more likely to be because they endorse its policy of independence or its commitment to Scottish interests. Conversely, many Scottish identifiers support other parties, one obvious reason being that they do not favour independence. This suggests that constitutional preference is a more powerful influence on party choice (Figure 5.2). Moreover, the patterns are rather more predictable than with national identity. Supporters of independence were a great deal more likely to vote SNP and rather less likely to support either Labour or the Conservatives. Those who favoured 'more powers' were especially likely to vote Liberal Democrat, in line with that party's prominent support for that option. However, Labour (and even to some extent the Conservatives) also won support from these voters, reflecting the size and heterogeneity of the 'more powers' group. In contrast, Labour did not win disproportionate support from those favouring the status quo, even though this was the party's position in

Figure 5.2 *Effect of constitutional preference on the odds of voting for each party*

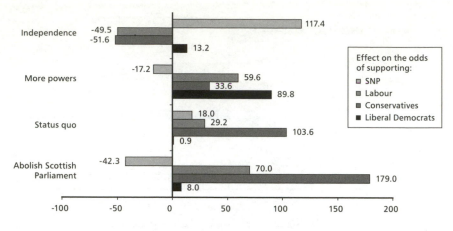

Percentage change in odds of supporting the party

Sources: Pre- and post-election surveys.

Figure 5.3 *Effect of perceptions of commitment to Scottish interests on the odds of voting for each party*

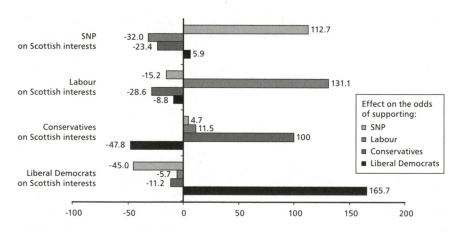

Percentage change in odds of supporting the party

Sources: Pre- and post-election surveys.

2007. It was the Conservatives who proved more popular among this group and, especially, among the (small) number of voters who would rather see a return to pre-devolution arrangements. Noticeably, however, Labour actually polled quite well in that group too, reinforcing the idea that in 2007 both parties were associated with a sceptical position on further devolution.

One striking aspect of these results is that the SNP was not heavily penalised for its pro-independence position by those favouring 'more powers' or even the status quo. Voters in neither of these groups were particularly unwilling to vote SNP. One plausible reason could be the earlier finding that supporters of all constitutional options were ready to acknowledge that party's commitment to Scottish interests. This presupposes that such a commitment is a vote winner, a point resoundingly confirmed here. Voters who regard a party as looking after Scottish interests were far more likely to support it, even after taking account of constitutional preferences and national identity as well as partisanship and a host of other variables (Figure 5.3).[8] This held true for all parties. Since the SNP was much more often credited with concern for Scottish interests, this translates into a major electoral advantage for the party. The only other point to note about Figure 5.3 is an interesting variation in the impact of these perceptions on other parties. The common view that the SNP was especially concerned with Scottish interests seems to have damaged Labour in particular. Yet the next cluster of bars shows that it was the Conservatives whose support was more affected by perceptions of Labour on this front. For some voters, then, a decision between the two leading Westminster parties looks to have been influenced by views about Labour's concern for Scottish interests. Meanwhile, the Liberal Democrats were the principal beneficiaries from widespread scepticism about Conservative commitment to Scotland. Finally, those assessing the Liberal Democrats' commitment appear to have regarded the SNP as the main alternative. These differences give an interesting insight into the different battlegrounds within the Scottish party system.

Conclusion

A central purpose of this book is to explain why a nationalist party won an election. Yet our account ends up relying surprisingly little on factors, such as national identity and constitutional preferences, that are most immediately associated with Scottish nationalism. There was no dramatic increase in Scottish national identity or of support for independence in 2007. The SNP did poll unusually heavily among those favouring independence, but, counter-intuitive as it may seem, that had little to do with constitutional politics. This is best shown by changing the question from 'why did so many independence

supporters vote SNP in 2007?' to 'why did so few do so in previous elections?'
The most plausible answer is that the SNP was not previously seen as a reasonably competent, moderate and united party willing and able to govern Scotland
under the given constitutional arrangements (and, of course, in UK general
elections the party was not a contender for government anyway). By 2007, the
party had improved its image sufficiently to claim the support of voters who, in
terms of constitutional preferences, should have been its natural constituency
anyway. That same improvement in the SNP's image, in particular its enhanced
credibility as a potential party of government, can explain why the party also
polled relatively strongly among the large numbers of 'more powers' voters
(who were probably less preoccupied by the constitutional question).

None of this is to argue that the Scottish dimension was irrelevant in
2007. As Miller (1981) demonstrated some 30 years ago, there is much more
to it than national identity or Scotland's constitutional status. One of the key
reasons why the SNP's vote outstrips support for its independence policy is
that it is widely seen as a party that promotes Scottish interests. Even before
devolution, parties in Scotland suffered if they were deemed to be anti-Scottish
in some way. In the context of an election to the Scottish Parliament, this
becomes especially important and perceptions of the parties' commitment to
Scottish interests proved a very powerful influence on party choice in 2007
(even controlling for a wide range of other factors). This will have worked to
Labour's considerable disadvantage in 2007, because the party trailed a long
way behind the SNP in the 'Scottish interests' stakes. That gap, combined
with the importance of the variable, is in itself enough to explain the election
outcome, given the narrow margin of SNP victory.

The vagueness of 'Scottish interests' makes it a malleable and contextual
concept. What it means to 'look after Scottish interests' will vary across individuals, across parties and over time. Indeed, Labour's poor ratings on Scottish
interests represented a sharp decline compared even with quite recent surveys
(Surridge, 2004) and the reasons for this decline are plainly worth investigating. The analysis in this chapter points to one noteworthy factor, namely that
Labour was the least willing of the four main parties to countenance further
devolution of powers to Scotland. Constitutional policy appears to send a
signal to voters about a party's commitment to Scottish interests. The campaign prominence of the constitutional question, coupled with the shortage
of other major ideological or issue differences between Labour and the SNP,
meant that one of Labour's most visible policy stances tended to magnify its
disadvantage in terms of Scottish interests. Another factor that may have dented
Labour's credentials in that respect is the party's long period in government
at Westminster and, more specifically, a perception that the UK government
had failed to govern in Scotland's interests. In the next chapter we consider

how much Labour in Scotland was tarred by that brush and, more generally, whether voters in 2007 were motivated by Scottish or British matters.

Notes

1 Unsurprisingly, British identity was much stronger among those identifying as Anglicans, although the numbers involved are small and hence this and other smaller religious categories are omitted from the table.
2 Given these results, it is little surprise that the idea of British 'nation-building' has become increasingly prominent in political discourse in Scotland. Gordon Brown literally flies the Union Flag outside his Fife home.
3 We also included a question about likely vote in a two-option referendum: status quo or independence. Respondents split almost exactly 2:1 in favour of the status quo.
4 For this analysis we use the five-option constitutional preference question and constituency voting in order to maintain comparability with previous surveys and with UK general elections. Hence the figures for 2007 vary slightly from those in the previous tables.
5 Multinomial logistic regression allows for simultaneous consideration of all the parties, and is therefore, strictly speaking, more appropriate for this kind of analysis. However, the repeated binomial approach taken here delivers very similar substantive results and is a good deal simpler to explain and to illustrate.
6 As previously, in order to maintain clean comparisons, we include all effects in the graphs, including some that were not statistically significant. The SES sample contained relatively few Conservative and Liberal Democrat voters, and strict application of the $p < 0.05$ criterion would very probably mean that substantively relevant differences were ignored. Significance levels can be checked in Appendix 3. To maximise sample size, we run these analyses on the constituency vote (in which most voters were obliged to choose one of the main parties).
7 As described in Appendix 3, logistic regression requires that one category of such variables be taken as the 'reference category', that is, as a comparison point. Here we select 'Scottish and British equally', the middle point, as that category. On the constitutional preference question, there were sufficient 'don't knows' for that to be used as the reference point.
8 Since the 'Scottish interests' variables were measured using a four-point scale rather than separate categories, the graph here shows the effect of moving one point along that scale on the probability of voting for each party. Consider two voters, one believing that the Liberal Democrats look after Scottish interests 'fairly closely', the other answering 'not very closely' to that same question. The odds of the former voter choosing the Liberal Democrats are more than 150 per cent greater than the odds of the latter voter doing so.

6

'Scottish not British'?
The election in multi-level context

Introducing the first legislative programme of the Scottish Parliament in June 1999, the then First Minister, Donald Dewar, described each measure in turn as 'a Scottish solution to a distinct Scottish need' (Scottish Executive, 1999). Evidently, if devolution is to achieve this ambition then the devolved institutions need sufficient powers to address these various needs. It is also important that voters have Scottish needs in mind when choosing MSPs to provide the solutions. If Scottish Parliament elections are used as opportunities to pass judgement on politics at Westminster or to express a preference on Scotland's constitutional future rather than on who should govern under the present arrangements, then the lines of electoral accountability are broken. Since voters' attention would be elsewhere, the outgoing Scottish government would not have been held responsible for its policies or performance. And the incoming government would owe victory not to its manifesto or policies but to the current popularity of the parties in a UK context. For these reasons, the question of whether 2007 was really a 'Scottish' election is more than a matter of academic or journalistic curiosity. In this chapter we address the question from a variety of angles, beginning with a discussion of the notion of 'second-order' elections.

Second-order elections and the Scottish Parliament

Background

It has long been obvious that some elections are more important to the electorate than others but the distinction between first- and second-order elections was first elaborated in a landmark article by Reif and Schmitt (1980). Each country, they suggest, has only one first-order election: the 'general' election to its dominant national legislative chamber. All other elections – municipal, regional, upper house, European and so on – are second-order elections. The crux of Reif and Schmitt's argument is that, because voters perceive less to be at stake in these second-order elections, their decisions are driven by factors inhering in the more important first-order arena. In the first place, they are less likely to vote at all in second-order elections, since it is thought that it will not make much difference whoever wins the election. If they do turn out, voters take the chance to have a mid-term say on the performance of the national government and this typically results in a poor showing for parties in office. Second-order elections also tend to see greater support for small parties, such as environmental or extreme right parties. This may be because voters really support these parties or simply because they want to 'send a message' to the mainstream parties (especially the party in government). Either way, voters can more easily afford to vote for small parties than in a first-order election, when, with more at stake, the opportunity cost of doing so is greater.

One limitation of Reif and Schmitt's distinction between first- and second-order elections is that it fails to capture the complexities of what is often called 'multi-level governance'. Like many countries, the UK has more than one sub-national level of government and how much is 'at stake' can vary substantially between different levels. This suggests that, rather than categorising elections on the basis of a first-order/second-order dichotomy, it might be more helpful to think of them as lying on a continuum ranging from purely first order, in which voters' decisions are driven entirely by factors pertaining to the particular political arena concerned, to purely second order, in which decisions are driven entirely by factors pertaining to another arena (van der Eijk *et al.*, 1996; Hough and Jeffery, 2005). For example, Heath *et al.* (1999) and Rallings and Thrasher (2005) have shown that, in Britain, arena-specific factors play a greater role in local than in European elections and conclude that voters must perceive that more is at stake in the former than in the latter. In other words, local elections are 'less second order' than European elections.

We would expect that on such a continuum Scottish Parliament elections would be still less second order. The devolved Parliament and hence the Scottish government have authority over a wide range of areas that are central to voters' concerns, including the NHS, education, crime and the environment. Indeed, one of the aspirations of the policy of devolution was that Scottish Parliament elections would come to rival UK general elections in importance, such that Scotland might even be said to have two sets of first-order elections (Cutler, 2008). The picture is further clouded in that both have a claim to be 'national' elections. Then again, key policy areas (such as immigration, social security and defence) are reserved for Westminster and the Scottish government also has very little fiscal or economic room for manoeuvre. Overall, then, Scottish elections look a lot more than simply second-order contests but voters could reasonably see less at stake than in Westminster elections. This is borne out in analyses of the 1999 and 2003

Scottish elections. According to Paterson *et al.* (2001: 44), 'the first Scottish election was neither clearly first order nor was it undoubtedly second order'. Curtice (2006: 107) concluded that in 2003 it was voters' views on the performance of the UK government that mattered most but that the Scottish Parliament elections cannot 'be simply described as second-order affairs in the manner that local and European elections often are'.

In both cases, the authors argue, the Scottish Parliament elections were essentially focused on the long-standing debate over the constitutional position of Scotland. Scottish voters strongly favoured a Scottish Parliament and, rather than fulfilling the main purpose of first-order elections – enabling the people to hold the government to account – the Scottish elections were something of a ritual providing legitimacy to the Parliament. Even in 2003, voters were still reaffirming their attitudes towards the Parliament and the possibility of further constitutional change when voting in the Scottish Parliament election. As we saw in the previous chapter, voters' constitutional attitudes remained a powerful predictor of their party choice in 2007 but there are two reasons why it would be misguided to infer from this a serious failure of accountability in that election. First, with the Scottish Parliament now firmly established, voting on the constitutional question is much more prospective than retrospective. That is, voters appear to be conveying preferences for Scotland's constitutional future rather than expressing their view on the initial policy of devolution. While alteration of the constitutional arrangements is a matter reserved, strictly speaking, to the UK government, it would be naive to deny that there is a link between the outcomes of Scottish Parliament elections and the prospects for constitutional change (whether full independence or further devolution). So voting on the basis of this issue cannot be regarded as simply a ritual affirmation of past support for, or opposition to, devolution.

The second reason is that, again as seen in the previous chapter, it was not the constitutional issue that decided the outcome of the 2007 election. There are entrenched and substantial minorities that are strongly for and against independence but their votes are relatively predictable. It is the voters who switch between parties who swing the election outcome and they tend to be less preoccupied by constitutional matters. Their decisions are driven by other considerations and a major question for this chapter is whether these considerations related mainly to the Scottish or to the UK context. We have already presented some relevant evidence in the chapters on leaders and issues, showing in each case that both arenas were in voters' minds in May 2007. In this chapter we address the question more directly and thereby enable some inferences to be made about the status and function of Scottish Parliament elections. The question becomes more pertinent with every passing Scottish election as the devolved institutions become ever more of a fixture on the

Scottish political landscape, as the consequences of Scottish government action (or inaction) have more and more impact on the electorate and as voters become used to more and more coverage of Scottish politics in the media.

Evidence from election results

We begin with the three features of election results that Reif and Schmitt specify as typical of a second-order election: lower turnout, weaker performance by the governing party, and more support for smaller parties.

Turnout is explored in more detail in Chapter 8 but three points can be made with respect to the discussion here. First, turnout in Scottish elections has consistently been lower than in the preceding UK general election (Table 6.1). Second, that gap is narrowing – it was 12.3 points between 1997 and 1999, 8.4 between 2001 and 2003 and 6.9 between 2005 and 2007. Third, turnout in Scottish Parliament elections is much greater than in European Parliament elections.[1] The implication is that the former fall a good deal nearer to the first- than the second-order end of the continuum and seem to be getting 'more first order' over time.

The other two features of second-order elections concern party vote shares and in this case comparisons are not straightforward due to the different electoral systems used in UK general elections and Scottish Parliament elections. Nonetheless, a reasonable initial comparison can be made on the basis of votes cast in the Scottish Parliament constituency contests and Table 6.2 shows, first, the decline in the share of votes obtained by Labour – which formed the incumbent UK government throughout the period – in each Scottish Parliament election as compared with the previous UK general election results in Scotland. There is indeed a decline, as second-order theory would predict, although the differences are not huge and are certainly smaller than is the case with European elections, in which incumbents at Westminster

Table 6.1 *Scottish turnout (per cent) in UK general, Scottish Parliament and European elections, 1997–2007*

	UK general	Scottish Parliament	European Parliament
May 1997	71.3		
May 1999		59.0	
June 1999			24.7
June 2001	58.1		
May 2003		49.7	
June 2004			30.6
May 2005	60.8		
May 2007		53.9	

Table 6.2 *Changes in vote shares for Labour and minor parties between general and Scottish Parliament elections, 1997–2005*

	1997–99	2001–3	2005–7
Change in Labour share (constituency)	–6.8	–8.7	–6.7
Change in 'others' share (constituency)	+0.8	+5.6	–1.7
Change in 'others' share (list)	+9.4	+18.6	+10.2

tend to suffer acutely.[2] Moreover, there is a problem with interpreting even these relatively small losses as second-order effects. Labour's lost votes were not spread to any great extent among small parties but seemed mainly to be to the benefit of the SNP. As Paterson *et al.* conclude (with respect to 1999 but, as we saw in the previous chapter, their argument remains valid for 2007), Labour's decline 'was not because the election was seen as a chance to cast a risk-free protest vote against the incumbent Westminster government. Rather, voters revealed that what they are looking for in a Scottish election are parties that are willing to use the devolved institutions to promote Scotland's interests' (2001: 44). On this argument, the decline in support for Labour in Scottish Parliament elections is not caused by voters believing that there is little at stake in these elections.

The second row of Table 6.2 shows the changes in support for minor parties (defined as those other than the main four) between UK general and Scottish Parliament elections. These data cast further doubt on a second-order interpretation of Scottish elections. There was a spike in support for 'others' in 2003 but in 1999 there was hardly any increase and in 2007 there was a decrease in minor-party support in the constituency contests. The latter is due mainly to the sharp decline in the number of 'other' candidates contesting constituencies (see Chapter 1). Yet this 'supply-side constraint' was itself probably motivated by a lack of demand – it reflects the minor parties' struggle to win significant shares of the constituency vote. It is a different matter, of course, in the list contests, for which figures are also given in Table 6.2. In these, all voters have the opportunity to support a range of parties and candidates and the reasonably proportional allocation means that such votes are less liable to be wasted. Hence the 'other' parties have taken a substantial proportion of regional list votes – and a much greater share than in UK general elections. Yet this cannot be readily attributed to a second-order effect, with voters freed by the relative unimportance of the election to cast an experimental or rebellious ballot. It may simply reflect the electoral system being used rather than the status of the election. We have no idea how well 'others' would be supported if there were party list voting in a UK general election.

Our purpose in this chapter is to assess whether it was the Scottish or the British context that had a greater influence on voters in 2007. If voters perceived very little to be at stake in elections to the Scottish Parliament we could reasonably expect that Britain-wide considerations would predominate. Judging by the evidence so far, Scottish elections are more like first- than second-order elections. Turnout is somewhat lower than in Westminster elections but the choices of those who did turn out do not suggest in any straightforward way that they regarded the elections as less significant. It is unwise, of course, to attempt to draw reliable inferences about the thinking of individual voters from aggregate election results – hence the ambiguity in interpreting the Labour losses and SNP gains in Scottish as compared with Westminster elections. We turn, therefore, to the SES data to look more directly at voters' perceptions of the status of Scottish elections.

Evidence from voters

Since devolution to Scotland was put into effect, most major surveys of the Scottish electorate have included the following question: 'How much of a difference do you think it makes who wins in elections: i) to the Scottish Parliament? ii) to the UK House of Commons?' The pattern of responses is now well established: respondents perceive Westminster elections as making slightly – but only slightly – more difference (Curtice, 2006). Results from the 2007 SES fit the pattern: 49 per cent thought that UK general election outcomes made 'a great deal' of difference, compared with 45 per cent for Scottish Parliament elections. (In each case only 11 per cent thought that election outcomes made 'not very much' or 'no difference at all'.) These data are certainly consistent with the earlier suggestion that Scottish elections fall close to Westminster elections, towards the first-order end of the continuum. That point is reinforced by the fact that, in a parallel question about local council elections, only 30 per cent thought those made 'a great deal' of difference while 17 per cent opted for 'not much' or 'none at all'.

However, there is a major problem in using these data to judge how voters assess the *relative* power and influence of the devolved administration and the Westminster government. If that were how respondents interpreted these questions, then we would expect there to be a clear negative correlation between evaluations of the importance of the two types of election. In fact, however, there is a very strong positive correlation ($r = +0.67$) between the two evaluations. In other words, voters who see Westminster elections as making a big difference are very likely to see Scottish Parliament elections as having a similar impact. Equally, those who think that Scottish Parliament elections are inconsequential are not bemoaning the weakness of Holyrood relative to Westminster – they tend to take the same view of UK general elections. Basically, it appears, these questions are measuring attitudes to elections (and perhaps also perceptions of the ideological and policy differences between the parties – see Chapter 8), rather than the way in which voters see power as distributed between different levels of government. That, in turn, means that we cannot use responses to the questions to infer the bases for vote choice. Respondents reporting that Scottish Parliament elections make a great deal of difference might nonetheless focus on the Westminster arena since the chances are that they see it as equally, if not more, powerful. In short, while most voters think that Scottish Parliament elections matter, this is not enough to guarantee that the elections will be 'truly' Scottish.

A preferable approach to the question of relative importance is to explore voters' attributions of responsibility – that is, which levels of government they see as primarily responsible for key policy areas. In Chapter 4 we reported voters' perceptions of party performance in six such areas: law and order, health, education, the economy, transport and the environment. Respondents were also asked for each issue whether it is mainly the responsibility of the UK government or of the Scottish Executive. This gets directly at voters' perceptions of the importance of the devolved administration relative to Westminster in determining what happens in Scotland. As Table 6.3 shows, although there was a fair amount of uncertainty, majorities of the electorate regarded the Scottish government as principally responsible for four of the six key policy areas. Since many of these were reported by voters as their 'most important issue' when deciding how to vote (see Chapter 4), we have solid grounds for thinking that the Scottish arena was uppermost in many voters' minds in 2007. Predictably, the one area in which most people ascribed responsibility to Westminster was the economy and the fundamental importance of that issue inevitably gives a second-order flavour to Scottish Parliament elections. Nonetheless, in a separate question which asked respondents about the absolute capacity of both Westminster and Scottish governments to affect Scotland's economic performance, almost half of the respondents (46 per cent) perceived the Scottish government as having 'a great deal' or 'quite a lot' of influence. Even in this policy area, therefore, what is at stake in Scottish Parliament elections is not negligible. That helps to explain why, in Chapter 4, we saw that economic evaluations were a powerful influence on party choice in 2007.

We are not primarily concerned here with the accuracy of voters' attributions of responsibility – which is very difficult to judge anyway – but it is worth noting the lack of consensus in Table 6.3. On all issues there were substantial minorities dissenting from the general view (and significant proportions of 'don't know' responses). This may simply reflect the haphazard guesswork of respondents unsure about where responsibility lies, which would be

Table 6.3 *Level deemed 'mainly responsible' for six key policy areas (percentage of respondents)*

	Law and order	Health	Educa-tion	Economy	Trans-port	Environ-ment
UK government	39	31	20	60	24	38
Scottish Executive	50	59	70	26	61	46
Don't know	11	10	10	14	15	16
N	1,872	1,872	1,872	1,552	1,552	1,552

Sources. Pre- and post-election surveys.

understandable given the relative novelty and flux of Scotland's constitutional arrangements. On the other hand, there may be more systematic disagreement. Different voters may simply have different views of the power of the Scottish Parliament and thus locate Scottish elections in a different position on the first- to second-order continuum. To begin to explore this possibility, in Table 6.4 we repeat the above analyses but, as in previous chapters, show figures separately according to party support (whether identification or leaning) and constitutional preference (measured via voting intention in the hypothetical three-option referendum). To simplify presentation, we exclude those who answered 'don't know' on any issue and report the proportion of respondents attributing primary responsibility for each issue to the Scottish Parliament.

The differences by party are fairly consistent across issues and so are well summarised by the mean percentage shown in the penultimate column. SNP supporters are markedly more likely to regard the Scottish Parliament as responsible for these issues. In the absence of an obvious alternative hypothesis, we suggest that here the wish is father to the thought: SNP supporters are also the most likely to want the Scottish Parliament to exert more influence. This line of argument can also explain why Conservatives and Labour supporters were least inclined to ascribe responsibilities to the Scottish Parliament. The Conservatives are traditionally the most unionist of the Scottish parties and Labour fought the 2007 campaign on a platform of opposition to further devolution. The breakdown by vote intention in a hypothetical referendum provides strong support for a 'wishful thinking' hypothesis. Those favouring independence were very likely to regard the Scottish Parliament as primarily responsible for each issue, with 'status quo' voters being much less likely to do so. Overall, then, those who ascribe greatest influence and power to the Scottish Parliament are those who would most like it to be true.

An interesting implication of the foregoing arguments is that Scottish elections may be first-order to some voters but second-order to others. More

Table 6.4 *Attributions of responsibility by partisanship and referendum vote intention*

	Percentage of respondents holding Scottish Executive mainly responsible						Mean %	N (min.)
	Law and order	Health	Educa-tion	Economy	Trans-port	Environ-ment		
Party support								
Conservatives	43	57	70	22	68	48	51	*162*
Labour	52	59	74	24	65	51	54	*344*
Lib Dems	53	69	84	27	79	63	62	*124*
SNP	74	84	91	44	79	68	73	*287*
Other	58	66	73	21	73	44	56	*62*
None	53	61	71	31	71	50	56	324
Referendum vote intention								
Status quo	38	53	71	11	60	43	46	*420*
More powers	63	71	81	38	76	59	65	*593*
Independence	74	83	89	43	81	65	72	*317*

Sources: Pre- and post-election surveys.

generally, an election's overall location on the continuum reflects an aggregation of what may be quite widely differing individual perspectives. We say more about this in the conclusion to this chapter. Meanwhile, we should not lose sight of the fact that, overall, in 2007 the Scottish Parliament election appears to have been much closer to the first- than to the second-order end of the continuum. Most voters thought that the outcomes of the election would make a difference and, judging by their attributions of responsibility, most believed that there was a good deal at stake in 2007. In particular, the attributions for health, education, law and order and transport allow ample scope for the kind of 'domestic' valence voting envisaged in Chapter 4, which involves voters evaluating the capacity of SNP- and Labour-led Scottish administrations to deliver on the key issues.

The basis for decision-making: Scottish or British?

The attribution of substantial powers to the Scottish Parliament is not a guarantee that the Scottish context will be uppermost in voters' decision-making. They might still be preoccupied by Westminster matters, either because they regard that sphere as even more important or perhaps because

UK-level issues and leaders remained prominent in campaigning and media coverage. We need to look more directly and more closely, therefore, at how and whether relevant factors influenced vote choice in 2007.

How voters saw their choices

As a first step, we consider what voters themselves say about the context on which they focused when deciding how to vote. In our post-election survey, those who reported voting were asked whether, in choosing their party, they had in mind mostly what was going on in Scotland or mostly what was going on in Britain as a whole. Identical questions were asked in the SSA surveys conducted in 1999 and 2003.[3] As seen in the left-hand portion of Table 6.5, the 2007 results are consistent with those of previous election surveys. A comfortable majority of voters report voting primarily on Scottish matters and the proportion looks to be rising steadily. To this extent at least, Scottish Parliament elections are increasingly acquiring a first-order character.[4]

We would expect answers to this question to be closely related to attributions of responsibility. Those who think the Scottish government can do more will presumably pay more attention to what it does. To test this hypothesis, we did a simple count of how many of our six issues (see Table 6.3) respondents thought were primarily the responsibility of the Scottish Parliament and categorised the degree of responsibility as low (0–2 issues), moderate (3–4 issues) or high (5–6 issues). Overall, these categories account for 29 per cent, 37 per cent and 34 per cent of respondents, respectively. The right-hand portion of Table 6.5 shows that, as expected, the more issues they attributed to the devolved administration, the more likely respondents were to report voting mostly according to what was going on in Scotland.

Table 6.5 *Basis for voting decision 1999–2007 and by attributions of responsibility (percentage of respondents)*

	All voters			2007, by number of issues attributed to Scottish Parliament		
	1999	*2003*	*2007*	*0–2*	*3–4*	*5–6*
Mostly Scottish context	62	67	71	55	72	81
Mostly British context	38	33	29	45	28	19
N	*878*	*736*	*1,091*	*278*	*414*	*390*

Note: The data refer to those who reported voting in the relevant election.
Sources: SSA (1999, 2003); SES pre- and post-election surveys (2007).

Nonetheless, attributions are clearly far from the whole story. Even among those who believed that the Scottish Executive had extensive powers, almost 20 per cent nonetheless paid more attention to British matters when voting in 2007. More strikingly, perhaps, of those who saw Westminster as responsible for the majority of the six issues, fully 55 per cent still had mainly Scottish matters in mind when deciding in 2007. This raises serious questions about the theory of second-order elections because it indicates that voters do not ignore a level of government that they see as subordinate. Westminster is still seen as the dominant arena by many voters but for plenty of them 2007 was, nevertheless, a Scottish election.

A different approach to the question of first- and second-order elections is to ask respondents what they would have done had it been a Westminster election on 3 May 2007. If virtually all voters would have behaved in exactly the same way then it is more difficult to maintain that this was a specifically Scottish election. Looking first at turnout, 96 per cent of those who reported voting in the Scottish Parliament election said that they would also have done so in a UK general election. Yet 48 per cent of those who stayed at home claimed that a Westminster election would have brought them to the polling station. This figure invites strong suspicion, since actual Scottish turnout in UK general elections is not that much higher than in Scottish Parliament contests (see Table 6.1). A rather more realistic picture is painted by responses to a pre-election survey question which simply asked respondents whether they would be more or less likely to vote if the upcoming election were a UK general

Table 6.6 *Likelihood of and reasons for turning out in a hypothetical Westminster election*

	% of respondents
If a UK general election on 3 May...	
More likely to vote	16
Less likely to vote	3
Makes no difference	81
N	*1,872*
Of those 'more likely to vote'...	
Westminster Parliament has more influence	61
More difference between the parties	16
Obvious who was going to win Scottish Parliament election	10
Prefer voting system for Westminster	11
Don't approve of Scottish Parliament	16

Source: Pre-election survey.

election. More than four in five of them (81 per cent) said that it would make no difference but almost all of the rest (16 per cent of respondents overall) said that they would be more likely to vote in a Westminster election (Table 6.6). These respondents were presented with a list of possible reasons for this and asked to tick any that applied to them. The second-order response – that the Westminster Parliament has more influence over people's lives – was by a long way the most common. Concerning the decision of *whether* to vote, then, there is clear evidence that Scottish elections are different, in the negative sense that a relatively small section of the electorate sees too little at stake to make turning out worthwhile.

We consider now the decision about *how* to vote and return to the post-election question asking respondents directly what they would have done in 2007 had they been voting in a UK general election. Of those who voted in the real election and would have voted in the hypothetical election, 76 per cent would have opted for the same party in their constituency.[5] When a parallel question was asked at the time of the 1999 Scottish Parliament election, 82 per cent reported that they would have supported the same party in a Westminster contest (Paterson *et al.*, 2001: 31). This is not a dramatic change, but it may suggest that individual voters are becoming more accustomed to choosing different parties in elections at different levels. At the same time, however, when we aggregate the individual decisions into overall vote shares on the basis of survey responses, the differences between Scottish Parliament and Westminster results are narrowing. In 1999, Labour's lead over the SNP was 11 percentage points among survey respondents in the Scottish Parliament contest but would have been fully 27 points had it been a Westminster election (Paterson *et al.*, 2001: 32). In 2007, the SNP's one-point lead would have been a six-point

Table 6.7 *Vote shares in a hypothetical Westminster election, overall and by actual 2007 constituency vote*

Hypothetical Westminster vote	Actual 2007 constituency vote (%)					Overall vote share (%)	
	Conser-vative	Labour	Lib Dem	SNP	Other	Holyrood	Westminster
Conservative	83	5	9	6	11	17	18
Labour	6	85	14	10	24	32	34
Lib Dem	2	4	63	5	16	16	14
SNP	3	3	7	75	13	33	28
Other	6	3	7	4	36	2	5
N	157	344	161	371	38	1,174	1,071

Source: Post-election survey, weighted by 2007 vote shares.

deficit in a Westminster poll (Table 6.7, right-hand panel). Labour continues to get more support relative to the SNP in Westminster elections than in Scottish Parliament elections but the differences are smaller than they were. Taken together, these results point to 2007 being a genuinely Scottish election and away from a second-order interpretation. A growing number of people vote for a different party but a shrinking number do so in the predicted second-order direction – supporting an opposition party for the Scottish Parliament but continuing to support the governing party for Westminster.

These data relating to party choice allow only for educated guesswork concerning the reasons behind voters' decisions. As with turnout, however, pre-election survey respondents were asked not only whether their vote intention would be different in a UK general election but also why. Again, several reasons were presented and respondents indicated which, if any, applied to them in 2007. There are two key differences compared with the equivalent data on turnout. First, as seen in Table 6.8, there was less of a consensus, with no reason being cited by more than one-third of 'switchers'. Second, there is little evidence of a second-order effect. Just 22 per cent of switches were

Table 6.8 *Likelihood of and reasons for vote switching between Scottish Parliament election and a hypothetical Westminster election (percentage of respondents)*

	All voters	Those intending SNP list vote
If a UK general election on 3 May…		
Vote for the same party	83	82
Vote for a different party	17	18
N	1,381	419
Reason for switching among those who would have voted differently [a]		
Prefer party in Scottish election that has no chance of winning in my Westminster seat	9	4
Prefer party in Scottish election that has no chance of forming a Westminster government	28	55
No single party has best policies for Scotland and Britain	33	29
Will use Scottish Parliament elections to send a message to London	22	26
N	232	76

Note: [a] Column percentages may sum to more than 100 because respondents could choose multiple reasons.
Source: SES pre-election survey, weighted by 2007 vote shares.

motivated by the desire to send a protest message to the (presumed first-order) Westminster government. This point is even clearer when we look specifically at those who reported an intention to vote for the SNP on the regional list.[6] Of those who intended to vote Nationalist in 2007 but would not have done so in a UK general election, only around a quarter (26 per cent) had London in their sights. Slightly more were looking to match policies to arenas, perhaps trusting the SNP to defend Scottish interests rather than endorsing the party's manifesto. The most common reason given, however, is the simplest: the SNP has no hope of forming a government at Westminster and so switching to another party in UK general elections makes tactical sense. These results are in harmony with the recurring theme of this chapter, namely that – unlike relatively low turnout – party choice in the 2007 Scottish election is not well accounted for by characterising it as a second-order election.

Factors predicting party choice

Traditionally, those involved in studying electoral behaviour pay rather little attention to survey respondents' own accounts of why they voted for a particular party.[7] Rather, they investigate characteristics, preferences, beliefs and attitudes that can predict party choice. In previous chapters we have already seen a range of such predictors and another approach to the question posed in this chapter is to assign those to the UK or Scottish context, with a view to comparing the overall predictive power of each arena. As far as the party leader analysis in Chapter 3 is concerned, this is quite straightforward. Evaluations of Tony Blair and Jack McConnell showed similar predictive power, indicating that the two arenas had roughly equal impact. However, with the issues examined in Chapter 4, matters become more complicated. As noted in that chapter, Iraq and Trident are two issues for which Westminster is obviously responsible but which resonate powerfully in Scotland due the involvement of Scottish regiments in the former and the fact that Trident has a Scottish base. Meanwhile, voters may be unimpressed by the Scottish Executive's performance on issues like law and order and health but deem Westminster ultimately responsible because the UK government holds the purse strings. In this section, therefore, we rely on the overall performance evaluations discussed in the latter part of Chapter 4. These questions are unambiguous, because they expressly instruct respondents which arena to consider, and are directly comparable, because they both ask respondents to evaluate Labour's performance (on the same scale).

Although reported prior to the elections, these evaluations will nevertheless be heavily influenced by partisan predispositions. Labour supporters are more likely both to evaluate the party's performance favourably and to vote

Table 6.9 *Evaluations of Labour performance (UK and Scottish levels) and Labour voting (percentage Labour constituency vote) in 2007 (all voters and previous Labour supporters)*

	All voters		Labour vote 2005		Labour vote 2003	
	UK	Scotland	UK	Scotland	UK	Scotland
Good	54	54	68	72	73	78
Neutral	24	26	51	58	57	60
Bad	6	5	32	23	29	23
N	1,190	1,164	406	401	335	330

Source: Evaluation of Labour from pre-election survey, votes from post-election survey.

for it. Hence the impact of performance evaluations on vote is liable to be seriously overstated unless – as later in the section – we control for partisan predispositions. That is less important at this stage, however, because the aim is not to estimate the overall impact of performance evaluations but to compare the relative impact of evaluations relating to the Scottish and UK contexts (and there is no reason to suppose that either of these would be significantly more affected by partisan bias). To give a simple indication of this impact, we begin by collapsing the five-point evaluation scale into three categories – good, neutral and bad – and then calculate in each category the proportion of respondents casting their constituency vote for Labour (see Table 6.9). Considering voters as a whole, the impact of the two arenas looks virtually identical: 54 per cent of those reporting favourably on Labour's performance at Holyrood voted for the party, as did the same proportion of those impressed by its performance at Westminster. In both cases, only a handful of those indicating negative evaluations (5 per cent for Scottish performance, 6 per cent for UK performance) did so.

The picture changes somewhat if we consider the sources of Labour's losses compared with previous elections.[8] The question now is whether those who defected from Labour were influenced more by the UK or the Scottish context and the data in Table 6.9 also bear on this. Looking first at those who reported having voted Labour in the 2005 UK general election, it is their evaluation of the Scottish Executive's performance that is the more powerful predictor of defection. Only 23 per cent of those taking a negative view of Labour's performance in Scotland went on to support the party in 2007, compared with 72 per cent of those taking a positive view. The difference is clearly narrower for the Westminster evaluations. One obvious objection to this argument is that the impact of poor performance by the UK government had already been felt by 2005 – an election in which Labour lost a significant amount of support – and so it is unsurprising that perceptions of performance in Scotland had a bigger influence on defections after that. The same pattern is evident, however, when Labour defections between the Scottish Parliament elections of 2003 and 2007 are examined. It appears, therefore, that Labour's losses in 2007 had more to do with its record in Scotland than its Westminster performance.

A more precise estimate of the relative impact of Scottish and Westminster evaluations requires us to control for other factors that might influence both these evaluations and vote choice. As in previous chapters, we can do this by using logistic regression analysis and, in the process, continue to build up the model of party choice that has been developed. Hence for this analysis we control for respondents' party identification and attitudes to the party leaders (Chapter 3), their issue opinions and policy positions (Chapter 4) and their national identity and constitutional preferences (Chapter 5). The full model is presented in Appendix 3 (Table A6.1) but here, as before, we present the key results graphically. Figures 6.1a and 6.1b illustrate the impact of evaluations of Labour performance within Scotland and in the UK context after taking account of the other influences just mentioned. On the constituency vote, evaluations at both levels prove to be significant and to have a more or less equal effect (Figure 6.1a). In the case of the regional list vote, however, evaluations of Labour in the Scottish Executive proved to be much the more important (Figure 6.1b), as shown by the markedly steeper slope of that curve. In particular, those with an unfavourable impression of Labour's Scottish performance were highly unlikely to cast a regional ballot for the party.

It is not easy to explain why the Scottish context should be particularly influential in respect of list voting. However, list voting is more purely 'party voting' than constituency voting. Not only is the full range of parties available but choices are largely unaffected by loyalties to particular candidates or preferences among them. In addition, list voting is the distinctive element in the Scottish electoral system and its purpose is to shape the overall distribution of seats among the parties in the Parliament (as opposed to electing a constituency representative). In these circumstances, it may be that more voters have the future government of Scotland in mind when casting their list vote than is the case in constituency contests.

The results for constituency voting suggest that evaluations of Labour's performances in Scotland and the UK as a whole had a roughly equal impact on party choice. This does not mean that all voters were affected equally by each arena. It is more likely that the lack of difference between the two suggested in Figure 6.1a reflects the cancelling out of voters' disagreements about attributions of responsibility. Other things remaining the same, we

Figure 6.1 *Evaluations of Labour performance at Holyrood and at Westminster and likelihood of voting Labour: (a) constituency vote; (b) regional list vote*

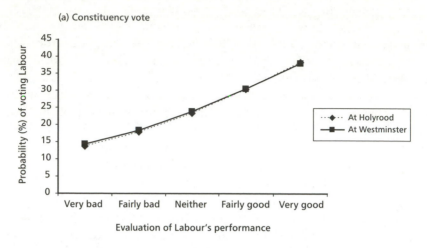

(a) Constituency vote

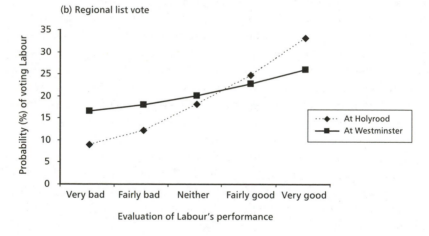

(b) Regional list vote

Source: Pre- and post-election surveys.

would expect those who regard Westminster as more powerful to be more influenced by their evaluations of the Blair governments, while those attributing more responsibility for key issues to the Scottish Parliament would be more influenced by the Scottish context. To test this hypothesis, the analysis follows the same pattern as above but focuses on the constituency vote, with respondents divided into two groups according to how many of the six key issues (Table 6.3) they viewed as primarily the responsibility of the Scottish Parliament. Broadly, the results support the notion that voters are influenced

Figure 6.2 *Evaluations of Labour performance at Holyrood and at Westminster and likelihood of voting Labour (constituency vote), by attributions of responsibility for key issues: (a) 0–3 issues; (b) 4–6 issues*

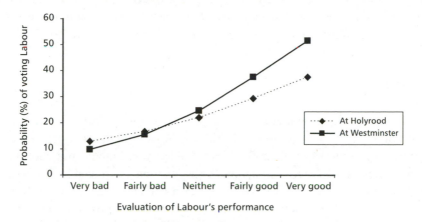

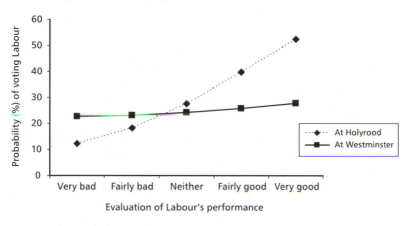

Source: Pre- and post-election surveys.

by the arena they regard as more important (see Appendix 3, Table A6.2 for details). Figure 6.2a shows that, among those assigning greater influence to Westminster, the line indicating the impact of evaluations at UK level slopes more steeply than the line relating to evaluations of the party's Scottish performance. Among those regarding the Scottish government as responsible for four or more of the issues in the analysis (Figure 6.2b), it is the slope for Scottish evaluations that is steeper. Another difference between the two graphs is worth noting, however. For those attributing issue responsibilities primarily to the Scottish Parliament, Labour's performance at Westminster seems to matter very little – the line barely slopes at all. Yet the party's performance in Scotland clearly influenced both groups. This reinforces a point made earlier, namely that voters are quite likely to pay attention to – and vote on – Scottish matters even if they regard the Scottish Parliament as less influential than Westminster. We discuss this further in concluding the chapter.

Conclusion

This chapter began by asking what appears to be a relatively simple question – was the 2007 election a 'Scottish' one? Answering it is altogether more complex. The results of the 2007 election reflect the thinking and choices of almost four million electors. Naturally, they exhibit considerable differences in perceptions of the influence of the Scottish Parliament and of the role and status of Scottish elections. Nonetheless, the evidence presented here does allow some conclusions to be drawn. First, there remained a second-order effect on turnout, with participation lower than in the 2005 UK general election and some non-voters reporting that they would have voted in a Westminster election but stayed away from the Scottish Parliament election because they believed that there was less at stake. Once people made it to the polls, however, their choices point to 2007 being a Scottish rather than a second-order election. A majority reported voting according to what was going on in Scotland and the evidence from the analysis of party choice bears this out, with Labour's Scottish performance tending to weigh more heavily in voters' decisions than the party's record at Westminster. This was especially true of those who had supported the party in previous elections and the resulting defections look particularly costly given the narrow margin of the SNP's victory.

The 'Scottishness' of the 2007 election is not surprising when we consider voters' assessments of where power and influence lie. While acknowledging Westminster's leading role in respect of the economy, most voters regard the Scottish Parliament as more influential in key areas such as crime, health and education. We should not overstate the case here as a substantial section of the electorate sees Westminster as clearly the more important arena. Nevertheless, those voters may attribute significant responsibilities to the Scottish Parliament. The theory of second-order elections has led to something of a fixation with *relative* importance but there is good reason to suppose *absolute* importance also matters – in this case, how much the Scottish Executive can do. Many voters saw plenty at stake in 2007 and hence Scottish issues and concerns strongly influenced their choices.

Perhaps the most telling indication that 2007 was basically a Scottish election came from asking our respondents how they would have voted if it had been a Westminster election. While one in five voters would have chosen a different party, there was little evidence of a flood back to Labour, as would be expected were this a second-order election. The clearest pattern was that some voters – though a smaller proportion than at previous elections – would vote for the SNP at the Scottish Parliament election but not a UK general election. This was rarely to do with sending a protest message to London, however. Rather, it was because the SNP, as a purely Scottish party, stands no chance of winning at Westminster and has policies that are geared towards Scottish rather than British interests and concerns. This reflects a wider point: for SNP supporters – and particularly those who favour independence or at least further devolution – Scottish Parliament elections have become the more important. Those voters are more likely to see the Scottish Parliament as influential and to report voting on Scottish matters. We referred to a 'wishful thinking' effect but it is perhaps more apt to see both the view that the Scottish Parliament matters more and the desire for it to matter even more as manifestations of giving a higher priority generally to Scotland and its politics. In contrast, those closer to the unionist end of the spectrum tended to be more focused on British issues when voting in 2007, perhaps again reflecting the prominence and priority of that arena in their political world view.

The embedding of devolution ensured that the 2007 Scottish Parliament election was unmistakeably more Scottish than the two previous contests. Other things being equal, we would expect the 2011 election to maintain the trend, as there will have been another four years of existence, activity and publicity for the Scottish government and Parliament. However, other things may not remain the same. One thing that will inevitably differ – from both 2003 and 2007 – is that the party in power in Edinburgh will not be that in power in London and, of course, 2011 may be the first Scottish Parliament election held with Labour in opposition at Westminster. These different per-mutations imply different campaigning strategies for the various parties and for some it may be advantageous to try to direct voters' attention to London. Another point worth noting is the very close contest in 2007, which served to focus attention on the race in Scotland rather than events at Westminster. This contrasts sharply with 2003, in which a drab Scottish campaign drifted to a predictable conclusion while media coverage was dominated by the fallout from the Iraq war. These points are important because the 'Scottishness' of any election in Scotland – whether to the Scottish Parliament or Westminster – is determined not just by voters considering what is at stake but also by how the election is presented to the electorate via parties' campaigning and media coverage. Indeed, one of the features of the 2007 election was the tussle between the SNP and Labour over the territory – Scotland or the Union – on which the campaign would be fought. In the next chapter we show how the SNP enjoyed the electoral spoils of that battle.

Notes

1   We use European elections rather than local council elections for comparison because council elections have been held on the same day as Scottish Parliament elections since 1999.

2   In both the 1999 and 2004 European elections, Labour's vote share in Scotland declined by 16.9 points compared with the previous UK general elections.

3   To make for cleaner comparisons, our analysis excludes the option 'other reasons' that was offered in all three surveys but was chosen markedly less often in the 2007 internet survey.

4   It might be thought that respondents simply avoided what they thought was a 'wrong' answer, that is, focusing on British matters at a Scottish election. Yet that suggestion sits uneasily with the fact that, when the same question was asked at the 2001 UK general election, 45 per cent of SSA respondents nonetheless gave the 'mostly Scottish' answer.

5   We have not used the list vote for this calculation because the different electoral system inflates the extent of 'switching'.

6   The question did not specify which of the two Scottish Parliament election votes was to be the basis for comparison and so we cannot be sure which respondents had in mind. Our analysis is based on the list vote.

7   The doubts are not so much about respondents' honesty but more about whether people really understand and can accurately report the reasons behind their thinking and behaviour (Nisbett and Wilson, 1977).

8   The importance of this analysis should not be overstated. As we saw in Chapter 2, and contrary to much of the post-election media reaction, 2007 did not see a major haemorrhaging of Labour support. Hence we are here exploring the reasons behind a relatively small number of defections.

7
Battling for votes: campaigning and its impact

In the weeks leading up to the 2007 Scottish Parliament elections, political activity across the country went into overdrive with, in effect, 82 different but simultaneous campaigns for these elections taking place: the national campaign dominated by the major parties and conducted via the national media; eight regional contests relating to the seats to be determined by list voting; and 73 individual constituency battles for the first-past-the-post seats. More than 1,000 candidates were competing for seats in the Parliament – 334 in the constituency contests and 715 in the regional list contests. At the same time, council elections were also being held in every local authority, giving rise to even more campaigning at ward level. For about a month, voters were being bombarded almost daily with election news and material – directly from parties and candidates and also in the media.

Election campaigns usually have two main aims. First, parties want to mobilise their committed supporters. This is particularly important in elections under systems of proportional representation. In first-past-the-post contests, parties are not rewarded for winning seats with large majorities or for losing seats narrowly, but under proportional representation every vote can count. The second aim is persuasion. While some voters will have made up their minds about which party to support before an election takes place (sometimes long before), others remain undecided until late in the day. Winning over these undecided voters can make the difference between success and failure.

In this chapter, we examine how the parties campaigned, how the campaigns were experienced by the voters and the effect, if any, that they had on their decisions. Our analyses draw on relevant aggregate data as well as the SES surveys. The latter are particularly valuable in this context, for two reasons. First, they give us insights into how voters experienced the campaigns – who contacted them and how – and also how they reacted to them. Second, the panel design of the surveys, with the same individuals being surveyed before and after the election, allows us to examine how effective campaigning was in influencing voters' choices in the election.

Electioneering: the wider picture

Election campaigns at national level involve major organisational efforts. Parties conduct extensive market research and, in an increasingly complex mass media marketplace, they require national communication strategies to get their messages across. This can involve relatively traditional forms of communication such as televised party election broadcasts (PEBs), streams of media events to highlight the issues and personalities that the party wants to emphasise (or to attack opponents) and the planning, production and placement of advertising material (including billboards and advertisements in the press). Since the mid-1990s, new forms of campaign communication have become increasingly important, including telephone contact with voters, the internet and direct mailings to voters, especially those in key seats (Denver *et al.*, 2003b). All of this requires considerable resources, as modern electioneering does not come cheap. Since the passage of the Political Parties, Elections and Referendums Act (PPERA) 2001, however, election campaigns in the UK have been subject to national expenditure limits.

In addition to the national campaign, in every constituency there are also local campaigns fought on behalf of individual candidates. From the advent of television in the mid-1950s, these local campaigns were conventionally seen as of limited electoral importance (Denver and Hands, 1997: ch. 2). After all, went the argument, almost all voters now follow election campaigns – if they follow them at all – via television and the national press. Very few attend local public meetings. Moreover, changes in party performance from election to election did not vary a great deal across constituencies. Under such conditions, the constituency campaign seemed to have become an empty ritual. However, an extensive body of work has provided persuasive evidence that this received wisdom is wrong (see, for example, Seyd and Whiteley, 1992; Denver and Hands, 1997; Pattie and Johnston, 2003). Intensive constituency campaigns can and do make a measureable difference to election outcomes, in terms of both turnout and party choice. Particularly in marginal seats, the difference between a well fought and a poorly fought campaign can easily be the difference between winning and losing.

Constituency electioneering is now explicitly built into national campaign strategies (Kavanagh, 1995; Norris, 2000; Denver and Hands, 2004b). Most effort is expended on the most marginal seats, with the parties making only token efforts in seats where they are bound to lose and being relatively relaxed about seats they seem sure to win by comfortable majorities. In the marginals, however, there is much to be gained or lost and so voters in these seats can expect a lot of attention from the parties. This extra attention begins long before the formal campaign (Johnston and Pattie, 2007) but intensifies once the election is called. National phone banks are used to canvass them, party leaders' election itineraries are focused on them and volunteers from less marginal seats in adjoining areas flock into them to help the campaign effort.

Like the national campaign, local electioneering also requires resources. Constituency campaign spending is tightly controlled by law (and has been since the 1880s). The maximum amount that each candidate in a seat is permitted to spend is a function of the size of the constituency's electorate and of whether the seat is a borough (largely urban) or a county (suburban or rural) constituency, the latter having slightly more generous spending limits. At the 2007 Scottish Parliament election, the average permitted campaign spending was £10,500 (ranging from £8,283 for the smallest constituency to £12,162 for the largest).

Most of the constituency effort rests on local voluntary activity – people are required to fill envelopes, deliver leaflets by hand, canvass voters at home, 'knock up' supporters on polling day and so on. It follows that local party members are an important campaign resource. They are a declining resource, however, as most parties have seen a substantial fall in membership in recent years (Fisher and Denver, 2008). This makes it more difficult to mount effective campaigns (Whiteley and Seyd, 2003; Fisher et al., 2006). In the light of this, a major advantage for the SNP in 2007 was that it had bucked the trend of declining membership and had seen a considerable increase following the introduction of a central membership register and Alex Salmond's resumption of the leadership.

Fighting the good fight?

The parties entered the 2007 Scottish Parliament election campaign with all to fight for. The SNP had an appreciable advantage over Labour in the opinion polls (Appendix 2) but most commentators expected the gap to narrow. The Conservatives and Liberal Democrats, in their turn, were vying for third place. Moreover, as the campaign began, many voters remained open to persuasion. In the pre-election survey, we asked SES respondents how likely they were to vote in the upcoming contest and whether they had decided which party or candidate to support. A substantial proportion of the Scottish electorate had still to make up its mind (Table 7.1). Of those who thought they were likely to vote, about a third (34 per cent) remained undecided. A sceptical view might be that most of these undecided voters would actually abstain when the election came along but this was not the case. If we limit analysis to those who reported after the election that they did vote, almost exactly the same percentage (32 per cent) had been undecided two weeks before polling.

Table 7.1 *Voters' decisions at the time of the pre-election survey (percentage of respondents)*

	All likely to vote	*All who did vote*
Decided	62	65
Not decided yet	34	32
Don't know	4	3
N	1,439	1,192

Source: Pre- and post-election surveys.

Thus, a third of voters were open to persuasion as the contest moved into its last and most intensive phase. Parties which could make a compelling case to these voters stood to make substantial gains.

Furthermore, many voters changed their minds during the campaign. We can compare respondents' pre-election intentions with how they reported voting afterwards and the resulting 'flow of the vote' matrix (using the list vote) reveals considerable 'churning' over the course of the campaign (Table 7.2). For instance, around 16 per cent of those who initially said that they had no intention of voting changed their minds in the event – with most of those who did vote giving their support in the regional ballot to Labour or the SNP. Most of those who said at the start of the campaign that they would vote for a particular party in the regional ballot actually did so: loyalty across the campaign ranged from 56 per cent among those initially intending

Table 7.2 *Flow of the regional vote from pre-election intention to actual ballot (percentage of respondents)*

Regional vote	Pre-election regional vote intention					
	Abstain	*Conservative*	*Labour*	*Lib Dem*	*SNP*	*Other*
Abstain	84	10	21	9	12	16
Conservative	2	68	1	5	1	4
Labour	4	3	64	10	2	4
Lib Dem	1	2	6	56	1	3
SNP	4	8	4	10	77	16
Other	6	9	4	11	7	56
N	114	171	300	145	385	185

Sources: Pre- and post-election surveys.

to vote Liberal Democrat to over three-quarters of all intending SNP voters. By the same token, however, substantial minorities of those intending to vote for each party did not actually do so. The biggest defection rates were to abstention. At the extreme, around one in five of those who initially intended to vote Labour did not in the event cast a regional ballot at all. However, all parties lost some voters to their rivals and all gained some too. In total, 32 per cent of our respondents changed their minds on how they would vote in the regional ballot over the course of the 2007 campaign. Analysis of the constituency-level vote produces a very similar picture.

The combination of many undecided voters and clear evidence of people changing their minds on how to vote during the campaign illustrates the potential for parties' campaign activities to affect the election outcome. If the campaigns could influence the eventual decisions of even a small proportion of these voters, then their efforts would have paid electoral dividends. Mounting strong campaigns was not easy, however. Although the UK-wide parties received help from London in funding their campaigning, these subventions were rather smaller than would typically be made available in UK general elections. Moreover, the frequency of major elections in Scotland after devolution risked serious 'campaign fatigue' on the part of local activists. In the 10 years from 1997, the Scottish parties had to mount campaigns in three UK general elections, a referendum, three Scottish Parliament elections, two European Parliament elections, and three rounds of local government elections (all on the same day as that year's Scottish Parliament election). The pressure on both national and local parties' campaign organisations was unrelenting.

This pressure, along with financial constraints, meant that parties were obliged to prioritise and, in particular, to decide where to defend (mobilising support to protect existing seats) and where to attack (winning over new support in target seats). The SNP's decision-making was informed by its new 'Activate' software system, which allowed for a sophisticated form of campaigning, combining telephone canvassing, constituency profiling and targeting. The 2007 election was the first major test of this new resource, although the party also anticipated that it would be able to build on – and profit from – the information collected in 2007 when running future campaigns. According to SNP strategists,[1] 'Activate' had given them early warning that the party was making limited headway in some of its main targets yet competing very strongly in seats previously seen as much more remote prospects. The SNP was thus able to divert resources into the latter seats and ultimately to make some surprise gains in seats such as Edinburgh East and Musselburgh, and Livingston. One reason why the party was not able to take some of its more prominent targets – such as Cumbernauld and Kilsyth, Aberdeen Central, and Linlithgow – was that Labour adopted a largely defensive approach, pouring resources into its more vulnerable marginals. The Liberal Democrats took a similar tack, focusing their efforts on a few seats – overwhelmingly those they had won in 2003. Nine of these were retained but two were lost, one of which – Roxburgh and Berwickshire – was the Conservatives' sole constituency gain (although the Conservatives also made considerable progress in areas that had been represented by the party in the past and will be targets in future elections).

Turning to the financial side, some impression of the extent of campaigning efforts can be gleaned from the accounts that parties are obliged to lodge with the Electoral Commission. A summary of national campaign expenditures is given in Table 7.3. As in UK general elections, national campaign spending was capped and the legal controls applied to all expenditure incurred in the four months before polling day. Each party contesting the election was allowed to spend a maximum of £12,000 for each constituency in which it had a candidate and £80,000 for each regional list on which it had candidates. A party contesting all seats and all regions could spend, therefore, a maximum of around £1.5 million on its national campaign. Although no party spent up to the permissible legal maximum, the 2007 election was the most expensive in recent Scottish history. In total, Scotland's four largest parties spent £3.4 million on their national campaigns, more than double their expenditure in 2003 (£1.65 million). Inevitably, there were significant differences between the parties. Labour and the SNP each spent over £1 million, comprehensively outspending the Conservatives and the Liberal Democrats. The latter were very much the poor relations, spending just under £300,000,

Table 7.3 *National 2007 campaign expenditure by party (£)*

	Conservatives	*Labour*	*Lib Dems*[a]	*SNP*
Party political broadcasts	29,338	59,685	15,381	90,726
Advertising	119,419	337,609	26,166	494,642
Unsolicited material to electors	247,521	270,020	98,323	323,580
Manifesto/party documents	9,134	17,525	6,905	56,999
Market research/canvassing	15,353	107,477	64,626	178,705
Media	17,957	29,710	29,481	45,041
Transport	2,243	72,366	29,635	52,239
Rallies and events	270	89,685	1,710	64,652
Overheads/general administration	160,747	118,789	25,345	76,146
Total	601,982	1,102,866	297,572	1,383,462
% increase on 2003	86.2%	51.8%	133.0%	192.4%

Note: [a]A further £6,168 of Liberal Democrat spending was disputed.
Source: Electoral Commission.

half the Conservatives' total. All four parties spent more than they had four years before but it was the SNP which saw by far the biggest proportionate increase, almost tripling its expenditure to become – for the first time – the biggest-spending party. On returning to the leadership, Alex Salmond had set his party the aim of having £1 million to spend on the 2007 election. At its pre-election conference in March, the SNP was able to announce that it had exceeded its target. Much media coverage focused on the contributions made by individual business people, and in particular on the hefty donation from Stagecoach tycoon Brian Souter. These large donations were seen by the SNP as important in signalling business support for the party (as well as swelling the coffers). In addition, however, a considerable part of the election fund was raised from the ordinary membership. Labour, on the other hand, spent just half as much again as it did in 2003. At the UK level the party was starved of funds – not least due to the continuing row about cash for honours – and Scottish Labour received less support than usual from London.

All four parties spent roughly the same relative amounts on their PEBs – between 5 and 6 per cent of total expenditure (although, of course, that translates into much more money for Labour and the SNP than for the other two) – and a substantial proportion of their budgets went on materials for electors (leaflets being particularly important). The Conservatives spent just over 40 per cent of their funds on this, the Liberal Democrats a third, and Labour and the SNP just under 25 per cent. There were wide variations, however, in the proportions of expenditure going on other forms of advertising (billboards, newspaper advertising etc.). The SNP and Labour dominated here, spending not only the largest absolute sums but also the largest relative amounts: each devoted around a third of its expenditure to advertising, compared with 20 per cent of Conservative funds and just 9 per cent of Liberal Democrat expenditure.

Total expenditures at constituency level are shown in Table 7.4. Compared with the national campaigns, much less was spent in the constituency campaigns of the major parties (£1.3 million in total). Labour's spending on constituency campaigns was just under 40 per cent of that on its national campaign while the equivalent figure for the SNP was just under 25 per cent. The smaller parties spent rather more, proportionately, on constituency campaigns: the Conservatives' local spending was 50 per cent of that at national level while the Liberal Democrats came closest to parity between national and local spending, with the latter being just under 80 per cent of the former. Unsurprisingly, the funding gap which was apparent in the national contest was also evident at local level: Labour was the largest spender on constituency battles (which is also not surprising, given that it already held most constituency seats and had to campaign hard to defend them), followed by the SNP and Conservatives, with the Liberal Democrats once again the poor relations.

Table 7.4 *Constituency campaign expenditure in 2007 by party and as a percentage of the legal maximum*

	Conservatives		Labour		Lib Dems		SNP	
Total spending	£302,099		£426,394		£235,141		£344,484	
% of legal maximum:	%	N	%	N	%	N	%	N
All seats	38.9	71	55.7	71	30.0	71	44.0	71
By 2003 marginality[a]								
Hopeless loss	31.9	62	18.9	16	19.4	57	37.5	51
Marginal loss	87.7	6	48.4	9	89.1	1	57.9	11
Marginal win	87.6	3	84.8	13	84.7	3	64.8	5
Safe win	–	–	62.6	33	67.9	10	62.8	4

Note: [a]Figures in this section of the table exclude Falkirk West, and Strathkelvin and Bearsden, both of which were won by independent candidates in 2003. The marginality categories are based on the difference between a party's 2003 vote share in a constituency and either (if the party won the seat) the 2003 vote share of the party in second place or (if it lost) the vote share of the winning party. A constituency is categorised as 'marginal' if this gap was less than 10 points, and otherwise as 'hopeless' or 'safe'.
Source: Electoral Commission.

The parties targeted their local efforts sensibly. Table 7.4 also shows the average constituency expenditure by each party as a percentage of the legal maximum, broken down by how marginal the seat was for a party. The figures show that all four major parties spent much less in seats that they were bound to lose. In part, this reflects most parties' weak grassroots organisations in such seats but spending was also lower in their safest seats than in marginals. Insofar as expenditure is an indicator of campaign effort, then, the greatest efforts were made in the seats that could yield the largest electoral dividends. Spending figures also confirm the defensive strategy adopted by Labour – much more was spent in seats that were narrowly held than in those where they were challenging – whereas the other parties appear to have made little distinction between the two.

The 2007 campaign from the voters' perspective

To investigate how voters experienced the election campaign, respondents to the SES post-election survey were asked about four possible types of campaign exposure: whether a canvasser called at their home; whether someone from a party telephoned them; whether they read an election leaflet that came through the door; and whether they saw any of the PEBs shown on television. In each

Table 7.5 *Voters' contacts with campaigns (percentage of respondents)*

	Any party	*Conservatives*	*Labour*	*Lib Dems*	*SNP*
Any campaign contact	83	64	73	66	73
Any constituency contact	78	58	66	60	66
Any canvassing	29	6	11	6	13
Canvassed in person	22	5	9	4	9
Read party leaflet	73	57	64	59	63
Telephoned	11	1	3	2	6
Saw party election broadcast	50	27	36	27	39
N	*1,552*	*1,552*	*1,552*	*1,552*	*1,552*

Source: Post-election survey.

case, if the answer was positive, they were asked which parties were involved. Few respondents were untouched by the parties' campaign efforts, with fully 83 per cent coming into contact with some aspect of at least one party's campaign (Table 7.5). Moreover, a majority of respondents encountered at least two of the major parties' campaigns and fully 56 per cent said they had noticed campaign activities from all four of these parties. More reported encountering the Labour and SNP campaigns (73 per cent in each case) than those of either the Conservatives or the Liberal Democrats, although the difference is relatively slight. Strikingly, while almost four out of every five respondents were exposed to some aspect of the constituency campaign (i.e. had read a leaflet, been canvassed or been telephoned by a party), only half had seen a PEB. As noted above, it was previously thought that the rise of television campaigning in Britain from 1959 had rendered local campaigning redundant but the growth of multi-channel TV since the 1980s has made it easy for viewers to avoid PEBs entirely by switching channels. The local dimension remains important in 'post-modern' political campaigning (Norris, 2000). Nonetheless, it was the relatively low-intensity aspects of constituency campaigning which were most widely experienced. Whereas almost three-quarters of respondents reported reading party leaflets, only around a quarter reported being canvassed and just over one in 10 reported being telephoned. This reflects both resource constraints, notably the lack of a large and active membership, and parties' strategies in targeting marginal seats.

As discussed in Chapter 1, there were marked differences between the leading parties in their approach to and tone of campaigning in 2007. Labour, on the back foot going into the election, made much of fears that an SNP win would be the first step towards independence, with particular emphasis on the alleged adverse effects on Scotland's economy. The SNP, on the other

Table 7.6 *Perceptions of party campaign tone (percentage of respondents)*

	Conservatives	*Labour*	*Lib Dems*	*SNP*
Very positive	6	3	5	22
Fairly positive	30	17	30	29
Neither positive nor negative	30	21	41	20
Fairly negative	23	25	18	15
Very negative	11	34	7	14
N	1,214	1,271	1,216	1,261

Source: Post-election survey.

hand, campaigned on the promise of a fresh start after the Labour years. 'Time for a change' was undoubtedly part of the SNP's appeal and, in general, the party sought to emphasise positive messages. These differences were noticed by voters. SES respondents were asked to rate the campaigns of the four main parties on a scale from 'very positive' to 'very negative'. Labour's campaign was assessed very unfavourably – almost 60 per cent of respondents who expressed a view thought that the Labour campaign was negative, a far larger proportion than for any other party's campaign (Table 7.6).[2] In stark contrast, just over 50 per cent of voters thought that the SNP campaign was generally positive. In short, the party's upbeat message got across. For the Liberal Democrats, the campaign challenge was to present themselves as an effective party of government (they had been a part of the Executive since devolution and could point to some achievements in office) while at the same time keeping some distance from Labour, their unpopular partner in the Executive. Clearly, this was a difficult tightrope to walk. Perhaps as a result of the difficulties the party faced, voters were less clear in their overall opinion of the tone of the Liberal Democrats' campaign than was the case for the other parties. The Conservatives' campaign, meanwhile, split opinion neatly into three parts: a third of the electorate thought that the party had campaigned positively, a third thought it had been negative and a third thought it had been neither. (Given the party's shaky standing with the Scottish electorate, these neutral ratings may well represent a relatively successful campaign.)

Did it matter? Measuring campaign effectiveness

In this section, we investigate the impact of the campaign on voters' opinions of parties and on voting in the constituency contest. Since part of the aim of a campaign is to improve a party's image with the electorate, we begin by

Figure 7.1 *The impact of campaign exposure on party likeability*

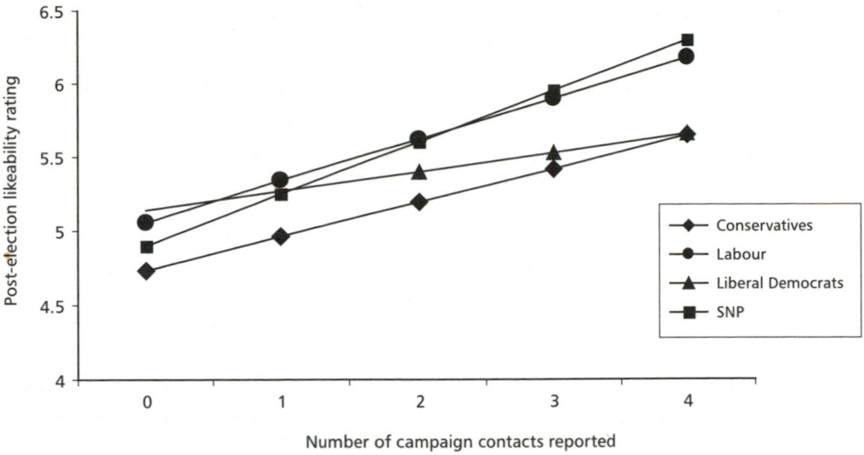

Source: Pre- and post-election surveys.

analysing changes in people's feelings towards the main parties over the course of the campaign. In both the pre- and post-election surveys, SES respondents were asked to rate each party on a like–dislike scale from 0 ('strongly dislike') to 10 ('strongly like'). To gauge the impact of campaigning on these ratings, we ran regression analyses predicting post-election likeability ratings on the basis of respondents' exposure to all measured aspects of each party's election campaign.[3] By also including the original likeability rating as a control, we can take account of voters' prior feelings towards the parties. This means that we are effectively measuring the extent to which exposure to each party's campaign increased its likeability. The full regression results are reported in Appendix 3 (Table A7.1) but the salient points are displayed in Figure 7.1, which shows the effects of exposure to a party's campaign on a hypothetical voter who gave each party a likeability score of 5 before the election.

The positive effects are clear from the upward slopes of the lines: the more someone was exposed to a party's campaign, the warmer they felt towards that party by the time of the election.[4] The steepness of the slopes indicates the effectiveness of campaigning in boosting each party's popularity and the graph suggests that the Liberal Democrats' campaign was somewhat less effective than those of the other parties. Indeed, unlike those of the other parties, the Liberal Democrat campaign did not have a statistically significant effect on the party's likeability rating.

Since voters are more likely to support a party that they like, these results suggest that campaigning by the parties did ultimately improve their electoral

Table 7.7 *Campaign exposure and party choice (regional list)*
(percentage of respondents)

| | Was respondent exposed to party's campaign? | | | | | | | |
| | Conservative | | Labour | | Lib Dem | | SNP | |
	Yes	No	Yes	No	Yes	No	Yes	No
Non-supporters	83	90	72	81	85	89	59	80
Defectors	5	4	8	9	6	3	6	9
Joiners	2	1	4	1	2	3	7	3
Loyalists	11	5	17	9	7	5	28	8
N	863	438	965	336	877	424	967	335
χ^2	**15.2**		**17.1**		7.6		**65.6**	

Note: χ^2 (chi-squared) values measure the statistical significance of differences by campaign exposure for each party; those in bold are significant at the $p < 0.05$ level.
Source: Post-election survey.

performance. We can test this suggestion more directly, however. Respondents were divided into four groups: those who neither intended to vote for a party (on the regional list) before the election nor did so in the election (non-supporters); those who initially intended to vote for the party but in the event did not, either voting for another party or abstaining (defectors); those who before the election said they would not vote for the party (indicating an intention either to vote for another party or to abstain) but who did so on polling day (joiners); and those who both intended to and actually voted for the party (loyalists). We compare how respondents split among those four groups depending on whether or not they were exposed to at least one of the four aspects of a party's campaign.

These results again suggest that campaigning yielded electoral benefits (Table 7.7). The proportion of 'loyalists' in each case is higher among those who were exposed to a party's campaign, strikingly so in the case of the SNP. For three of the four parties, the ratio of joiners to defectors is also greater among those who experienced some aspect of the parties' campaigning. In other words, the more voters that those parties reached in the campaign, the better they did out of the (extensive) switching during that period. The exception is again the Liberal Democrats, for whom, as before, there is no evidence of statistically significant campaign effects. More broadly, there are clearly limits on the beneficial effects of campaigning, given that the tendency to defect from a party differs little according to whether respondents were exposed to its campaign. A voter reached is not necessarily a voter retained.

However, we need to be mindful of the biasing effects of partisanship on these results. Those with a prior attachment to a party, even if it is weakening, are more likely both (to choose) to be exposed to that party's campaign and to recall such exposure. Even if campaigns had no impact on party choice, the effects of selective exposure and selective recall would lead us to expect a disproportionate number of defectors as well as joiners and loyalists in the 'exposed' group. This reinforces the need to test for campaign effects while controlling for partisan predispositions and other influences on party choice.

The need to control for partisan bias is even more pressing when we are trying to assess whether voting behaviour is affected by electors' perceptions of campaign tone. Identifiers are inclined to see their own party's messages as especially positive and those of rival parties as unduly negative. Nonetheless, the differences between the parties' ratings in Table 7.6 suggest that these evaluations also have an objective component, independent of partisanship. This gives them the potential to influence voting behaviour. To assess whether this potential was fulfilled, we divide the electorate into three groups based on

Table 7.8 *Perceived campaign tone and party choice (regional list) by party support ('identifiers' and 'leaners') (percentage of respondents)*

Party support	Regional vote	Party running more positive campaign		
		SNP	*Neither*	*Labour*
SNP	SNP	95	55	40
	Other	5	36	0
	Labour	0	9	60
	N	*213*	*22*	*5*
Labour	SNP	24	4	0
	Other	35	22	11
	Labour	41	74	89
	N	*66*	*142*	*135*
Other	SNP	26	5	0
	Other	72	92	77
	Labour	1	4	23
	N	*140*	*108*	*61*
None	SNP	47	18	0
	Other	42	52	46
	Labour	11	30	54
	N	*138*	*107*	*37*

Sources: Pre- and post-election surveys (weighted by vote shares).

the ratings for Labour and the SNP: those regarding the SNP's campaign as more positive, those regarding Labour's as more positive and those who rated the campaigns as equally positive or negative. Comparing the voting behaviour of these groups gives an indication of the impact of campaign tone. In order to control for partisan predispositions, we run the analysis for four types of voter – SNP supporters (identifiers and leaners – see Chapter 3), Labour supporters, other party supporters (combined) and those who reported no partisan leaning (Table 7.8).

The results for SNP supporters are not especially interesting because the vast majority of them thought their party's campaign more positive than Labour's and went on to vote for the SNP. Labour supporters who rated their party's campaign tone as more positive were also overwhelmingly likely to vote for it. Yet well over half of Labour supporters felt unable to claim that their party's campaign was more positive and their support clearly could not be counted on. Those Labour supporters who regarded the SNP's campaign as more positive voted in significant numbers for that party. Those seeing no difference between Labour and the SNP in campaign tone were reluctant to support the latter but around a quarter defected to other parties. As would be expected, most of those who supported parties other than Labour and the SNP voted for neither. Among the exceptions, however, there is a clear association between perceptions of campaign tone and party choice. The same is true among the group of non-partisan voters and it is noteworthy that this group was especially unlikely to see the Labour campaign as the more positive.

On the basis of this evidence, then, the SNP's considerable advantage over Labour in terms of campaign tone looks as if it yielded electoral benefits in 2007. Once again, however, we need to add a word of caution about controls. Although these results take account of partisanship, there are other factors that might be important. A supporter of independence, for example, is unlikely to have been impressed by the tone of the Labour campaign in 2007 but then was probably unlikely to vote for the party anyway. A more precise estimate of the effect of campaign variables – both exposure to the campaign and perceptions of tone – requires these sorts of factors to be added to the models of party choice built up over previous chapters and, since these are the final variables to be added, this is done in Chapter 10.

The local battle

In addition to the national campaign, largely conducted via the mass media, there were, of course, local campaigns in each of Scotland's 73 constituencies. We have already touched on aspects of local campaigning (canvassing, leaflets and so on) but in attempting to assess the impact of individual constituency campaigns we reach the limits of the SES data. The surveys were designed to yield information about the Scottish electorate as a whole: they do not provide significant samples of respondents in each constituency. To analyse constituency campaign effects, therefore, we turn to constituency campaign expenditure data, which provides a proxy measure of parties' campaign effort in individual seats (Johnston and Pattie, 2006). Using these data, a regression model was fitted for each party. In each model, the dependent variable is the party's share in 2007 of the constituency electorate (i.e. the proportion of those registered to vote in a constituency who voted for the party). Since parties tend to do best where they are strong already and worst where they start weak, the relevant party's share of the constituency electorate at the 2003 Scottish Parliament election is included as a control. The other independent variables are the amount spent by each party in the relevant constituency as a percentage of the legally permitted maximum.

Full results for the regression models are given in Appendix 3 (Table A7.2) but what they reveal about the impact of constituency campaign spending on party support is illustrated in Figure 7.2. This shows how many percentage

Figure 7.2 *The impact of constituency campaigning on constituency share of the electorate*

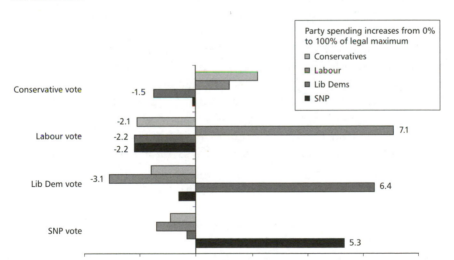

Note: Where the size of the increase or decrease in electorate share is given, this indicates a statistically significant effect.

points each party's share of the electorate in the 2007 constituency contest would have changed had that party gone from making no effort locally to spending up to its legal limit in the constituency and had the other parties in the seat failed to campaign at all. This is an unrealistic scenario, to be sure, but it does give us some idea of the potential size of constituency campaign effects. For example, the top four bars in the figure illustrate the effect of local campaigning on the Conservatives' share of the electorate (controlling, of course, for that party's performance in 2003). Other things being equal, and assuming the other parties did not campaign, if the Conservatives stepped their local campaign spending up from 0 per cent of the maximum to 100 per cent, then their share of the electorate would have increased by 2.2 percentage points. Had the Liberal Democrats increased their local campaign to the maximum possible, however, the Conservatives would have suffered, and their electorate share would have dropped by 1.5 percentage points.

Overall, the story that emerges is relatively straightforward. First, the harder that parties (except the Conservatives, for whom the difference failed to reach statistical significance) campaigned locally, the better they did in the constituency contest. Labour, the Liberal Democrats and the SNP all benefitted substantially from intense local campaigns. Second, in general, a party's performance in a constituency was also affected by the strength of the local campaigns mounted by competitors. Thus, support for the Conservatives was adversely affected by strong Liberal Democrat campaigning, support for Labour by the campaigns of the other three major parties and support for the Liberal Democrats by effective Labour local campaigning. Only the SNP was not significantly affected by rival parties' local campaigns. All the relevant effects are negative but none is statistically significant.

This sort of analysis is not novel (except in being applied to a Scottish Parliament election): it is familiar in the context of UK general elections. Under the Scottish Parliament electoral system, however, the regional list contests offer an opportunity for further analysis, since they raise the possibility of split-ticket voting (see Chapter 2). An additional potential function of party campaigns in these circumstances is to try to maximise gains (or minimise losses) from ticket-splitting. Effective constituency campaigns might boost the viability of their candidate as the best option for tactical voters and thus persuade some voters to abandon the party they supported in the regional ballot. At the same time, parties work hard to persuade their constituency voters not to defect (for example to a minor party) in the list contest, in which every vote won could be vital. Previous analyses of constituency campaigning in other AMS elections have shown that effective campaigns can help parties benefit in the constituency contest both from split-ticket voting and from

Figure 7.3 *Constituency campaigning and the difference between regional and constituency shares of electorate, 2007*

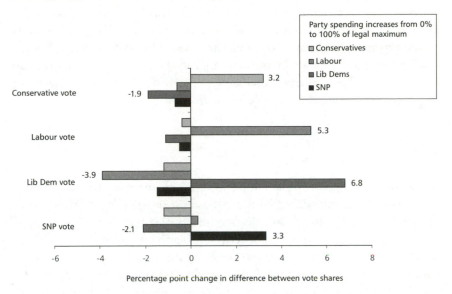

Percentage point change in difference between vote shares

encouraging their regional voters to remain loyal in the constituency vote (Johnston and Pattie, 2003; Gschwend *et al.*, 2003).

To address this question in respect of the 2007 Scottish Parliament election, we once again employ regression analyses. We know, for each party in each constituency, the votes received as a percentage of the constituency electorate in both the list and the constituency contest. Subtracting the former from the latter gives a measure of how much better (or worse) a party did locally in the regional list than in the constituency contest. That measure constitutes the dependent variable in these analyses. The independent variables are, as before, the four parties' 2007 constituency campaign expenditures, as a percentage of the legal maximum. The results (detailed Appendix 3, Table A7.3) provide support for the hypothesis that stronger local campaigns help parties benefit from ticket-splitting (see Figure 7.3, which employs the same conventions as Figure 7.2). The harder each party campaigned locally in 2007, the greater was the improvement in its performance from the regional to the constituency vote. The effect was particularly conspicuous for the Liberal Democrats. Other things being equal, in seats where the party's constituency campaign hypothetically spent up to the limit, its constituency vote (as a percentage of the electorate) would have been on average 6.8 percentage points higher than its regional vote. In addition, on the whole, the harder parties fought locally, the more effective they seem to have been in preventing their rivals from holding on to their supporters in the regional contest. Thus, strong Liberal Democrat campaigning made for poorer Conservative and SNP performances in terms of ticket-splitting and where Labour hypothetically campaigned up to the limit the difference between the Liberal Democrats' constituency and regional votes would have been almost 4 percentage points smaller than where Labour did not campaign at all. The impact of campaigning on constituency performance, therefore, is partly explained by its impact on ticket-splitting between the two levels of election.

Conclusion

Inevitably, the outcome of the 2007 Scottish Parliament election owed much to the politics of the preceding four years. Yet, as this chapter has shown, during the campaign itself a significant minority of voters were still making up their minds about how to vote. Moreover, given the unprecedented closeness of the contest between Labour and the SNP, the parties' efforts to persuade voters during the campaign took on even greater significance than normal. For the 'big two' especially, the election could potentially be won or lost on how effectively they campaigned.

It is hardly surprising, therefore, that Labour and the SNP expended considerable resources on their election campaigns. The Liberal Democrats and Conservatives also had much to win or lose but neither could remotely match the war chests available to their larger rivals. Both, therefore, had to be more circumspect in their efforts. All parties focused their efforts on key marginal constituencies but the operation of the AMS electoral system meant that they could not neglect the national and regional contests.

Our evidence suggests that the efforts made by the parties – all the exhausting work of leafleting, canvassing, telephoning, printing and display-ing posters, together with election broadcasts – made a difference. At the simplest level, over 80 per cent of voters recalled some sort of contact from the main parties. While in some cases the only contact (apart from news stories in the press and on television) came from seeing PEBs, others were contacted in a variety of ways. While we do not know how informative voters found the campaigns, the parties did at least achieve the minimal threshold of being widely visible during the election. More importantly, the evidence suggests that the parties' campaigns influenced vote choices. The more voters saw of a party's campaign, the more likely they were to support it. This worked in a variety of ways. The more voters noticed a party's campaign, the more their opinion of the party improved, making a vote for the party more likely. Strong campaigns also encouraged those already predisposed towards a party to actually turn out and vote for it. They also helped to minimise defection and maximise retention between the list and constituency contests. It is the case, of course, that each party's campaign efforts were to some extent counteracted by the campaigns of its rivals, so that the net effect was often limited. However, the effects of campaign tone did not cancel out in this way. If a party's overall campaign approach tends to repel rather than to attract voters, then its efforts on the ground are likely to be undermined. Certainly there is clear evidence in this chapter that Labour lost out on polling day due to the widespread perception that it ran a negative campaign. In a closely contested election, with significant proportions of the electorate making up their minds late in the day, this may have been enough to swing the outcome away from the party.

Notes

1 Personal communication with authors.
2 Predictably, partisan respondents were more likely to credit their party with a positive approach. Yet this was true of only 43 per cent of Labour identifiers, well adrift of the corresponding proportions for the other parties, all of which exceeded three-quarters.
3 An 'index of exposure' for each party was calculated by counting whether a respondent was canvassed, telephoned or leafleted, or had seen its PEB. It ranges from 0 (no contact with a party's campaign) to 4 (experienced all four of these campaign activities).
4 As expected, the more someone liked a party before the election, the more they liked it after. The coefficients for pre-election likeability scores are all strongly positive but they are all less than 1.0, implying that had the parties not campaigned at all, voters would have liked them less at the end of the campaign than at the start.

8
Turnout and turning out: a normal election?

It almost goes without saying that elections are central to democracy. Yet, in all political systems (including those in which voting is compulsory by law) not all eligible citizens take the opportunity to participate in what H. G. Wells called 'democracy's feast' (see Weisberg, 1995: 1). Exploring turnout and abstention has become a particular preoccupation of electoral analysts in the UK since the plunge in general election turnout from 78 per cent in 1992 to 59 per cent in 2001. It is useful to distinguish two distinct analytical approaches to the topic. The first focuses on 'turnout' – the aggregate percentage of the eligible electorate voting in an election. In the UK, this varies between different types of election and also over time, while in any one election it varies from place to place. There is a considerable literature focused on explaining these sorts of variations (see Denver, 2007b: ch. 2). The second approach focuses on individuals – some turn out in an election and some do not, and the key questions to be considered in this case are who votes, who doesn't and why? In this chapter we look first at turnout patterns in Scotland before going on to consider whether Scotland displays any distinctive patterns in respect of who votes and why. We pay particular attention to comparisons with turnout in the 2005 UK general election, in both Scotland and the rest of Britain, and consider whether turnout decisions in 2007 were driven by the same kinds of factors that operate in different electoral contexts.

Turnout trends in Scotland

Over the post-war period, turnout in British general elections in Scotland has been very close to the levels recorded in the rest of country and the trends in turnout are more or less identical (Figure 8.1). This implies that the reasons for turnout variation over time in Scotland are the same as those that apply in Britain as a whole. These include the expected closeness of the election contest in question and the extent to which the major parties were perceived

Figure 8.1 *Turnout in general elections in Scotland and the rest of Britain, 1950–2005*

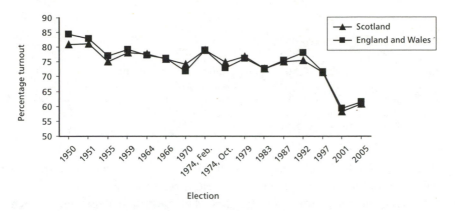

Table 8.1 *Turnout in Scotland, 1997–2007 (%)*

	1997	1999	2001	2003	2005	2007
UK general elections	71.3	–	58.1	–	60.8	–
Scottish Parliament elections	–	59.0	–	49.7	–	53.9

as offering significantly different choices (Heath and Taylor, 1999), as well as steady declines in the strength of party attachments and sense of civic duty (Clarke *et al.*, 2004: 261–74).

For convenience, Table 8.1 again presents the turnout figures discussed in Chapter 6. In British general elections, turnout in Scotland, as in Britain as a whole, dropped sharply between 1997 and 2001 but recovered a little in 2005. In Scottish Parliament elections turnout has consistently been lower than in the preceding British general election, and fell below 50 per cent in 2003. This is the 'second-order election' effect on participation noted in Chapter 6. There was a clear increase in turnout in the 2007 election compared with 2003, however, probably due to widespread anticipation of a close contest between Labour and the SNP.

Constituency variations

Around these overall figures, turnout varies a great deal from constituency to constituency and (even more so) from ward to ward. In the 2007 Scottish Parliament election, for example, turnout ranged from 38.0 per cent in Glasgow

Table 8.2 *Correlations between constituency turnouts, 1997–2007*

	1997*	*1999*	*2001**	*2003*
1999	0.904			
2001*	0.952	0.912		
2003	0.844	0.921	0.904	
2007	0.803	0.912	0.860	0.944

Notes: Figures for the asterisked years refer to UK general elections, the remainder to Scottish Parliament elections. The N for coefficients involving UK general elections is 72; otherwise $N = 73$. All coefficients are statistically significant ($p < 0.01$).

Shettleston to 64.8 per cent in Eastwood. Moreover, the pattern of variation is very consistent in election after election. Table 8.2 shows Pearson correlation coefficients measuring the association between constituency turnouts in each pair of elections since 1997 (excluding the 2005 UK general election, which was fought on different boundaries from the rest). All the relationships are very strong, including those which compare constituency turnouts in UK general elections with those in Scottish Parliament elections. No matter the type of election or the overall level of turnout, the same constituencies tend always to have either relatively high or relatively low turnouts.

What explains the pattern of variation in constituency turnouts? In general terms, two main factors have been found to influence turnout levels – the socioeconomic character of constituencies and the extent to which constituencies are competitive between parties or safe for one party or another (marginality). Thus a combination of social and political factors is involved. The significance of socioeconomic context at the aggregate level derives from the fact that different social groups display different propensities to turn out. Marginality is important largely because parties campaign more intensively in more marginal seats, so that electors are more successfully mobilised to go to the polls (see Denver *et al.*, 2003a).

Table 8.3 shows, for elections between 1997 and 2007, bivariate correlations between turnout and various sociodemographic characteristics – plus the marginality – of Scottish constituencies.[1] These data make it clear that there has been consistent and systematic variation in turnout across constituencies in both Scottish Parliament and UK general elections. Turnout is significantly higher in seats with larger proportions of owner occupiers, people with an affiliation to the Church of Scotland, people in professional and managerial occupations and people employed in agriculture. In more recent elections the percentage aged 65 and percentage with a degree have become more significant. Three variables (percentage of manual workers – defined here as social grades C2 and D; percentage with no religious affiliation; percentage of

Table 8.3 *Bivariate correlations with constituency turnout in elections, 1997–2007*

	1997 general	1999 Scottish	2001 general	2003 Scottish	2005 general	2007 Scottish
% owner occupiers	0.717	0.760	0.768	0.749	0.814	0.795
% Church of Scotland	0.629	0.591	0.667	0.577	0.502	0.467
% professional/managerial	0.385	0.448	0.414	0.445	0.644	0.560
% employed in agriculture	0.327	0.294	0.387	0.357	0.280	0.293
% aged 65+	0.175	0.200	0.281	0.336	0.261	0.226
% with degree	0.089	0.214	0.145	0.268	0.475	0.402
% manual workers	0.046	−0.028	0.037	−0.061	−0.275	−0.147
% no religion	0.033	−0.014	−0.016	−0.047	0.131	0.065
% private renters	−0.276	−0.195	−0.208	−0.091	−0.006	−0.010
% with no car	−0.749	−0.737	−0.788	−0.704	−0.707	−0.705
Persons per hectare	−0.673	−0.626	−0.684	−0.593	−0.468	−0.527
% social renters	−0.550	−0.635	−0.643	−0.681	−0.768	−0.756
% ethnic minority	−0.484	−0.484	−0.531	−0.408	−0.354	−0.347
% aged 18–24	−0.478	−0.450	−0.500	−0.428	−0.345	−0.348
% Catholic	−0.350	−0.367	−0.397	−0.393	−0.435	−0.415
Marginality in previous general election	0.535	0.566	0.604	0.628	0.582	
Marginality in previous Scottish Parliament election				0.329		0.514
N (constituencies)	72	73	72	73	59	73

Note: Coefficients in bold are significant at the $p < 0.05$ level.

private renters) have no consistent significant relationship with turnout. On the other hand, there are consistent and strong negative relationships with percentage of households having no car, number of persons per hectare (which taps a rural–urban dimension) and the proportions of social renters (local authority or housing association tenants), ethnic minority residents, young people (aged 18–24) and Catholics. The higher the scores on these variables, the lower is the turnout. Previous marginality also correlates consistently and significantly with turnout as expected – more marginal seats tend to have higher turnouts than safer seats. Previous work on the 1999 and 2003 Scottish Parliament elections has shown that the pattern of relationships revealed by Table 8.3 is broadly replicated when analysis is carried out at ward level (Denver and Hands, 2004a).

While bivariate correlations provide interesting and important information about the characteristics of constituencies associated with turnout variations, their usefulness has limits. One problem is that the various measures of social composition are themselves highly interrelated. For example, areas with large proportions of owner occupiers tend also to have relatively large proportions in professional and managerial occupations and small proportions of social renters and households without a car. Furthermore, bivariate analysis provides no clue as to the joint impact of a number of variables or to the impact of any particular variable once others are taken into account. We might want to know, for instance, how much of the variation in turnout is explained by class and housing tenure together, or whether the proportion of Catholics affects turnout once the class composition of the constituency or ward is taken into account.

We can deal with these issues by undertaking multiple regression analysis. Such an analysis shows that just two measures of the social make-up of constituencies (percentages of owner occupiers and of people aged 65 and over) plus marginality in the previous Scottish Parliament election accounted for more than 70 per cent of the variation in constituency turnouts at the 2007 election. (For details see Appendix 3, Table A8.1.)

It has to be emphasised, of course, that analysing aggregate turnout does not tell us anything definitive about how well or badly the various groups identified in Table 8.3 turned out. Although constituencies with larger proportions of owner occupiers have higher turnouts, this does not necessarily mean (although it might be true) that owner occupiers themselves have a higher turnout than average. The aggregate data analysed refer to the characteristics of – and thus enable us to talk about – constituencies. In order to talk about the turnout of various groups of voters, we need to turn to individual-level data collected in surveys of the electorate. In the next section we use the 2007 SES data for that purpose.

Who votes and who doesn't? Social characteristics

Not having the resources to check whether SES respondents actually voted by consulting marked electoral registers, we have to rely on their own reports of whether or not they voted. On the face of it, the fact that 78 per cent of respondents claimed to have voted might be thought to undermine these reports, given that the actual turnout was just 54 per cent. Yet this kind of gap is not unusual: surveys routinely find that the proportion of respondents claiming to have voted in an election is much larger than the actual turnout (Heath and Taylor, 1999). However, false claims typically account for only a small part (typically only around a quarter) of the gap. Most of the difference is due to the fact that non-voters, mainly because of their lack of political interest, are less likely to respond to surveys (Swaddle and Heath, 1989). Thus, self-reports of non-voting are reasonably accurate and we have enough self-confessed non-voters in our sample to draw reliable conclusions about abstainers. Nonetheless, in what follows we weight the data according to turnout in order to yield more realistic estimates.

The question of who votes and who doesn't has been investigated over a lengthy period. The subject is of some theoretical importance, since socially skewed patterns of participation could pose problems for those who view extensive citizen involvement via elections as a defining characteristic of democracies. The first significant survey study of non-voting in Britain was published in the late 1970s (Crewe *et al.*, 1977). The authors investigated the effects of a series of social variables on propensity to vote and found that, contrary to common assumptions and to well established results from other countries, most had little effect. Only four (interconnected) social factors were associated with poor turnout: being young (the most important), being unmarried, living in privately rented accommodation and being residentially mobile. Crewe and his colleagues explained higher levels of non-voting by these groups in terms of isolation from personal and community networks, which encourage conformity with the norm of voting.

In a later analysis, Swaddle and Heath (1989), making use of the official turnout records of survey respondents for the first time, broadly confirmed for the 1987 UK general election the results originally reported by Crewe *et al.* with respect to social influences on the propensity to vote. In addition, they found that class and income appeared also to influence turnout, with manual workers and poorer people having lower turnouts than average. In the 1992 general election, however, from a restricted set of social variables (not including marital status or length of residence in the community, for example), Pattie and Johnston (1998) found that only age and tenure affected electoral participation, while class and education did not.

To sum up, then, it appears that at UK level there is strong and consistent evidence that propensity to vote varies by age, marital status, housing tenure and residential mobility. The evidence about class is mixed. No other social characteristic appears to make a consistent difference. We now consider the extent to which this is true of Scotland at the start of the twenty-first century. First, Table 8.4 shows the turnout of a variety of social groups in the 2007 Scottish Parliament election and the 2005 UK general election in Scotland. The 2005 data are derived from the Scottish sample interviewed face to face in connection with the 2005 British Election Study (BES) survey. In that case, reported turnout was validated by reference to the relevant electoral registers but the data have again been weighted to reflect actual turnout.

Table 8.4 *Turnout by sociodemographic group, 2007 Scottish Parliament election and 2005 UK general election*

	2007 Scottish Parliament election		2005 general election	
	%	N	%	N
Age				
18–24	35	222	42	114
25–34	40	325	49	163
35–44	48	285	59	195
45–54	57	267	69	162
55–64	66	366	79	138
65+	62	130	76	189
Sex				
Males	55	728	63	451
Females	48	868	63	509
Occupational class				
Professional/managerial	60	558	75	245
Other non-manual	49	526	64	288
Manual	49	355	54	352
Tenure				
Owner occupiers	56	979	70	665
Rent from local authority	47	184	53	151
Rent privately	42	203	42	52
Rent from housing association	40	96	37	73
Marital status				
Married/widowed	57	831	72	594
Live with partner	34	253	46	102
Separated/divorced	56	125	56	71
Single	48	387	46	194
Highest educational qualification				
None	40	341	60	298
Degree	61	412	76	147
Professional/teaching	59	298	66	186
School certificate	44	346	55	176
Vocational/technical/other	51	200	62	152
Religious affiliation				
None	44	1,005	56	435
Church of Scotland	69	272	72	301
Catholic	54	155	63	128
Other	63	143	65	97

Note: Data are weighted to reflect actual turnout in the election.
Sources: Pre- and post-election surveys; BES 2005.

Although turnout was higher in the general than in the Scottish Parliament election, the pattern of variation across different social and demographic groups is very similar in both cases. Among the well established social influences on turnout, age, marital status and tenure show the anticipated effects. Older voters, the married (or widowed) and owner occupiers clearly turn out more than other groups. In addition, however, the data suggest that among Scottish electors there are significant differences related to class, education level and religious affiliation. The only example of a difference between the general and Scottish Parliament election concerns sex. In the Scottish Parliament election men were significantly more likely to vote than women but in the 2005 UK general election – and, for that matter, the two previous Scottish Parliament elections – there was no significant gender gap in turnout. In the absence of any obvious explanation for the unusual result in 2007, it is tempting to conclude that the sex difference here is simply a statistical blip.

Simple cross-tabulations suffer from some of the same drawbacks as simple bivariate correlations – most notably, they do not allow us to assess the impact of a single variable while simultaneously taking account of others. However, we can employ the same logistic regression technique used in previous chapters. Here we are analysing the independent impact of the social characteristics listed in Table 8.4 on the likelihood that an individual turned out to vote. We conducted separate analyses for turnout in the 2007 Scottish Parliament and the 2005 UK general elections. The full results of each are provided in Appendix 3 (Table A8.2). Here we present a chart showing the effect on the likelihood to vote, at both the 2007 and the 2005 elections, of each social characteristic that had a significant impact (at the $p < 0.05$ level) in either of the analyses.

Considering first the 2007 Scottish Parliament election, perhaps unsurprisingly age is the most important of these characteristics affecting turnout, taking all the others into account (Figure 8.2). The odds ratios show that those aged 35–54 were around twice as likely to vote as those aged 18–34 and those aged over 55 three times as likely to do so. Also in line with expectations, people with a degree or professional qualification had a significantly higher turnout than those with no educational qualification. People affiliated to a religion or Christian denomination were more likely to vote – especially those with a Church of Scotland attachment – than those without and women were significantly less likely to vote than men. Those who cohabit with a partner were less likely to vote than married or widowed people and, finally, as far as tenure is concerned, the significant difference is between owner occupiers and those who rent from a housing association. Summarising drastically, then, we can say that the archetypal non-voter in the 2007 Scottish Parliament elections was a woman aged less than 35, with no educational qualifications and no religious affiliation, living with a partner in rented accommodation.

Figure 8.2 *Effects of social characteristics on likelihood of turning out, 2007 Scottish Parliament election and 2005 UK general election*

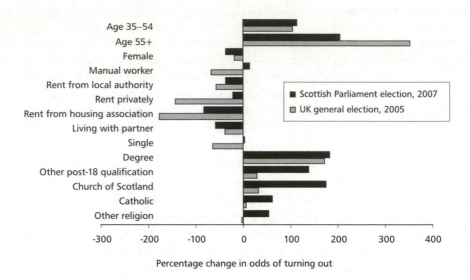

Percentage change in odds of turning out

Sources: Pre- and post-election surveys; BES 2005.

The analysis of voting in Scotland in the 2005 UK general election shows some similarities and some differences from that for the 2007 Scottish Parliament election. In both cases, older people voted to a much greater extent than younger voters, owner occupiers more than renters and those with a degree more than those without educational qualifications. On the other hand, in the UK general election there was no significant difference in the voting rates of men and women or on the basis of religious affiliation. To some extent, this reflects the smaller number of cases available in the 2005 data, since in many instances the effects in the two elections are similar but fail to reach conventional significance levels for the 2005 election. In the case of marital status, it was lower rates of voting by single people (rather than cohabiters) that was significant. In 2005 manual workers were less likely to vote than those in professional and managerial occupations, whereas in 2007 occupational class proved not to have a significant impact on to turnout once the other factors were taken into account.[2]

A final point, not so clearly conveyed by the chart, concerns the combined impact of these social characteristics. A 'model improvement' statistic can be calculated, showing the increase in the percentage of respondents correctly predicted to be voters or non-voters based on the sociodemographic information in the regression models. The baseline for this calculation is the percentage that would be correct on the basis of simply assigning all cases to the largest category ('voted' in this case). In the 2007 analysis, these social characteristics allow us successfully to assign 66.1 per cent of respondents as voters or non-voters, an improvement of almost 13 percentage points compared with simple allocation to the largest category. The corresponding improvement in the 2005 UK general election analysis was only seven points. We can conclude that voting versus non-voting in the Scottish Parliament election was more predictable on the basis of social characteristics than it was in the case of the 2005 UK general election. This is as expected. Where turnout is lower – as in Scottish Parliament elections – the fall-off is usually greatest among groups which have a weaker propensity to vote in the first place. Nevertheless, despite the small differences revealed by the analysis, it appears that there was not a great deal that was particularly novel about the social pattern of who voted and who did not in the Scottish Parliament election.

Political commitment and attitudes to elections

In their pioneering article referred to above, Crewe *et al.* (1977) went on from considering social characteristics to compare what they called the 'political commitment' of voters and non-voters. They found (as have all subsequent survey studies of turnout) that voting is strongly related to strength of party identification, with people who did not identify with any party having much the weakest propensity to vote. In addition, the measures of political commitment used by Crewe *et al.* included the extent to which respondents perceived differences between the parties, cared who won the election in question, were interested in politics and talked about politics. Although the SES has no measure of the *strength* of party identification or of the frequency of talking about politics, respondents did indicate whether or not they were party supporters and we also have a measure of general interest in politics. Turnout is fuelled not only by general political commitment but also by attitudes to elections and voting more specifically, and we have survey data measuring several of these attitudes. One such is citizens' judgements of how much it matters who wins elections and another (closely related) is their perception of differences between the major parties. Respondents were also asked whether they agreed or disagreed with the statement that 'it is every citizen's duty to vote'. Voting is in itself a culturally valued activity – the good citizen, it is widely believed, goes to the polls – and it has been suggested that a decline in sense of civic duty (due largely to generational replacement within the electorate) is a prime cause of declining turnout in Britain (Clarke *et al.*, 2004: 269–73).

Table 8.5 *Turnout by political commitment, 2007 Scottish Parliament election and 2005 UK general election*

	2007 Scottish Parliament election		2005 general election	
	%	N	%	N
Party supporter				
Yes	65	652	73	504
No	41	944	52	456
Interest in politics				
Great deal	78	199	81	64
Quite a lot	70	399	76	233
Some	53	515	68	329
Not very much	28	326	50	278
None/don't know	14	157	25	57
Matters who wins Scottish Parliament elections/care who wins UK general election				
Great deal	71	542	82	464
Quite a lot	61	389		
Some	43	235		
Not very much	38	137	45	233
None/don't know	15	293		
Difference between Labour and SNP				
Great deal	67	327		
Quite a lot	59	558		
Some	53	298		
Not very much	50	137		
None/don't know	16	275		
It is every citizen's duty to vote				
Agree	66	1,077	72	745
Neither agree nor disagree	23	255	38	105
Disagree	18	146	27	112

Note: Data are weighted to reflect actual turnout in the election.
Sources: Pre- and post-election surveys; BES 2005.

Parallel measures are also available in the 2005 BES, and so we can exam-ine the impact of political commitment and attitudes to elections on turnout in the most recent Scottish and UK general elections. The relationships are very much as expected (Table 8.5). In both cases, party supporters are clearly more likely to vote than those who disclaim any such identification, while turnout increases steadily along with respondent's interest in politics and their view of how much it matters who wins the election in question. In the Scottish Parliament election, the less difference that respondents perceived between Labour and the SNP, the less likely they were to turn out. No question like this was asked in the face-to-face UK general election survey but respondents to the mail-back questionnaire were asked to indicate whether they agreed or disagreed with the proposition that the main parties offer little or no choice to the voters. Among those who agreed ($N=395$) 64 per cent voted, while turnout among those who disagreed ($N=155$) was 81 per cent. Finally, belief in voting as a duty is strongly linked to turning out in both elections. It is a testament to the strength of the norm in favour of voting that only small minorities (9 per cent in 2007 and 12 per cent in 2005) could bring themselves to express explicit disagreement with the statement that there is a duty to vote.

It should be said that using some of these variables to explain voting as opposed to non-voting appears to come perilously close to tautology. It is not in the least surprising that those declaring a great deal of interest in politics turn out in greater numbers than those who say that they have no interest, still less that those who see a duty to vote are disproportionately likely to do so. Nonetheless, even among those who are interested in politics, who think it matters a lot who wins and who see voting as a duty, not everyone votes. Equally, some of those with little interest in politics and no sense of duty to vote still make it to the polls. More generally, social scientists have long found that attitudes are far from a perfect predictor of behaviour. Since these variables are only part of the explanation of turnout, it is necessary to include them alongside other factors in a more comprehensive model of voting versus non-voting. We come to that task shortly. Before that, however, we consider two final motivations for voting.

Marginality and mobilisation

It has been shown that elections in which the overall outcome is thought likely to be close have higher turnouts than those in which an easy victory for one party or another is anticipated (Clarke *et al.*, 2004: 261–8). In the 2007 SES pre-election survey, respondents were asked whether they agreed or disagreed that it was obvious who was going to win the Scottish Parliament election. Turnout was 65 per cent ($N=862$) among those who disagreed but only 35 per cent among those who agreed ($N=206$). There was no comparable question in the 2005 BES survey. However, in both surveys respondents were asked in advance of the election how likely each party in turn was to win their own constituency and, separately, how likely each was to win the election overall. By combining responses for the different parties we can create a new variable

Table 8.6 *Turnout by perceived closeness of local and national race, 2007 Scottish Parliament election and 2005 UK general election*

	2007 Scottish Parliament election		2005 general election	
	%	N	%	N
Constituency outcome				
Easy winner	56	198	67	153
Clear winner	60	443	69	308
Competitive	62	614	69	177
Other/don't know	18	308	50	12
Overall outcome				
Easy winner	51	107	69	190
Clear winner	56	401	67	307
Competitive	64	731	68	166
Other/don't know	22	357	47	15

Note: Data are weighted to reflect actual turnout in the election.
Sources: Pre- and post-election surveys; BES 2005

indicating the extent to which respondents thought that their constituency was safe or competitive and whether they thought the election would be a one-horse race or not. These perceptions do seem to have had an effect on behaviour in 2007 (Table 8.6). The impact was quite limited at the constituency level, although those who regarded the local contest as competitive were somewhat more likely to vote that those who thought that it would be a one-horse race (and very much more likely to turn out than the large minority who could not offer an opinion on the matter). Perceptions of the likely overall outcome had a stronger effect, with a 13-point difference in turnout between those who thought that the outcome would be close and those who expected an easy victory for either Labour or the SNP. The figures for Scottish voters in the 2005 UK general election, on the other hand, suggest that perceptions of the electoral context – whether local or national – made little difference to turnout. It would appear that instrumental considerations relating to the electoral context played a greater part in influencing the decision to vote or not in the Scottish Parliament election than in the UK general election. This may be because citizens feel a greater duty to vote in UK general elections – irrespective of the electoral context – than in Scottish Parliament elections.

As described in the previous chapter, a major feature of constituency campaigning is a 'get out the vote' operation on polling day. Having tried to identify potential supporters during the campaign, party workers seek to contact them on the day of the election and encourage them to vote by knocking on doors, telephoning, offering lifts to the polls and so on. We have divided respondents to both surveys simply according to whether they were canvassed (by any party, on the doorstep or by telephone) or not. The figures show a turnout of 60 per cent among those who were canvassed in the Scottish Parliament election ($N = 407$) as against 50 per cent among those who were not ($N = 775$). In the UK general election the difference was more spectacular – a turnout of 59 per cent among the non-canvassed ($N = 775$) and 79 per cent among those canvassed ($N = 186$). In both cases, the differences are statistically significant. There are issues about selective memory here, of course. It is likely that those who are more interested will more readily remember being canvassed than those with little interest. In the next section we examine the effect of canvassing on turnout after controlling for political interest and other background variables.

Who votes and who doesn't? A composite model

We can explore the cumulative impact of the various factors influencing turnout, and also assess their individual effect when taking account of all the others, by including all of them in an extended version of the logistic regression analysis described earlier and reported in Figure 8.2. First, we look closely at the Scottish Parliament election of 2007, and illustrate all of the factors that had a significant impact on the likelihood of turning out in that election. (The full results of the analysis are reported in Appendix 3, Table A8.3.)

Before considering the results in the chart (Figure 8.3), it is worth listing those variables discussed earlier that do not appear here: sex, housing tenure, marital status, being a party supporter, and perception of the difference between Labour and the SNP. When all the other variables are taken into consideration these no longer contribute significantly to differentiating between voters and non-voters. Those which are listed, however, enable us correctly to designate 76 per cent of respondents as voters or non-voters. This represents a marked improvement of 23 points on simply assigning all to the largest category (although it remains the case that, even knowing so much about their backgrounds and attitudes, we are still unable accurately to predict turnout for a quarter of respondents).

The strongest influences on turning out are the attitude variables, and in particular whether or not an individual considers voting a matter of civic duty. Other things remaining the same, those who agreed that it is a citizen's duty to vote were around five times as likely to vote as those who disagreed. Even under a partly proportional electoral system, one vote makes so little difference

Figure 8.3 *Effects of significant predictors of voting versus non-voting, 2007*

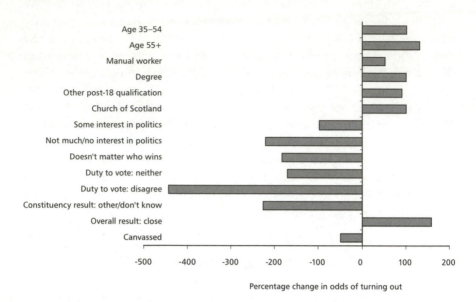

Percentage change in odds of turning out

Source: Pre- and post-election surveys.

to the electoral outcome that, following Downs's (1957) famous argument, voting can be seen as an irrational act. What has sustained reasonable turnout levels in Britain, it seems clear, is the fact that many people believe they have an obligation to vote, whether or not their vote makes any difference to the result. As noted above, a decline in this sense of duty goes a long way to explain Britain's declining turnout.

As might be expected, level of interest in politics in general is also strongly associated with turnout, and people who thought it mattered a good deal who wins Scottish Parliament elections were more likely to vote than those who did not. We suggested above that the increase in turnout in 2007 as compared with 2003 was almost certainly due to the fact that a close contest between Labour and the SNP was widely expected (and transpired) at the later election. This finds an echo in the survey data, as respondents who anticipated this close contest were significantly more likely to vote than were those expecting a wider margin of victory. At constituency level, however, the only significant difference is that those who had no idea about the likely outcome (and perhaps did not care) were less likely to vote than those interested enough to be able to give an opinion.

The effect of social characteristics was somewhat weaker, but still age, religious affiliation and education had an independent impact on turnout in the Scottish Parliament election. Holding all other variables constant, it remains the case that young people vote less than their elders, those affiliated to the Church of Scotland vote more than others and those with higher educational qualifications more than those with none. Although they are (just) statistically significant, the results for canvassing and occupational class are rather odd, suggesting that respondents canvassed during the election campaign were less likely to vote, while manual workers were more likely to vote than professionals and managers. We return to these unexpected results below.

Is Scotland different?

In this section we elaborate on the comparison between Scottish turnout in 2007 and in the 2005 UK general election but also compare Scotland with the rest of Britain. This focus addresses not only the question of how 'normal' the 2007 election was in terms of turnout but also whether there is anything distinctive about voting and non-voting in Scotland. As noted at the outset, aggregate turnout in Scotland at UK general elections is normally at a very similar level to that found in England and Wales and, over time, follows a similar trajectory. The question arises, however, of whether the bases of constituency variations elsewhere in Britain are the same as those which apply within Scotland. If we use the variables that best predicted constituency turnout at the Scottish Parliament election (marginality, percentage of owner occupiers and percentage aged 65 and over) to predict constituency turnout in England and Wales at the 2005 UK general election, then the results are closely comparable. All three variables have a highly significant effect and together they explain 66 per cent of turnout variation (see Appendix 3, Table A8.1). There is clearly nothing unusual about the pattern within Scotland.

Turning to the individual-level factors that predict voting versus non-voting, to allow for comparison we replicated the SES analysis reported in Figure 8.3 with BES data from 2005, first on Scottish and then on English and Welsh respondents. The full results are given in Appendix 3 (Table A8.3), while Table 8.7 reports a summary. The positive and negative signs denote whether respondents in that category were more or less likely to turn out than those in the comparison group (specified in parentheses alongside each variable). Doubled signs indicate a statistically significant difference (at the $p < 0.05$ level).

In predicting voting in the 2005 UK general election, whether in Scotland or elsewhere in Britain, the mixture of duty, 'political' variables and social

Table 8.7 *Factors affecting propensity to turn out in Scotland and in England and Wales*

Individual-level factor (comparison group in parentheses)	Scotland		England and Wales
	2007 Scottish Parliament election	2005 general election	2005 general election
Age (18–34)			
35–54	++	+	++
55+	++	++	++
Sex (Male)			
Female	–	–	++
Occupation (Professional and managerial)			
Other non-manual	+	+	–
Manual	++	–	– –
Tenure (Owner occupier)			
Rent from local authority	–	– –	–
Rent from housing association	–	– –	–
Privately rented	–	–	– –
Marital status (Married/widowed)			
Partner	–	–	–
Separated/divorced	–	–	–
Single	–	+	– –
Highest educational qualification (None)			
Degree	++	++	++
Professional/diploma/teaching	++	+	+
School certificate	+	+	+
Vocational/technical	+	+	+
Religious affiliation (None)			
Church of Scotland/Anglican	++	+	–
Catholic	+	– –	–
Other	+	–	+
Party supporter (No)			
Yes	+	++	++
Political interest (Great deal/quite a lot)			
Some	– –	–	–
Not much/none	– –	–	–
Party difference (Great deal/quite a lot)			
Some	– –	–	–
Not much/none	+	–	–
Matters/cares who wins (Great deal/quite a lot)			
Some	–	n/a	n/a
Not much/not at all	– –	– –	– –
Voting is citizen's duty (Agree)			
Neither	– –	–	– –
Disagree	– –	– –	– –
Likely constituency result (Easy winner)			
Clear winner	–	+	+
Close	–	++	+
Other/don't know	– –	–	+
Likely overall result (Easy victory)			
Clear victory	+	–	+
Close	++	–	+
Other/don't know	++	–	+
Canvassed (No)			
Yes	– –	++	++

Sources: Pre- and post-election surveys; BES 2005

characteristics is much the same as for the 2007 Scottish Parliament election. Comparing first the two Scottish elections, there are very few differences and most of these are quite predictable. In the 2005 general election in Scotland, the surprising result for manual workers is not replicated and the canvassing variable works as expected, with those having been canvassed more likely to vote, all things considered, than those who did not recall being canvassed. Party supporters were also significantly more likely to vote, again in line with expectations. In the 2005 analysis, it is the closeness of the constituency rather than the overall race that has a greater influence on turnout, which makes sense given the nature of the Westminster electoral system.

Overall, the factors which account for variation in the propensity to vote in Scotland are not very different from those which apply in the rest of Britain. In Scotland, as elsewhere, turnout is clearly higher among those who have a strong sense of civic duty, among those who think it matters who wins the election, among older people, and among those with higher educational qualifications. While the evidence is slightly less strong, it is also the case in both Scotland and the rest of Britain that, all things considered, the politically interested vote more than the less interested, those who identify themselves as party supporters vote more than those who do not, owner occupiers vote more than renters, and married and widowed people vote more than those who are single, separated or divorced or living with a partner. Those expecting a close constituency race are more likely to vote in Scottish, English and Welsh constituencies alike.

Nonetheless, there are a few ways in which voting patterns in Scotland differed from those found in the rest of the country in 2005. In the latter case, women were more likely to vote than men whereas sex made no statistically significant difference in Scotland. By contrast, religious affiliation had no effect on propensity to turn out in England and Wales once other factors are taken into account, while in Scotland those affiliated with the Church of Scotland were significantly more likely to vote than those with no religious attachment. This reinforces previous evidence showing that turnout in Scotland is higher among Protestants than among Catholics but lowest among those professing no religious affiliation (Bennie *et al.*, 1997: 114; see also Denver and Hands, 2004a: 538). It is not clear whether some aspect of Scotland's distinctive religious tradition is responsible for this persistent turnout effect.

Then there is the striking difference in the effects of occupational class. While manual workers were significantly less likely than professional and managerial groups to vote in England and Wales, they were significantly more likely to do so in the Scottish case. It is tempting to attribute this to a distinctive political culture in Scotland in which, for a variety of reasons, the working class is more politicised than in England. Yet no such pattern appears in the analysis of UK general election voting in Scotland, so it is more likely that the electoral context of 2007 explains the relatively high rates of participation by manual workers. The election was a close contest between two left-of-centre parties vying for support among working-class voters, whom they both would have sought to mobilise. In particular, manual workers disillusioned by Labour's performance in office could make their protest, not by staying away from the polls, but by turning up and supporting the SNP, which is widely seen as an acceptable alternative to Labour in a way that the other parties are not.

The other unusual result in the Scottish Parliament 2007 election, the apparent negative impact of being canvassed, is less easily explained. Our simple bivariate analysis showed that, as expected, those who reported being canvassed turned out to a greater extent than those who did not. Once all the other variables are taken into account, however, the relationship is reversed. In what may be a quirk of this particular analysis, other factors are 'washing out' the influence of canvassing. What we have here is likely to be a statistical blip of no substantive significance.

Conclusion

To sum up, then, with some minor variations relating especially to the influence of religious affiliation, in general there is nothing very distinctive about turnout patterns in Scotland. The same sorts of people vote and the same sorts of people don't vote as in the rest of Britain. Equally, the same sorts of places consistently produce higher turnouts and the same sorts of places consistently produce lower turnouts. There remains a small but clearly discernible gap between Scottish Parliament and Westminster election turnouts, reflecting the perception of some voters that there is less at stake – or perhaps a less established obligation to vote – in the former elections. Yet that gap is narrowing, and for the most part the factors predicting voting versus non-voting in 2007 were just the same as drive turnout in 'normal' elections.

Our survey data are inevitably better suited to exploring the causes rather than the consequences of turnout levels in 2007. One question that we can address, however, is whether relatively low turnout affected the results of the 2007 Scottish Parliament election. There is circumstantial evidence to suspect so. In Chapter 3 we saw that Labour identifiers were markedly more likely to abstain than those of any other party, notably the SNP. Given this, it might be thought that a boost to turnout would have helped Labour in particular. Moreover, our knowledge of the social correlates of voting and of the geography of turnout frequently leads people to assume that, in broad terms, Labour will benefit (and the Conservatives suffer) by getting non-voters to turn out. Yet the evidence seldom supports such inferences and the 2007 election is no exception to that general rule. Non-voters were asked which party they would have supported in the constituency and regional list contests if they had voted. The largest proportions (35 per cent and 31 per cent respectively) didn't know. Among those who did indicate a party, however, the distribution of support among the major parties was remarkably similar to the actual election result. In the constituency vote, the preferences of non-voters were Conservative 14 per cent, Labour 35 per cent, Liberal Democrat 11 per cent and SNP 36 per cent ($N = 510$); in the regional list vote, the respective percentages were 14, 33, 10 and 32 ($N = 535$). The same reasons that led erstwhile Labour sympathisers to abstain would also, it seems, have deterred them from supporting the party if they had voted. The data strongly suggest that had turnout in the election been higher, the outcome would not have been significantly different.

The wider consequences of low turnouts are unclear, although this is not for the want of attention from politicians and commentators, as well as academics. What seems clearer is that relatively high levels of abstention look set to be the norm in Scottish Parliament elections. Following the record low turnout in the 2001 UK general election, Anthony King (2001) sounded a reassuring note: 'Just provide the voters with a closely fought election at which a great deal is at stake and, make no mistake, they will again turn out in their droves'. At least as far as Scottish elections are concerned, this confidence looks questionable. The 2007 election was very closely fought and, as we saw in Chapter 4, more than two-thirds of SES respondents saw either 'a great deal' or 'quite a lot' of difference between Labour and the SNP. Yet turnout increased by only four points to the still unimpressive level of less than 54 per cent. This suggests few grounds for optimism about future turnout.

Notes

1 The sociodemographic variables are all taken from the 2001 census.
2 One possibility is that the single people and manual workers in YouGov's internet panel are atypical, being more politically engaged and hence more likely to vote than the average person in these categories.

9

Scotland's hanging chads: rejected ballots in 2007

Mundane matters of electoral administration rarely make front-page news. Perhaps the most glaring exception to this general rule is the US presidential election of 2000, particularly in the very closely contested state of Florida, where various aspects of electoral process were exposed as seriously faulty – if not actually fraudulent – and the outcome was eventually determined by the Supreme Court (see Issacharoff *et al.*, 2001; Hasen, 2004). In the course of the controversy, even casual observers became familiar with the obscure terms used by American election administrators such as 'hanging chads' and 'pregnant chads'.[1] In subsequent US elections there has been more suspicion attached to electoral administration – and the parties and candidates have made efforts to ensure that the election process is carefully monitored. In Britain, too, there have been examples of electoral administration being called into question, for example in relation to postal voting fraud (Stewart, 2006). Generally, however, elections in the established democracies of Europe and North America are widely regarded as free and fair and this helps to explain the general readiness of election losers to accept defeat gracefully (Anderson *et al.*, 2005).

In the Scottish Parliament elections of 2007, however, a largely unanticipated aspect of the results catapulted administration of the elections to the forefront of discussion: the number of ballots that were rejected as invalid and, therefore, did not count towards electing a candidate. Many more ballots were rejected than had been the case hitherto, the proportions increasing very sharply in 2007, to 2.88 per cent of all ballots in the regional list voting and 4.08 per cent in the constituency contests (Table 9.1). Some ballots are rejected in all elections but these proportions are very much greater than those recorded at UK general elections – the comparable figures for Scotland in 2001 and 2005 were 0.18 per cent and 0.20 per cent respectively – and are also well in excess of the proportion of rejected ballots in the contemporaneous local elections (1.83 per cent), at which an unfamiliar electoral system involving preferential voting (STV – single transferable vote) was in use for

Table 9.1 *Rejected ballots in Scottish Parliament elections, 1999–2007*

	1999	*2003*	*2007*
Constituency contests			
Number	9,210	12,810	85,644
% of all ballots	0.39	0.66	4.08
Regional list voting			
Number	7,268	12,482	60,455
% of all ballots	0.31	0.67	2.88

Source: Denver (2007a).

the first time. In addition, in New Zealand and Germany, two countries which also use AMS, the proportions of invalid votes are smaller (Lundberg, 2008).

In the Scottish Parliament elections a ballot can be rejected for one of four reasons: lacking the official mark stamped on at the time of voting; containing material which might identify the voter; having votes for more than one candidate; or being unmarked or unclear as to the voter's intention. The published results show that the rejection of ballots for the first two reasons was extremely rare, accounting for only 0.15 per cent of those rejected in constituency contests and for only 0.21 per cent in the list voting. In the constituency contests almost all ballots rejected were deemed unmarked or unclear as to the voter's intention (96.8 per cent). In the list voting, however, almost a third (30.1 per cent) contained votes for more than one party/candidate, while 69.6 per cent were unmarked or unclear.[2]

The unforeseen increase in rejected ballots, together with a number of other administrative problems – especially related to the electronic counting of votes – led to a furore in the Scottish media and provoked much recrimination among the political class. On 5 May, the day after the results were announced, the newspaper headlines included 'The worst poll debacle in the history of British democracy' (*Scotsman*) and 'Who is to blame when everyone involved says it's not their fault?' (*Herald*). In response, the Electoral Commission set up a special committee of enquiry chaired by Ron Gould, 'an international expert in electoral administration' (Electoral Commission, 2007: 3). In his report, published in October 2007, Gould declared that in the planning and administration of the elections 'the voter was treated as an afterthought' (*ibid*.: 120) and his conclusion on the causes of the increased numbers of rejected ballots is unequivocal (if ungrammatical): 'The main reason there were much higher rates of rejection in the 2007 Scottish parliamentary elections than in previous elections was a result of the combined ballot paper' (*ibid*.: 52).

In the two previous Scottish Parliament elections, voters were handed two differently coloured ballot papers by polling station staff – one for the constituency contest and one for the regional list vote. The printed instructions on each reminded them that they should vote for one candidate or party list. In 2007, however, there was a single ballot paper, with the list contestants printed on the left-hand side and constituency candidates on the right. The instructions indicated that the elector had two votes and (in most cases – see below) there were arrows to indicate that one vote should be cast in the left-hand column and one in the right-hand column. The official explanation for the change in the layout of the ballot paper was that it would help dispel the notion, widespread in the two previous elections and actively encouraged by the campaign appeals of some small parties, that the list vote is a 'second' vote which is somehow less valuable or important than the 'first' (constituency) vote (Scotland Office, 2006).

The Gould committee had available to it greater details on rejected ballots than were published along with the election results. It found that 50 per cent of ballots which were rejected in either the constituency or the list election had a list vote only, while 25 per cent had a constituency vote only. Thus three-quarters of all rejected ballots had only one vote marked rather than one on each side of the ballot paper. In addition, about 15 per cent had two votes indicated on the list ballot and none on the constituency side (Electoral Commission, 2007: 50; see also appendix D of the report). The report noted that analysis of the rejected papers could not indicate why so many voters did not vote correctly – it 'reveals what they did but not why they did it' (Electoral Commission, 2007: 50). However, two reasons why most rejected ballots had only one vote marked were suggested. First, some voters might have deliberately abstained on one side of the ballot or the other. Second, some voters might not have understood that they had two votes and in some cases this might have been because the two ballots were read as one continuous list. This might have been due to a lack of instructions or to a lack of motivation or cognitive ability on the part of voters. Analysis of the variation across constituencies in the proportion of ballots rejected can throw some light on these explanations.

Variations in rejected ballots across constituencies

The sharp increase in rejected ballots between 2003 and 2007 occurred across the entire country (although with marked constituency variations, as noted below). This reinforces the suggestion that the nationwide shift to a combined ballot sheet was responsible. In turn, it perhaps explains why the Gould report

Table 9.2 *Correlations between percentage of constituency ballots rejected and list minus constituency vote share of minor parties*

	Correlation
Socialist Labour Party	**0.838**
Solidarity	**0.760**
British National Party	**0.615**
Scottish Socialist Party	**0.542**
Christian Peoples Alliance	**0.313**
Scottish Green Party	0.103
Scottish Senior Citizens' Party	−0.012
Scottish Christian Party	−0.221
UK Independence Party	−0.423

Note: Coefficients significant at the $p < 0.05$ level are in bold.

paid relatively little attention to *where* larger and smaller numbers ballots were rejected. Yet there were considerable geographical variations. The proportions of constituency votes rejected were unusually large in Glasgow (7.9 per cent) and Lothians (5.2 per cent). At constituency level, only 1.9 per cent were rejected in Stirling compared with 12.1 per cent in Glasgow Shettleston. The variation in the case of list votes was smaller (1.7 per cent in Gordon to 5.9 per cent in Shettleston) but still significant.

In line with the arguments above, there are three plausible explanations for these variations and each warrants some discussion. The first derives from the fact that significant minor parties, such as the Greens and Solidarity, competed on all regional lists but had few constituency candidates or none. It is conceivable that those who voted for these parties on the lists deliberately abstained on the constituency ballot because they had no candidate to vote for. If this occurred to a significant extent, we would expect the percentage of rejected ballots in the constituency contests to be positively associated with the difference in the level of support for these parties in the list voting and constituency contests. Table 9.2 shows the relevant correlation coefficients for groups and parties that contested all lists but, at best, only a few constituencies in 2007.

The expected relationships are very strong in the cases of the radical left parties and for the British National Party. Yet the coefficient for the Green Party is very weak (0.103) and not significant. For the Scottish Christian Party and the UK Independence Party the relationships are in the 'wrong' direction. This mixed picture tends to contradict any simplistic notion that rejected ballots resulted from deliberate abstention by supporters of minor

Table 9.3 *Correlations between socioeconomic indicators for constituencies and the proportions of list and constituency ballots rejected*

	List	*Constituency*
% of households with no car	**0.644**	**0.770**
% social renters	**0.528**	**0.653**
Number of persons per hectare	**0.391**	**0.579**
% ethnic minority	**0.394**	**0.377**
% owner occupiers	**−0.545**	**−0.629**
% professional/managerial	**−0.479**	**−0.433**
% employed in agriculture	−0.175	**−0.385**
% with degree	−0.276	−0.276

Note: Coefficients significant at the $p < 0.05$ level are in bold.

parties. Moreover, the strong relationships for the left parties may be partly spurious; that is, there may be some other reason why rejected ballot rates were highest where the radical left performed relatively well.

One such reason might be the socioeconomic make-up of constituencies. Studies in the United States have routinely found that rejected ballot rates are higher in more deprived areas (Knack and Kropf, 2003; Sinclair and Alvarez, 2004). Although we know of no published study that has examined British data, a simple analysis suggests the same conclusion. In the 1992 general election, for example, across all British constituencies ($N = 634$) there are significant positive relationships between the proportion of ballots rejected and the size of the local ethnic minority population (0.520), the percentage of households with no car (0.301) and the percentage renting their homes from the council (0.108). Given the relative difficulty of completing the AMS ballot correctly compared with a first-past-the-post ballot, we would expect an accentuation of this pattern in Scottish Parliament elections, since indicators of social deprivation are probably proxies for the general level of political interest and awareness – and general cognitive abilities – that help voters to cast a ballot accurately reflecting their preferences. Table 9.3 reports correlation coefficients measuring the association between various indicators of the social composition of constituencies and the proportions of rejected constituency and list votes in 2007.

The relationships are clear and consistent. The proportion of rejected ballots in both list and constituency contests was greater in more deprived areas (households without a car), where there were more social renters (homes rented from the council or a housing association), in heavily urban areas (more persons per hectare) and in areas with more ethnic minority residents. On the other hand, rejected ballots were less frequent in constituencies with larger proportions of owner occupiers, professional and managerial workers and people with a degree-level qualification, and in rural areas.

In 2003, only two of the above variables were significantly correlated with rejected ballots in constituency contests – the proportion of households with no car and of professional and managerial workers (correlations of 0.276 and –0.350, respectively) – while for the list voting there were no significant correlations in the expected direction. The clear implication of this is that the change in ballot design for 2007, by making the task of voting more complex, had a disproportionate impact on those least well equipped for that task (Carman *et al.*, 2008).

Beyond level of support for minor parties and the socioeconomic composition of constituencies, there is a third explanation for the abundance of rejected ballots in Glasgow and Lothians. There was a limit to the size of ballot papers that the electronic counting machines were able to process. This became important in Glasgow and Lothians because in both these regions there was an unusually large number of contestants (23 in both cases) in the regional lists. A last-minute decision was taken by officials that the only way to meet the size limit was to abbreviate the instructions section at the top of the ballot paper. Hence, in those regions, the arrows intended to guide the voter were omitted.[3] On its own, the requirement to have both list and constituency votes registered on the same ballot paper caused problems for some voters; the removal of the visual prompts indicating where to register these votes surely compounded the difficulty.

Assessing the relative and cumulative importance of deliberate non-voting by supporters of the minor parties, the socioeconomic character of the constituencies and the special weakness in ballot design in Glasgow and Lothians requires multivariate analysis, which takes account of the fact that the variables concerned are themselves inter-correlated. The results of the relevant regression analyses are shown in Appendix 3 (Table A9.1). As far as constituency contests are concerned, the analysis shows that simply being located in Glasgow or the Lothians resulted in a significant increase in the proportion of rejected ballots. Over and above that, the more middle-class people there were in a constituency, the smaller was the proportion of rejected ballots. There is also evidence consistent with deliberate abstention in the constituency ballot by supporters of left parties in the list voting. Together, the five variables included in the final model account for 83 per cent of the variation in the proportion of ballots rejected at constituency level. In the model for list voting, the five significant variables explain 55 per cent of the variation. Even taking account of residence in Glasgow or Lothians, there were more rejected ballots in poorer areas but fewer in other urban areas and more in rural areas.

Voters' awareness of administrative problems

The discussion in the previous section tells us about variation in rejected ballots across constituencies. As almost every analysis of aggregate electoral data notes, at best this is suggestive of the behaviour of individuals, but no more. In order to draw conclusions about the latter we require survey data and for the remainder of this chapter we use the SES surveys, in particular the third survey wave, undertaken in December 2007, specifically to explore in more detail the question of rejected ballots.

Two preliminary points need to be made about the December survey. First, it is a commonplace in electoral research that voting is not a hugely important activity for most people. Given that we asked respondents relatively complicated questions about voting some seven months after the event, it should be borne in mind that – while the broad picture painted by the answers is likely to be accurate – recall of what they did and thought at the time of the election is likely to have been somewhat hazy for some. It could also be argued that the extensive post-election public discussion of administrative failures will have coloured voters' perspectives on the various issues raised and this creates problems for analysts. It is a misconception, however, to suggest that voters have 'true' attitudes that can and should be elicited before any exposure to political or media messages on a topic. Rather, voters' views are formed through that sort of public discourse. Hence a survey in December 2007, when debate was dying down following the publication of the Gould report, is actually well timed to gauge the impact of the election problems on voters' perceptions and attitudes.

Second, survey data cannot enable us to detail the characteristics and attitudes of those who voted but whose ballots were rejected. It is in the nature of things that the vast majority of those whose votes were rejected simply have no way of knowing whether or not this was the case. Apart from a small minority who might have deliberately spoiled their ballots – and there is little sign of such voters among the survey respondents – rejected ballots were caused by errors of which voters would have been unaware. Equally, some of those who were very confident that their vote was not rejected might be in a state of blissful ignorance. Nonetheless, we can use survey data to analyse voters' awareness of and reactions to the issue.

In the survey carried out immediately after the Scottish Parliament election – which was planned, of course, before it was realised that rejected ballots would become a major issue – respondents who had voted were asked how difficult they had found it to fill in the ballot paper. Responses are shown in Table 9.4, together with the distribution of responses given to the same question in relation to the Parliament elections in 1999 and 2003. For a

Table 9.4 *Reported difficulty of completing ballot papers, 1999–2007 (percentage of respondents)*

	1999	*2003*	*2007*	*2007 local*
Very difficult	1	2	1	2
Fairly difficult	9	12	11	12
Not very difficult	39	33	26	25
Not at all difficult	52	52	62	60
N	*805*	*868*	*1,181*	*1,181*

Sources: SSA 1999 and 2003; SES post-election survey 2007.

different comparison, the final column of the table reports responses to a parallel question about completing the STV ballot paper for the local elections.

There is no evidence here that the 2007 Parliamentary ballot caused greater difficulty than usual. Indeed, a larger proportion than previously (62 per cent) reported that they found no difficulty at all. Overall, the combined ballot paper was rated as slightly easier than the ballot papers in previous years. (It would be interesting to compare these figures with reactions to voting in a first-past-the-post election, such as a general election, but, as far as we aware, there are no relevant data.) There was very little evidence of specific sociodemographic groups finding voting particularly difficult. No significant differences appeared on the basis of sex, age, education, housing tenure and whether respondents were party identifiers or not.

The unprecedented number of rejected ballots was not the only administrative problem that afflicted the 2007 elections. Electronic counting, introduced to facilitate the more complex STV counts for the council elections, was responsible for several of these. The counting machines could not cope with ballots that had been folded by mistake and some broke down altogether. A number of counts were abandoned overnight and so the outcome remained uncertain well into the day after polling (SPICe, 2007: 51) – something that is now very rare in British elections. Other problems could not be blamed on the authorities: bad weather delayed the collection of ballot boxes from outlying islands and in an Edinburgh polling station some ballot papers were damaged by a vandal wielding a golf club. Isolated incidents such as these happen in any election; in 2007 they were woven immediately into the broader story of an election descending into farce. Indeed, such an impression may have been developing even before polling day, as there had already been complaints about the late delivery of postal voting forms: some did not turn up at all; many arrived so late that recipients were effectively disenfranchised (Electoral Commission, 2007: 64–7).

Table 9.5 *Perceptions of problems with different aspects of election adminis-tration (percentage of respondents)*

	Postal voting	*Electronic counting*	*Number of rejected ballots*	*New system for local elections*
Very serious problems	18	38	69	33
Quite serious problems	31	34	19	36
Not very serious problems	25	13	3	16
No problems at all	8	3	1	5
Don't know	18	12	8	10
N	*1,166*	*1,166*	*1,166*	*1,166*

Source: Third survey wave.

In the light of all this, it is worth considering whether survey respondents recognised that rejected ballots were a particular problem or whether they simply dismissed the entire election as an organisational disaster. We asked if they thought there had been problems with postal voting, the electronic counting machines, the number of rejected ballots and the new STV electoral system for council elections. It is striking that even seven months after the elections, almost nine out of 10 respondents thought that the number of rejected ballots had been a very or quite serious problem (Table 9.5). Given the high-profile difficulties with the electronic counting machines, it is not surprising that a large majority of respondents remembered this. Less clear is why so many respondents believed that there had been problems associated with the introduction of STV, since the administrative arrangements for the local elections appeared to proceed relatively smoothly. Nonetheless, in the post-election debate various commentators and politicians suggested that it was simply confusing for the electors that the two elections, using differ-ent electoral systems, were held on the same day, and this may underlie the perception that the new electoral system caused problems. Postal voting was perceived as the least troubled aspect of the election. Although, as noted above, there were problems in this area, these could easily have passed un-noticed by the large majority of voters with no direct experience of postal voting – only 11 per cent of the Scottish electorate were registered for postal votes in 2007. Nonetheless, almost half of the respondents thought that there had been serious problems with postal voting arrangements.

Also in the third survey wave, we presented respondents with a list of poss-ible causes of the large number of rejected ballots and asked them to indicate which they thought were the two most important. Whether influenced or not

Table 9.6 *Perceived reasons for the increase in rejected ballots (percentage of respondents)*

	Most important	*Second most important*
Putting both votes on the same ballot paper	31	24
Electronic machines not reading votes properly	11	17
Council elections on the same day	20	23
Not enough public information for voters	9	12
Lack of instructions on the ballot papers	9	14
Many voters too dim to get it right	14	10
Don't know	7	2
N	*1,166*	*1,082*

Source: Third survey wave.

by the Gould report, more than half of the respondents (55 per cent) regarded the combined ballot paper as either the most or the second most important cause (Table 9.6). However, alternative explanations also received support, the most popular being the fact that local council and Scottish Parliament elections were held on the same day. Gould concluded that there was 'very little evidence to support the argument that the simultaneous local government election using STV contributed substantially to the higher rejection rates in the Scottish parliamentary election' (Electoral Commission, 2007: 52), although he did accept that this 'added complexity to the voting process' (*ibid*.: 36). In this case, however, the aggregate evidence available to Gould is simply not up to throwing light on whether voters found it confusing to vote in two separate elections, using two different electoral systems, during a single visit to the polling station. The survey evidence showing that 43 per cent of respondents thought that this contributed importantly to the large number of rejected ballots suggests that the 'coupling' of the two elections may have contributed to mistakes being made on the Scottish Parliament ballot.

Significant proportions of respondents blamed the authorities in other ways, citing the use of electronic counting, the lack of public information prior to the election or the lack of instructions on the ballot papers. In addition, almost a quarter (24 per cent) thought that, to some extent, the rejected ballots problem was the fault of the voters themselves, rather than the administrative arrangements. The underlying sentiment among these respondents appears to be that what voters were being asked to do was not particularly difficult and that most should have been able to handle it. All of these factors can operate in combination. Thus, the impact of having a single ballot sheet was exacerbated by the inadequate instructions on the sheet, which led to mistakes by less attentive voters. Holding contemporaneous local elections using a new electoral system tended to obscure the messages of public information campaigns. This makes it difficult for respondents, as well as analysts, to disentangle the impacts of the various contributory factors.

Consequences: confidence in the electoral process

In a cross-national study of popular confidence in electoral processes, Sarah Birch comments that 'when citizens lack full confidence that elections in their countries are free and fair, the result can be a decline in levels of voter participation ... confidence in electoral processes is arguably a precondition for popular support for the other institutions of representative systems' (Birch, 2008: 305). This is an area on which there has been very little published academic work (see Alvarez *et al.*, 2008) but there are clearly important broader implications if confidence in elections in a mature democracy can be shaken by administrative problems.

In the December survey, we asked those who voted how confident they were that their ballot was counted (as opposed to being rejected) and the results show quite widespread doubts. Only 47 per cent of respondents declared themselves 'very confident' that their vote had been counted, 30 per cent were 'quite confident', 10 per cent 'not very confident' and 8 per cent 'not at all confident'. Plainly, given the actual rejection rate, this pattern of responses reflects an undue pessimism. Although some groups felt more confident about their votes than others – men, the better-educated, the more politically interested and knowledgeable – this seems likely to be a

Table 9.7 *Perceived fairness of the 2007 election and other elections (percentage of respondents)*

	2007 Scottish Parliament election	*Scottish Parliament elections in general*	*Westminster general elections*
Very fair	12	22	23
Quite fair	39	48	47
Not very fair	27	16	17
Not at all fair	12	6	5
Don't know	11	8	8
N	*1,166*	*1,166*	*1,166*

Source: Third survey wave.

function of general self-confidence about politics. Certainly, we cannot tell whether it reflects real patterns in the distribution of ballots that were rejected. Nonetheless, it is clear that the potential impact of the rejected ballot problems on voter attitudes goes well beyond the relatively small number of those whose votes actually went uncounted.

Respondents were also asked how fair they thought the 2007 election had been and (separately) how fair they thought Westminster elections and Scottish Parliament elections in general were. Table 9.7 reports the results. While it is impossible to know what respondents had in mind when assessing fairness, the figures describing reactions to the 2007 Scottish Parliament elections are strikingly out of line with those for Westminster elections or Scottish Parliament elections in general. Moreover, the problem with rejected ballots was a major cause of damaged public confidence in the 2007 contest. Among those respondents – a large majority – who had identified 'very serious problems' with rejected ballots, fewer than half (47 per cent) described the 2007 election as very or quite fair. Among the remaining respondents, the corresponding figure was 68 per cent.

There are two approaches to determining whether the rejected ballots issue may affect participation in future elections. One simple strategy is to ask respondents directly whether, all things considered, the problems that arose in 2007 had made them less likely to vote in future (or made no difference). In Table 9.8 we present the responses to this question, first for all respondents and then divided according to whether the respondents voted in 2007. At first glance, the figures for all respondents are rather worrying – only four in five said that the events of 2007 made no difference to the likelihood of their voting, with 14 per cent saying that the likelihood had been reduced. Looking at the other two columns, however, it is apparent that it was mainly non-voters who were likely to say that 2007 had made them (even) less

Table 9.8 *Reported impact of the 2007 problems on likelihood of voting (percentage of respondents)*

	All	*Voted 2007*	*Did not vote 2007*
Makes no difference	81	89	49
Slightly less likely to vote	10	5	27
Much less likely to vote	4	3	11
Don't know	5	3	13
N	*1,019*	*808*	*211*

Source: Third survey wave.

likely to vote. Only 3 per cent of those who voted said that they were now much less likely to vote and one would expect that even this would decline as memories of 2007 fade. Judging by these data, the negative effect of the 2007 problems on turnout in future Scottish Parliament elections seems likely to be minimal. Nonetheless, since turnout in Scottish Parliament elections is not particularly good (and fell below 50 per cent in 2003) and policy-makers are concerned with tempting non-voters back into participation, the figures in the right-hand column should not be dismissed as irrelevant. The administrative failures in 2007 may well have reinforced a conviction among some people that abstention is a sensible course of action.

There are reasons to doubt the validity of the kind of self-reports presented in Table 9.8. Having answered a series of questions about major administrative problems in 2007, some respondents may have felt it perverse to report themselves unaffected. Others may have wanted to present themselves as rather more stalwart voters than is truly the case. The second approach to the question of future participation offers a way round these problems. At the very outset of the December survey – that is, before any indication that it concerned the 2007 election and its problems – respondents were asked how likely they would be to vote in a hypothetical Scottish Parliament election held 'tomorrow'. The question was asked using a 0–10 scale but to simplify presentation we collapse this into a two-category variable: likely to vote (those choosing '10') and not likely to vote (all other respondents).[4] For this analysis we focus only on those who voted in 2007 and explore whether their willingness to continue to turn out has been affected by their evaluations of the election. Table 9.9 shows the relationship between willingness to vote and two such evaluations: perceived fairness of the election and confidence that their ballots counted.

Table 9.9 *Evaluations of the fairness of the 2007 Scottish Parliament election and likelihood of voting in a hypothetical election (2007 voters only) (percentage of respondents)*

Likely to vote if election tomorrow?	How fair do you think the 2007 election was?		How confident are you that your vote counted?	
	Very/quite	*Not very/ not at all*	*Very/quite*	*Not very/ not at all*
Yes	85	77	83	76
No	15	23	17	24
N	*442*	*324*	*625*	*143*

Source: Third survey wave.

Those who regarded the 2007 election as unfair were less inclined to say that they would vote in the hypothetical election than those who were less critical in this respect. The same is true of those who seriously doubted whether their vote had counted, compared with those with few doubts. There is evidence here, then – which is also borne out by more advanced analyses of these and other data from the surveys (Carman and Johns, 2008) – that negative evaluations of the electoral process in 2007 reduced some respondents' willingness to participate in a future election. Two caveats need to be registered, however. First, these effects are not very large and, second, we have no means of knowing their durability. Certainly, we are in no position to make predictions about the effects of 2007 on turnout in the next Scottish election, in 2011.

Conclusion

The Scottish Parliament elections of 2007 thrust matters of electoral administration and, in particular, ballot design on to the public agenda. The fact that an unusually large proportion of ballots was rejected raised important questions about electoral processes and the relevant election data have been subject to much detailed analysis. It is widely accepted that a new ballot design was the main cause of the upsurge in wasted votes and that the problem was particularly acute where there was an unfortunate abridgement of the ballot paper instructions, as well as in areas of low social status. All that, while undoubtedly important, tells us little about how voters reacted to the problems in 2007. This chapter has provided additional information from surveys, although precisely who failed to vote correctly and the nature of their misunderstanding of what was required remain something of a mystery.

The public reaction to the major administrative problems in the 2007 elections produced rapid action by the authorities. The newly elected Scottish Parliament very quickly determined that local and Parliament elections would be 'decoupled', thus removing one possible source of confusion, and it also seems highly likely that there will be a return to separate ballot papers (Ghaleigh, 2008: 144). If that occurs, then the chances are that widespread problems with rejected ballot papers are unlikely to recur in the next elections. Whether the same applies to other aspects of administration – notably the electronic counting of votes – remains to be seen.

Notes

1 In many cases, it seems, the voting machines used in Florida failed to punch a proper hole in the punch cards used to record votes but left the 'chad' (the part to be punched out of the card) attached. These, as well as those where the chad was indented but not removed ('dimpled' or 'pregnant'), were not counted by the counting machines.

2 It should be emphasised that the phrase 'rejected ballot' does not indicate that the entire ballot paper is rejected. If a voter left the constituency side of the ballot paper blank but cast a valid vote on the regional list ballot, then that regional vote would be counted as normal even though their constituency ballot would be rejected.

3 Carman *et al.* (2008) discuss this in more detail and provide images of the different ballot papers.

4 The basis for this decision is the observation in previous studies that the proportion of respondents choosing the highest point on the scale tends to match actual turnout quite closely.

10
Why did the SNP win?

Over two million people voted in the 2007 Scottish Parliament election. It follows that explaining why the election was won and lost is not straightforward. Some voters made up their minds long before the campaign began; others did so on the way to the polling station. Some will have been concerned about a single key issue; others had a range of considerations in mind. Some split their tickets between the constituency and list contests; others registered two votes for their favourite party. Some voted as they always had; others switched from a previous loyalty. This list could be extended but the point is that the size and heterogeneity of a mass electorate mean that any explanation for an election outcome will inevitably involve considerable simplification. In this chapter, we seek to highlight the most important reasons for the SNP's victory and to work these into a plausible account of the election outcome.

In previous chapters, using data from the SES surveys, we have investigated and estimated the importance of a wide range of factors that might have influenced voting in 2007. Some have proved to be less influential than might have been expected but the list of apparently influential variables is lengthy and, reflecting the diverse electorate, quite disparate. There are core demographics (such as age), policy preferences (such as attitudes to the council tax), performance evaluations (such as of the parties' economic competence) and contextual factors (such as whether a voter was directly canvassed). To identify the key reasons for the SNP's victory we need to assess the relative importance of these different influences on party choice. That requires testing comprehensive statistical models in which all of the variables are included and we present the results of such analyses for each of the four major parties. We combine these results with material from earlier chapters to explain how the SNP came from a long way behind to win in 2007. Finally, we consider the implications of our study for the future of Scottish electoral politics.

Modelling party choice in 2007

So far, we have examined separately various clusters of influences on party choice. Here, however, we include all relevant variables in logistic regressions and hence gauge whether each still improves our prediction of party choice when all the others are taken into account. Only if a variable is shown to have such a separate and independent impact can it be deemed significant in explaining the election outcome. As in Chapter 5, we present the results of a regression analysis for each of the four major parties. Full results for both constituency and list voting are reported in Appendix 3 (Tables A10.1 and A10.2) but we focus on the key results of the list vote here, using illustrative charts. These show the variables with a statistically significant effect (at the $p < 0.05$ level) on the likelihood of voting for the party concerned and also indicate the relative importance of these variables.[1] It should be emphasised that the length of the bars in each chart represents the extent of each factor's importance. In order to assess the overall impact of each factor, we need also to consider earlier evidence about parties' ratings on that variable. For example, all the charts show a positive effect for 'Scottish interests', indicating that each party was rewarded by those voters perceiving it as looking after those interests – and punished by those who doubted such commitment. Read in conjunction with the evidence on Scottish interests from Chapter 5, these results are good news for the SNP, which will have been more often rewarded than punished, and not such good news for Labour, to which the reverse applies.

Figure 10.1 shows the results for voting SNP. It can be seen, first, that the age difference observed in Chapter 2 remains significant: older voters were more likely to vote SNP. The fact that this remains true even after taking account of a whole variety of other variables means that age had a genuine and independent effect. Given that previous election studies suggested that younger voters were more likely to vote SNP, this is an intriguing finding. One possibility is that the emphasis placed by the SNP on its opposition to the council tax proved particularly popular or contributed to an image as sympathetic to the interests of older voters. Second, party identification has the expected effects but they are not dramatic. In most analyses of British electoral behaviour, the impact of partisanship dwarfs that of more or less everything else but in this case it looks like just another variable. That reinforces the suggestion that the SNP's success in 2007 was based less on its core vote and more on winning over non-aligned voters (or even erstwhile supporters of other parties). Third, insofar as issues helped the SNP to do this, they were valence rather than position issues. There was considerable public opposition to the council tax, the Iraq war and the replacement of Trident but none of these gave a significant boost to SNP regional list support. What mattered

Figure 10.1 *Effects of significant variables on the probability of voting SNP in the regional list ballot*

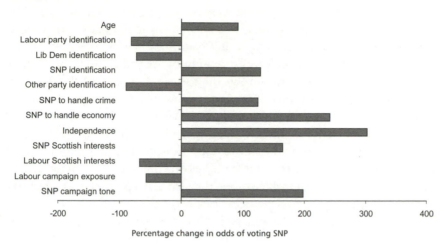

Sources: Pre- and post-election surveys.

more was how voters expected an SNP-led administration to handle crime and the economy. Fourth, the campaign mattered. The more that voters saw of Labour's campaign, the less likely they were to vote SNP. There remains the question of whether this reflects genuine campaign effects or the fact that those willing to be exposed to a party's campaign are already among its supporters. However, given the extensive controls here – for partisanship and much else – there are quite strong grounds to suspect the former. With respect to the SNP's own campaign, it was tone rather than exposure that mattered, with the party polling markedly better among the large group of voters perceiving the campaign as positive. Given the number of controls, the size of the campaign tone effect is striking and underlines the importance of the image that the party projected in 2007.

Turning to the Scottish dimension, there are three main points to note. Predictably, support for independence had a huge effect, making a voter almost 300 per cent more likely to cast a list vote for the SNP. Second, even controlling for constitutional preferences, the SNP enjoyed markedly stronger support among those who trusted the party to look closely after 'Scottish interests'. As we saw in Chapter 5, such trust was more readily placed in the SNP than in Labour, even by those preferring more devolved powers over independence. If, for such voters, constitutional preferences mattered less than how each party would operate under current arrangements, an SNP vote could be an appropriate response. Third, as might have been anticipated given the results in

Chapter 5, national identity has no significant effect. Once party identification, constitutional preferences and other variables are held constant, voters from across the Scottish–British spectrum were roughly equally likely to vote SNP.

Evaluations of Alex Salmond are also missing from the chart. Other things being equal, opinions of the SNP leader had no significant effect on willingness to vote for his party. This was true in both list and constituency voting, although it is especially surprising in the former case, given Salmond's star billing on the top of that side of the ballot paper (see Chapter 3). This result confounds any simple attribution of the SNP victory to the leader's personal popularity at the time of the election. It does not, however, rule out an indirect effect. Insofar as Salmond was responsible for laying the cornerstones of the party's success – its favourable ratings on competence, commitment to Scottish interests and campaign tone – then he may still have had a key role in the SNP's victory.

Regression results for Labour voting are summarised in Figure 10.2. All things considered, the party retains some of its traditional strength among Catholics but no other socioeconomic group is significantly more or less likely to vote Labour. There was a tendency for tabloid readers to vote for the party, although pending closer examination this constitutes no more than circumstantial evidence of newspaper influence on party choice. Party identification has the expected effects and the relative impact of partisanship is greater than in the SNP analysis, reflecting the latter's broader coalition

Figure 10.2 *Effects of significant variables on the probability of voting Labour in the regional list ballot*

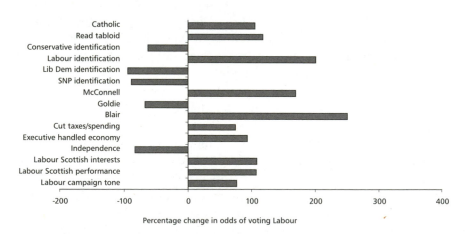

Percentage change in odds of voting Labour

Sources: Pre- and post-election surveys.

of support. As far as leadership effects are concerned, those giving positive ratings to Jack McConnell and – even more so – Tony Blair were significantly more likely to vote Labour. The problem for the party was that the electorate as a whole rated both relatively poorly. Those rating Scottish Conservative leader, Annabel Goldie, more positively were less likely to vote Labour. Again, however, ratings of Alex Salmond had no significant impact – there is certainly no evidence here that his personal popularity eroded support for Labour.

As with the SNP, support for Labour was driven more by performance and image than by policy. Evaluations of Labour's overall performance in the Executive and specifically of its economic record had a significant influence on choice. The latter effect was markedly smaller than the corresponding impact in the SNP analysis, reflecting voters' greater concern with the economic credentials of the less experienced party. Holding all else constant, whether voters saw Labour as committed to Scottish interests proved a powerful influence over willingness to vote for the party. As noted above, this will not have worked to the party's advantage in 2007.[2] There is also evidence that the perceived negative tone of Labour campaigning cost the party some support.

At various points we have emphasised that Labour did not lose a great deal of support between 2003 and 2007. One reason for this – confirmed by their absence from Figure 10.2 – is that prominent campaign issues, notably the council tax but also Iraq and Trident, cost the party much less than might have been supposed. With other variables held constant, those favouring local income tax over council tax were no less likely to vote Labour in the list contests. Local taxation thus looks to be an issue, rather like Iraq in the 2005 general election (Whiteley et al., 2005), that turns out in retrospect to have been more important in campaigning and the media than it proved for voting behaviour. Predictably, Labour was less popular among voters favouring Scottish independence but, as we have seen, this was not a very large proportion of the electorate. Labour's problem was not so much that unpopular policies drove away core supporters but more that it lost out to the SNP in the competition for short-term support based on leadership, performance in office and party image.

Like those of Labour, the social roots of Conservative support in Scotland no longer seem to go very deep (Figure 10.3). In Chapter 2 we saw that in 2007 the Conservatives lost more ground among Church of Scotland voters and this analysis confirms (by the relevant variable's absence) that the latter are no longer disproportionately likely to vote Conservative. There is evidence of a geography (if not a sociology) of Conservative support, however, with the party polling particularly well among voters living outside the central belt. It is, though, the effect of party identification that stands out. This is much greater than that of all the other variables in this analysis and also greater than

Figure 10.3 *Effects of significant variables on the probability of voting Conservative in the regional list ballot*

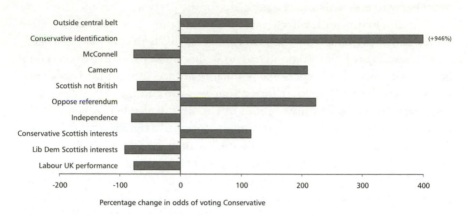

Percentage change in odds of voting Conservative

Sources: Pre- and post-election surveys

the corresponding effects of partisanship in the SNP and Labour results. At +946 per cent, the impact is literally off the scale (which we maintain at –200 to 400 in each chart in order to aid comparison across analyses and between smaller effects in the same model). This does not mean that the Conservatives were especially good at converting identification into votes; as seen in Chapter 3, this was not the case in 2007. Rather, it means that the other variables do little to explain the partisanship effect. If, for example, Conservative partisans tended overwhelmingly to regard the party as very closely concerned with Scottish interests, then the independent impact of partisanship would be limited in a model including the latter variable. Hence the huge impact of Conservative identification indicates that the party gave loyal supporters relatively few other reasons to vote for it. In that sense, partisanship was especially important for its vote in 2007.

In Chapter 3 we saw that Annabel Goldie was more popular than her party in 2007 but there is no evidence here that she proved a significant electoral asset. On the other hand, voters were more likely to support the Conservatives if their assessment of Jack McConnell was unflattering. Yet, as far as leaders are concerned, it was views about David Cameron that mattered most for voting Conservative or not. This was not especially good news for the Conservatives, given that Cameron was slightly less popular than the party's Scottish leader. The greater significance of UK-level leadership in this case may not be a matter of voters regarding the Scottish arena as secondary but is, rather, better explained by the much greater chance of Cameron becoming Prime Minister than of Goldie becoming First Minister. Nonetheless, the Conservatives drew particular support among voters unimpressed by Labour's performance at Westminster.

All of the remaining effects relate to the specifically Scottish aspects of this election. The Conservatives were significantly less popular among those disclaiming any British identification and likewise among supporters of independence. However, they did not enjoy a corresponding advantage among voters at the British or the anti-devolution ends of these dimensions (although they were relatively successful among voters opposed to an independence referendum). Finally, Conservative support depended to a significant extent on how closely voters thought that the party – and also the Liberal Democrats – looked after Scottish interests. Since the Conservatives scored worst in that regard (see Chapter 5), lagging some way behind the Liberal Democrats, this almost certainly swung votes from the former to the latter. Unlike Labour, whose negative campaign focus on independence and the perception that the party failed to stand up for Scottish interests seem to have weakened what was a previously reasonable reputation for looking after Scottish interests (see Surridge, 2004), the Conservatives have long suffered from being perceived as an anti-Scottish party. Certainly, voters seem to have made up their minds about the party well before polling day, since none of the campaigning variables had any significant effect on voting for it.

Studies of UK general elections have shown that, compared with the other major parties, it is more difficult to predict Liberal Democrat voting (Fieldhouse and Russell, 2001) than voting Conservative or Labour. That also proved true in 2007: even with a great deal of information about voters, it still proves much more difficult to predict support for the Liberal Democrats than is the case with the other parties. Nonetheless, we still have quite a long list of variables that at least proved to have a significant effect on the likelihood of voting Liberal Democrat (Figure 10.4). It is consistently found that voters with a degree are more likely to support the party and this held true in 2007 as well, although the effect is fairly small.[3] Another consistent, though more specifically Scottish, tendency is for the Liberal Democrats to poll more heavily outside the central belt and this analysis shows that the geographical effect is not simply due to the different characteristics, attitudes and perceptions of voters in the different regions. It holds even after controlling for all of that.

As in the Conservative analysis, the effect of party identification here is extremely strong (and the changes in probabilities are therefore specified rather than illustrated). A parallel argument can be made: partisanship was extremely important for Liberal Democrat support in 2007, not because all the party's identifiers voted that way but because many of those who did so

Figure 10.4 *Effects of significant variables on the probability of voting Liberal Democrat in the regional list ballot*

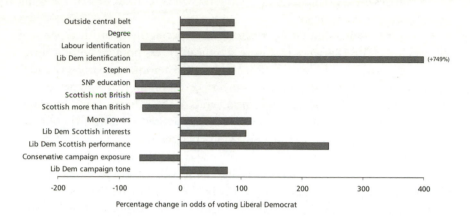

Sources: Pre- and post-election surveys.

were often supporting the party out of loyalty rather than for other reasons. Nonetheless, Liberal Democrat support was at least partly dependent on evaluations of the party's Scottish leader, Nicol Stephen.

By 2007, the party had been in coalition government in Scotland for eight years and, not surprisingly, evaluations of Liberal Democrat ministers' performance in office proved a relatively powerful predictor of support. Since those evaluations were fairly neutral on the whole (see Chapter 4), this is unlikely to have won or lost the party many votes but the size of the effect – controlling for partisanship and other evaluations of the party – points to a degree of electoral accountability within the coalition. While the Liberal Democrats were clearly the junior coalition partner, their contribution nonetheless seems to have been considered by at least some voters when voting in 2007. Perhaps that contribution was thought strongest in the area of education: certainly those with qualms about likely SNP performance on that issue were significantly more likely to vote Liberal Democrat.

Patterns of Liberal Democrat support also emphasise the far from perfect correlation between national identity and constitutional preferences. The party was the most prominent advocate of more powers for the Scottish Parliament in 2007 and profited from this at the ballot box. At the same time, the party was significantly less popular among those reporting a primarily Scottish identification. This perhaps implies ambiguity about the party's claim to 'Scottishness'. What is clear is that, as with all the other main parties, those who trusted the party to look after Scottish interests were considerably more likely to vote for it regardless of their own national identity and constitutional preferences. The party also benefited from the broadly favourable evaluations of the tone of its campaign. The run-up to polling day was not a period of untroubled vote-gathering for the Liberal Democrats. The party was vulnerable wherever voters were exposed to Conservative campaigning.

Why did the SNP win (and Labour lose)?

In explaining the SNP's success in the general election of October 1974, Miller (1981: 258–9) argued,

> the purely party, as distinct from policy characteristics of the SNP were far from repulsive. While the party might never have been able to take up a large measure of its natural support without the help of conditions such as those in 1974 which predisposed people throughout Britain towards deserting the old governing parties, the SNP had the image, the organization, and the enthusiasm to take the opportunity....

We suggest that this also applies to the 2007 Scottish Parliament elections. Voters' lukewarm reaction to Labour's performance in office created the opportunity and the SNP took it. However, the SNP did not win due to its policy stances, whether on the constitution, council tax or anything else. Rather, it overtook Labour by persuading enough voters that it was a credible and competent party of government and that it offered a more positive and Scottish-oriented agenda than its chief rival. It is worth emphasising the ordinariness of this explanation. Elections are quite often won by parties with ideological and policy stances at odds with those of the average voter (see Heath *et al.*, 1991). They are seldom won by parties whose competence to govern is widely mistrusted. This, then, was a normal election, in that voters were choosing between contenders for government on the basis of their capacity to deliver in office. In explaining the outcome, the key is to explain how the SNP persuaded an unprecedented number of voters – and just enough for victory – to choose it.

In providing an answer, we first examine how the SNP came from some way behind to compare favourably with Labour in terms of governing competence and then explore how the Scottish dimension influenced the outcome in 2007; we argue that the same basic notion of capacity to deliver, albeit with a distinctively Scottish aspect, is again the fundamental reason for the SNP's success. As a preliminary, however, we should acknowledge that our focus on the SNP and Labour, and reference to voters 'choosing a government' or parties 'winning the election', may seem at odds with Scotland's multiple parties and proportional electoral system, which together mean that the chances of any single party winning a parliamentary majority are remote. However, for some years Scottish opinion polls have shown that Labour and the SNP dominate the Scottish party system almost as much as Labour and the Conservatives do at UK level. No government was conceivable without one of these two parties (and, in 2007 at least, there was little prospect of their forming a coalition with each other). Yet any government including either of them would inevitably have been dominated by it. In practice, then, the 2007 election was going to produce an SNP-led or a Labour-led administration and, as noted in the opening chapter, that is broadly how the election was portrayed to voters, both by the leading parties in their campaigns and by the media. It is not unreasonable, therefore, to characterise the decisions of a good proportion of the electorate in 2007 as a choice between two rivals for government.

'Performance politics' in 2007

The core of the valence model of party choice is that voters assess the likely performance in office of the leading contenders. In evaluating Labour, Scottish voters had plenty to go on, the party having been in power in Scotland for eight years and at Westminster for 10. Although evaluations varied slightly across different issues, they were, on balance, somewhat negative. The average voter was unimpressed by Labour's performance and the average non-partisan voter was still less complimentary. The same applies to assessments of First Minister Jack McConnell. Since voters might reasonably have expected more of the same had Labour won in 2007, it is not surprising that such negative ratings cost the party support. In Chapter 1 we noted the common view that oppositions do not win elections but governments lose them. In 2007, Labour was holding a losing hand.

Arguably, that was also true in 2003, when there was little enthusiasm for the party's record in Scotland, the invasion of Iraq was fresh in voters' memories and Labour lost considerable support to the minor parties. On the other hand, the party had then served only one term in power, during which some significant policy innovations had been introduced, which allowed the party to present itself as defending Scottish interests. The SNP's 2007 slogan, 'It's time', probably resonated more clearly with the electorate in 2007 than it would have done in 2003. Put another way, the window of opportunity for an opposition party had been open in 2003 but was open much wider in 2007. Crucially, however, for power to change hands, it requires *both* the government to lose the election *and* the opposition to win it. The chief difference between 2003 and 2007 was the ability of the SNP to take advantage of Labour's difficulties.

Why did the SNP's challenge strengthen significantly between the two elections? According to SES respondents, an SNP-led administration would have outperformed Labour on health, transport and (especially) law and order, and the party was rated as equal to Labour even on the latter's flagship policy of education. Clearly, the SNP was quite widely regarded as able to deliver on key issues. Given that the SNP had no experience of power beyond some very limited experience in local government, we might ask how these optimistic expectations emerged. Denied any direct evidence, voters were obliged to infer likely SNP performance from their more general impressions – that is, from the party's image. The fact that party image is a rather vague concept does not make it any less useful in explaining voting behaviour. Most voters lack detailed information on parties' policies and records but have a broad sense of their priorities and likely performance, and it is these overall impressions that influence choices. Clearly, the SNP projected a positive image in 2007 and this is likely to have boosted its claim to be a reliable government in waiting.

We can identify four key elements underpinning this positive image. The first is simply the existence of the Scottish Parliament and the SNP's presence in it as the second-largest party. This in itself is likely to have increased the credibility of a party which, until devolution, had managed to get only small numbers of representatives elected at UK level. Yet that proved little help to the SNP in 2003. The second key element in 2007 was Alex Salmond's resumption of the party leadership. Although this triggered an upturn in SNP popularity in opinion polls, we have seen that Salmond was not the direct electoral asset that many have assumed. Nonetheless, few would dispute that his leadership contributed to perceptions of the SNP as a capable and credible party. Though it probably went undetected by voters, the SNP was far better organised (not least due to the work of John Swinney, Salmond's predecessor as leader). Third, the party handled the constitutional issue effectively in 2007, managing to come across as a party with independence as a clear medium- to long-term goal but conditional on public support, and with plenty of other things to say and do in the meantime. It is almost a truism in British politics that a moderate party is more readily trusted to govern than an extreme party and, by signalling a willingness to govern under current arrangements rather than dismantling them as soon as possible, the SNP was able to show such moderation. The fourth point, concerning the tone of the SNP's campaign, is closely related. An emphasis on its own plans rather than the past record of its opponents probably helped to persuade voters of the party's preparedness for office. It is likely that the ratings given for the tone of the parties' campaigns – powerful predictors of support for every party – were not based on close attention to the campaigns but in part reflect evaluations of broader party images. The SNP's impressive rating indicates a party credited with a strongly positive agenda.

There is an important distinction to be made between explaining voting behaviour and explaining an election outcome. Our argument is not that all voters are preoccupied by performance and that the electorate gravitates *en masse* towards the party that most effectively projects an image of competence and delivery. In 2007, as at every election, there were plenty of strongly partisan electors who would pay no heed to the SNP's changing image. The valence variables – performance, competence and party image – are more suited to explaining the behaviour of swing voters and, in this case, to explaining the large movement to the SNP between 2003 and 2007. Further evidence, albeit indirect, that these valence variables hold the key to the 2007 outcome is the uniformity of that movement across the partisan and social board. Performance and competence are neutral notions, in that there is little reason to suppose them to matter much more to certain social or political groups. Consequently, the SNP won over voters of all classes, from all parties and from all sides of the constitutional issue. The SNP was not a different kind of party with a different kind of support in 2007: it was just more successful at building on that support.

We should remember, however, that the SNP's margin of victory was slender and that also needs to be explained in accounting for the 2007 election outcome. One reason is that many voters were less convinced by the SNP's readiness for office – indeed, it is only with hindsight that we can conclude that 'enough' were persuaded. There were particular doubts about the party's economic credentials and the analyses in this chapter confirm that these evaluations mattered at the ballot box. Equally, not all voters found fault with Labour's record in office – on balance, the party received favourable evaluations of its performance on both education and the economy. Moreover, Labour went into the 2007 election with a clear advantage in terms of party identification. This head-start had been narrowing over the past few elections but in 2007 it meant that the SNP had to outpoll Labour substantially among non-partisans in order to win. Coupled with the fact that the SNP was a long way behind in 2003, that is why a distinct improvement in the party's image was required to achieve even a narrow victory.

'Performance politics' and the Scottish dimension

There is nothing very remarkable in our contention that the winning party in 2007 was the one which convinced more voters of its ability to run the country. This has not been the dominant theme in studies of previous Scottish Parliament elections, however, which focused instead on how party choice was influenced by beliefs about and attitudes towards the new Parliament and its powers (Paterson *et al.*, 2001; Bromley *et al.*, 2006). This made sense at a time when the constitution had so recently been in flux but in 2007, with the Parliament under no threat and the Scottish Executive's policies reaching further into voters' lives, voters' attention was likely to turn to the question of which party could best govern Scotland. On the other hand, the constitutional question can hardly be regarded as having been settled when one of the main contenders in 2007 had a long-standing commitment to independence and there is evidence that the public wants further devolution. Plainly, this issue mattered a great deal in the election: independence was mentioned far more often than anything else when respondents were asked to name the most important issue in the election and, other things remaining the same, supporters of independence were much more likely to vote SNP (and less likely to vote Labour or Conservative) than were others. Nonetheless, this does not invalidate the arguments relating to performance or imply that the constitutional issue was itself pivotal in the election outcome.

The most obvious point to make is that support for independence remained largely static between 2003 and 2007. The considerable increase in the SNP vote cannot be ascribed to a swelling of support for independence. For one thing, as previously noted, those with strong views on the issue are less likely to switch votes and hence less likely to determine the election outcome. Moreover, the SNP's strategy was expressly designed to ease those fears about independence which had kept voters from supporting the party in the past. Thus the party effectively raised the ceiling of its potential support and was able to maximise the electoral benefit of its advances in terms of competence and credibility. The SNP's approach to independence in 2007, if anything, enhanced the importance of 'performance politics'.

This is not to say that the Scottish dimension was unimportant in the election. The analyses earlier in this chapter highlighted the importance to all parties of being seen to look after Scottish interests. Since the overwhelming majority of voters identify themselves as Scottish to at least some extent, support for Scottish interests is, in effect, a valence issue. While there may be disagreement about how Scottish interests are best served, there is no significant section of the electorate that does not want them served. To pursue the valence interpretation, the implication is that judgements about a party's willingness and ability to look after Scottish interests play a key role in overall assessments of its likely performance in office if elected.

As with party image, the fact that 'Scottish interests' is a rather hazy notion does not reduce its electoral significance but it does mean that voters need simple ways of estimating parties' commitment in this regard. Given that standing up for Scotland's interests is part of the SNP's *raison d'être*, the party probably has an in-built advantage. As we have seen (Chapter 5), this was acknowledged even by voters who themselves oppose independence. Labour is the more interesting case in 2007 because the party's Scottish credentials were widely questioned. In Chapter 5 we suggested that one reason for this might be the party's constitutional stance. There is good reason at least to suspect that Labour's conspicuous unwillingness to see further devolution could have raised doubts about the party's commitment to Scottish interests. Certainly it did nothing to hamper the SNP's attempts to characterise its chief opponent as 'London Labour'. Labour may then have exacerbated its problems with a campaign focused squarely on the constitutional question. Relentless reference to the risks posed by independence not only accentuated a negative tone but also served as a constant reminder of Labour's own hesitancy with respect to further devolution. In short, Labour's campaign tended to tarnish rather than enhance the party's image and, like its perceived weakness in terms of Scottish interests, the perceived negativity of Labour's campaigning also cost it votes.

The 'London Labour' problem for the party was reinforced by the prominence of Westminster politicians in the campaign and, in particular, Tony Blair's visits. The performances of Blair himself and of Labour at UK level were both negatively evaluated and cost Labour significant support. This was not, however, a reflection of voters deeming the Westminster arena to be more powerful or important than the Scottish. More simply, having featured in the campaign, UK-level factors were in many people's minds at the time of polling. Voters' assessments of party image and performance remain the key to understanding party choice. As far as the Conservatives, Labour and the Liberal Democrats are concerned, however, these assessments are influenced by policies, events and personalities on both sides of the border.

In summary, the SNP triumphed over Labour for the most mundane but important reason: it convinced enough voters that it would do a better job than Labour if elected as the Scottish government. In the Scottish context, performance has two aspects. There are the usual concerns of governing competently and handling key issues effectively. In addition, in a devolved polity, there is the question of representing Scottish interests. The SNP had an unusually clear advantage on the second count in 2007 and was also able to compete with Labour on the first, partly because the incumbent coalition's performance was not rated very highly and partly because the Nationalists effectively projected an image of competence and moderation. As the election approached, many were expecting the SNP's opinion poll advantage to be eroded, with voters beginning to subject the untested opposition's credentials to closer inspection. In the event, the party's 'valence credentials' stood up to this scrutiny and, in any case, much of the campaign was fought on the 'Scottish interests' aspect of performance. Thus, the SNP was able to carry its advantage through to polling day.

Prospects for Scottish politics

None of this can tell us what will happen at the next Scottish election. However, 2007 was important in one respect that will have a bearing on the next election and potentially on elections thereafter. Inevitably, the focus is on the SNP. There are three reasons for this. First, in 2007 it became for the first time both Scotland's largest party and a party of government. Second, the SNP has always been the main engine of constitutional change in Scotland, even if it has not always been in the driving seat. Third, 2007 confirms a pattern of party politics that became evident only in the first elections to the Scottish Parliament: there are two main parties, the SNP and Labour, competing either to form a minority government or to be the dominant partner in a coalition government which excludes the other.

Sartori (1976) identified two resources of relevance for a political party: governing potential and blackmail potential. Until devolution, the SNP had only blackmail potential. The electoral threat posed by the party proved decisive in pushing devolution up the political agenda but at no stage was there ever any prospect that it had governing potential. This limited its appeal. Devolution changed this situation but, while it offered the Nationalists the possibility of governing, the party took some time to realise that potential (Mitchell, 2009). One key problem was that the SNP had no experience to call upon, no record for voters to judge (outside of its performances in local government). It had to convince voters that it was competent to govern at all, let alone more competently than Labour. Choosing an SNP government, therefore, involved a leap of faith. Given the party's radical constitutional aim, it was easy for its opponents to equate this with a leap in the dark and very difficult for the Nationalists to counter this image.

The chief significance of the 2007 election, therefore, is that the SNP has broken through to become a party of government. This is, in itself, enough to make it a historic election. In keeping with the analysis that has informed this book, it is competence – or otherwise – in government that will determine whether 2007 proves crucial in establishing the SNP as a credible party of government or pushes the party back into opposition. There is also, of course, the Scottish dimension to consider. The 2007 election gives the SNP the opportunity both to prove whether it is capable of governing and to show how it intends to combine that with support for independence. It might be thought that competence in government and pursuit of independence will pull the SNP in opposite directions. One implies the pursuit of stability, the other risk-taking. However, this tension – the same one faced by any party pursuing some kind of major constitutional, social or political change – should not be exaggerated. The SNP's strategy is clear: it hopes to make the case for independence *through* competent government. Yet there is no inevitability about this connection. Effective performance may mean that the SNP becomes a credible party of government even without it ever achieving its constitutional goal. On the other hand, it does seem likely that failure in government would not only make it difficult for the party to win again but would also undermine the SNP's long-term ambitions for independence. The link between competence and constitutional change is complicated and asymmetric. For this reason, while the 2007 election may ultimately have a decisive effect on Scotland's constitutional status, its clearest impacts at this stage are on the Scottish party system and the SNP's prospects for government in the future.

Conclusion

In his victory speech after being elected in the Gordon constituency, Alex Salmond asserted that the election results meant that 'a new dawn' was breaking in Scottish politics. The outcome of the 2007 election was certainly remarkable – it demonstrated that a party explicitly committed to independence could win power in Scotland. If we have emphasised the ordinary rather than the extraordinary in discussing the election, then the reason lies in the distinction drawn at the very beginning of the book between the outcome of an election on the one hand and the choices of voters – our main focus – on the other. In 2007 it was the former and not the latter that was remarkable. The SNP's victory was unprecedented, but the way in which it won – by persuading enough voters that it was the party best equipped to govern – is anything but. It was a straightforward example of 'performance politics'.

There are several reasons why performance has become – and can be expected to remain – a decisive factor in Scottish elections. Voters regard Scottish Parliament elections as important, and a growing share of the electorate bases its choices on what is going on in Scotland. This makes sense as the devolution settlement becomes better established and the Scottish government – as it is now invariably known – reaches further into people's lives. Since the Parliament is not seen as merely a 'talking shop', what matters is not just what parties say but what they do. Moreover, as the government does more, voters have a clearer basis for judging performance and for forming images of the contending parties: their capacity to govern, their reliability and their willingness to stand up for Scottish interests. A second reason is ideological convergence. Aside from the constitutional question, voters saw little policy difference between any of the major parties, but especially between Labour and the SNP. This restricts voters to deciding which party is best placed to deliver generally agreed outcomes. Third, and related, voting behaviour in

Scotland is increasingly being loosened from its social and partisan moorings and so the group of non-partisan or 'floating' voters is large and growing. These voters are more responsive to short-term factors, notably party performance and image, and so large swings – like that to the SNP between 2003 and 2007 – are likely to be increasingly common.

Performance politics has not supplanted or even suppressed the Scottish dimension, however. Instead the two share a complex and reciprocal relationship. In 2007, the SNP's pledge of a referendum (and generally positive agenda) eased fears about independence, thereby enabling the party to maximise its advantage over Labour in terms of governing competence. Once in office, the SNP had an additional incentive – beyond the usual desire for re-election – to maintain a reputation for competence. By governing effectively and responsibly, the party will hope to convince voters that it could do the same in an independent Scotland, and thus to persuade them to support independence.

Notes

1 In comparing the impact of the different factors, there is a problem given that some are yes/no variables (e.g. does the respondent favour independence?) whereas others have more options (e.g. how does the respondent rate Alex Salmond on a 0–10 like/dislike scale?). A shift of one category on the first variable is obviously much more important than such a shift on the second. There is no clean solution to this problem, but our compromise is to show for the first type of variable the effect of being in the named category, and for the second type of variable the effect of moving from one standard deviation below to one standard deviation above the mean.

2 Recall that the length and direction of these bars needs to be considered in conjunction with earlier evidence on parties' ratings. Naturally, the effect for 'looking after Scottish interests' is positive, because those who thought that Labour would do so were more likely to vote for the party. However, the corollary is that those who doubted Labour's commitment to Scottish interests were significantly less likely to vote for the party. And, as shown in Chapter 5, the latter group is a good deal larger.

3 The simpler analysis in Chapter 2 showed that more graduates actually voted Conservative than Liberal Democrat. However, that does not show a direct link between higher education and Conservative support; it may be that Conservative voters have the kind of social background from which people tend to go to university. Here, controlling for some of those other socioeconomic variables, it becomes clear that the education effect is indeed the other way round: those with a degree are less likely to vote Conservative and more likely to vote Liberal Democrat.

Appendix 1. Technical details of the Scottish Election Study surveys

The 2007 SES involved major surveys of the Scottish electorate before and after the Scottish Parliament elections on 3 May 2007. It was funded by the Economic and Social Research Council (ESRC) (ref. 000-22-2256), directed by the present authors and based in the Department of Government at the University of Strathclyde. Modelled on recent British Election Studies, the project's aim was to explore and explain voting behaviour in the election. The questionnaires and the survey data are publicly available via the project website (www.scottishelectionstudy.org.uk) and have also been lodged with the UK Data Archive (study number 6026, accessible via www.data-archive. ac.uk). Both sources also offer detailed guidance to assist users of the data.

Data collection

The surveys were conducted via the internet, fieldwork being undertaken by YouGov, Britain's leading internet survey agency. The initial sample – selected so as to be demographically representative of the Scottish electorate – was drawn from YouGov's panel of subscribers resident in Scotland (further details on YouGov's fieldwork methods can be read at www.yougov.co.uk/corporate/ about). The study was originally designed as a two-wave panel survey, with the same respondents surveyed before and after the election. These two waves are the basis for investigating electoral behaviour in 2007. However, in the light of the unforeseen problems surrounding the elections (notably the large number of rejected ballots), the ESRC agreed to fund a third wave of data collection. Therefore, in December 2007 we returned to our panel respondents in order to explore their perceptions of the elections and the problems that arose. Table A1.1 summarises the key information about each wave of data collection.

Table A1.1 *Details of the three waves of SES data collection*

Wave	Prefix in archived datasets	Fieldwork dates (% of responses in first three days of period)	N	Response rate (denominator)
1 – pre-election	pre_	17–23 April 2007 (86%)	1,872	71.5% (contacted respondents)
2 – post-election	post_	4–10 May 2007 (90%)	1,552	83% (pre-respondents)
3 – third wave	post2_	12–24 December 2007 (80%)	1,166	62%[a] (pre-respondents)

Note: [a] For the follow-up wave we sought responses from all pre-election respondents, even if they had not participated in the post-election wave. Thus 62 per cent is an overall figure, representing a 66 per cent response rate among pre–post respondents and a 47 per cent response rate from pre-only respondents.

Representativeness and weighting

In order to counteract non-response biases, we apply weighting variables when analysing the data. For the most part we rely on YouGov's standard weight, which adjusts the data so that they reflect the target sample in terms of a range of demographic and attitudinal variables, including age, gender, social class, region, newspaper readership and past vote. In analyses involving only one wave of the survey, we use the weight calculated for that particular survey sample. In analyses involving multiple waves, we use the weight corresponding to the latest of the survey waves. Even so, our samples do not exactly match the Scottish electorate in terms of voting in the election (Table A1.2). In appropriate analyses, therefore, we also weight the data by turnout or by party choice, thus ensuring that the reported findings match the actual election results.

Table A1.2 *Party choice in the post-election sample and in the election*

	Constituency votes		Regional list votes	
	SES sample	Election result	SES sample	Election result
Conservative	14.2	16.6	12.8	13.9
Labour	27.2	32.2	22.5	29.2
Lib Dem	16.5	16.2	11.9	11.3
SNP	37.9	32.9	34.2	31.0
Others	4.2	2.1	18.6	14.6

Note: The SES sample results are calculated using YouGov's standard demographic and attitudinal weight.

Appendix 2. Opinion polls in Scotland, 2003–7

Table A2.1 lists the voting intentions recorded in all polls conducted by established and reputable polling companies (MORI, Populus, ICM, YouGov and TNS/System 3) between the 2003 Scottish Parliament election and the start of the 2007 campaign on 3 April. Both constituency and regional list voting intentions are reported (except in two cases where no list voting figures were reported). Table A2.2 shows the results of polls by the same companies during the election campaign in 2007 (with more specific dates of fieldwork).

Table A2.1 *Constituency and list voting intentions in Scottish opinion polls, August 2003–March 2007 (percentage of respondents)*

Date	Firm	Constituency vote					Regional list vote				
		Con	Lab	LD	SNP	Other	Con	Lab	LD	SNP	Other
2003											
Aug.	System 3	13	31	15	31	9	9	26	16	27	22
Sep.	System 3	10	33	16	31	9	9	26	15	28	22
Oct.	System 3	12	32	15	31	9	8	25	20	25	22
Nov.	System 3	11	35	17	29	8	11	25	16	30	18
Dec.	System 3	15	35	11	30	9	13	28	14	28	17
2005											
Jan.–Mar.	MORI	16	36	21	20	7	14	31	18	24	13
Apr.–Jun.	MORI	13	40	21	22	4	11	37	23	23	6
Aug.–Sep.	MORI	16	40	17	21	6	14	34	18	24	10
2006											
Jan.–Mar.	MORI	14	38	17	24	7	16	33	18	23	10
Apr.	YouGov	14	30	20	26	10	–	–	–	–	–
Apr.–Jun.	MORI	15	28	19	30	8	16	26	19	28	11
Jul.	TNS/ System 3	11	37	14	31	7	9	29	17	33	12
Aug.	TNS/ System 3	13	37	14	29	7	10	29	15	32	14
Aug.	TNS/ System 3	12	36	17	28	7	11	28	19	27	15
Sep.	YouGov	14	30	18	29	9	14	27	15	29	15
Oct.	ICM	14	30	15	32	9	14	28	17	28	13
Oct.	TNS/ System 3	12	38	14	30	6	9	30	17	33	11
Nov.	YouGov	15	32	15	32	6	17	29	15	28	11
Nov.	YouGov	14	29	16	36	5	15	26	15	30	14
Nov.	ICM	13	29	17	34	7	12	26	19	31	12
Nov.	TNS/ System 3	11	35	14	32	8	11	32	15	30	12
2007											
Jan.	YouGov	14	31	14	33	8	15	28	11	33	13
Jan.	YouGov	13	29	18	35	5	14	30	14	32	10
Jan.	TNS/ System 3	11	38	14	33	4	–	–	–	–	–
Jan.	ICM	13	31	17	33	6	14	27	17	33	10
Feb.	ICM	16	29	16	34	3	15	28	17	33	7
Mar.	Populus	14	28	15	38	6	14	30	14	35	7
Mar.	TNS/ System 3	13	34	11	39	3	11	25	13	36	15
Mar.	YouGov	13	29	14	35	9	15	27	12	33	13
Mar.	YouGov	13	27	16	36	8	14	26	14	33	11
Mar.	ICM	13	27	19	32	9	14	26	14	33	11

Note: No Scottish Parliament voting intention polls were reported during 2004.

Table A2.2 *Constituency and list voting intentions in Scottish opinion polls, election campaign 2007*

Date	Firm	Constituency vote (%)					Regional list vote (%)				
		Con	Lab	LD	SNP	Other	Con	Lab	LD	SNP	Other
12–17 April	Populus	13	30	18	34	5	14	27	18	34	7
18–20 April	YouGov	14	30	15	37	4	13	28	13	35	11
24–26 April	YouGov	13	30	15	39	3	13	27	11	31	18
25–30 April	Populus	13	29	15	33	10	14	28	15	31	10
29–30 April	ICM	13	32	16	34	5	13	29	16	30	12
1–2 May	YouGov	13	31	14	37	5	13	27	11	32	18

Appendix 3. Full results of regression analyses

This Appendix contains the full results of the various multiple regression analyses reported in the book. Tables are numbered according to the chapters to which they principally relate (for example, Table A3.1 relates to the presentation in Chapter 3). Two types of multiple regression are used: ordinary least squares (OLS) and logistic regression. In the OLS regression equations, the unstandardised coefficients (the B values reported) indicate the change in the dependent variable resulting from a unit change in that particular independent (or 'predictor') variable. For instance, as the percentage of owner occupiers in a constituency increases by one point, the turnout in that constituency in the 2007 election was, on average, 0.441 percentage points higher (Table A8.1). In some cases we also report standardised (or beta) coefficients, which indicate the relative impact of each variable on the dependent variable. Tests allow us to determine whether the effect of a variable is statistically significant and coefficients significant at the $p < 0.05$ level are highlighted in bold.

In logistic regression, things are rather more complicated. The treatment of variables depends on whether they are categorical (such as social class) or measured via response scales (such as how closely each party is thought to look after Scottish interests). With categorical variables, a reference category for each independent variable (shown in parentheses after the variable name) is selected. The figures given for each remaining category are odds ratios, which indicate how more or less likely someone in that category was to vote for that party – or, in the turnout analyses, to vote – than someone in the reference category. A ratio of less than 1 means that, holding all other variables in the analysis constant, people in the category were less likely to vote that way than those in the reference category; a ratio of more than 1 means that they were more likely to do so. For example, in 2007, those in the 55+ age bracket were roughly three (3.044) times more likely to turn out to vote than those in the reference 18–34 bracket, holding constant other demographic and socioeconomic characteristics (Table A8.2). With response scale variables, the odds ratio indicates the average change in the likelihood of voting for that party resulting from a unit shift along the scale. For example, those who rated the SNP's campaign as 'very positive' were 1.730 times more likely to cast a regional list vote for the party than those who rated the campaign as 'fairly positive' (the next point down in the scale) (Table A10.1). Odds ratios in bold indicate differences between individual categories and the reference category that are statistically significant at the $p < 0.05$ level.

Various measures of the overall or combined effect of the variables are available. In the OLS regressions we report R^2, which is a measure of the proportion of variation in the dependent variable accounted for by the variables in the analysis. This cannot be calculated precisely for the logistic regressions but the Nagelkerke R^2 gives an estimate of the proportion of variance explained. In addition, we can calculate the percentage of respondents correctly classified (as voters or non-voters, or as voters for or against a particular party) on the basis of the relevant logistic regression equation. This can then be compared with the percentage that would be correctly classified on the basis of simply assigning all cases to the largest category. The difference between the two is the percentage point improvement achieved by the variables in the analysis.

Table A3.1 *Logistic regression of Labour voting by party identification and leader evaluations*

	List vote	*Constituency vote*
Party identification (Other/none)		
Conservative	**0.329**	**0.539**
Labour	**4.393**	**5.283**
Lib Dem	**0.112**	**0.256**
SNP	**0.029**	**0.074**
Other	1.038	1.214
Leader evaluation scales		
McConnell	**1.226**	**1.204**
Blair	**1.302**	**1.181**
Brown	1.028	1.078
N	1,238	1,238
Nagelkerke R^2	0.560	0.510
Original % correct	81.8	76.7
Model % correct	87.4	84.7
Improvement	5.6	8.0

Table A4.1 *Logistic regression of Labour constituency voting by issue opinions (with controls): (i) versus all other parties; (ii) versus SNP*

	Labour versus all parties	Labour versus SNP
Party identification (None)		
Conservative	**0.301**	1.226
Labour	**4.371**	**6.584**
Lib Dem	**0.241**	1.031
SNP	**0.161**	**0.264**
Other	1.154	1.164
Leader evaluation scales		
McConnell	**1.184**	1.104
Salmond	**0.820**	**0.806**
Blair	**1.182**	**1.206**
Brown	**1.105**	1.082
Issue opinions		
Cut taxes/spending (0–10 scale)	1.051	1.062
Tough on criminals (0–10 scale)	1.030	1.058
Supports Iraq war	1.133	1.214
Supports Trident	1.127	1.211
Prefers council tax	**1.612**	1.260
Performance evaluations:		
(i) Executive, (ii) Executive versus SNP		
Crime	1.270	1.052
NHS	1.134	1.107
Education	1.183	**1.508**
Economy	**1.708**	**2.442**
N	1,238	748
Nagelkerke R^2	0.563	0.774
Original % correct	76.7	58.3
Model % correct	85.2	89.4
Improvement	8.5	31.1

Table A5.1 *Logistic regression of constituency voting (versus not voting) for each party by national identity, constitutional preferences and Scottish interests (with controls)*

	Odds of voting versus not voting for party			
	Con	Lab	LD	SNP
Party identification (None)				
Conservative	**5.064**	**0.337**	**0.127**	0.503
Labour	**0.185**	**3.804**	**0.497**	**0.188**
Lib Dem	**0.163**	0.310	**5.969**	**0.211**
SNP	0.634	**0.220**	**0.229**	**4.395**
Other	2.048	0.722	0.837	0.640
Leader evaluations				
McConnell	1.000	**1.215**	0.922	0.915
Salmond	0.936	0.937	**0.885**	**1.211**
Goldie	1.020	0.960	1.024	0.938
Stephen	0.990	**0.872**	**1.156**	1.030
Blair	**0.869**	**1.158**	0.915	1.008
Brown	1.037	1.063	0.981	0.958
Cameron	**1.173**	0.978	1.111	0.961
Issue opinions				
Cut taxes/spending	1.051	1.037	**0.909**	1.042
Tough on criminals	1.003	0.981	1.035	0.996
Opposes Iraq war	1.118	0.895	0.947	1.007
Opposes Trident	0.899	0.939	0.926	**1.254**
Opposes council tax	1.429	0.756	1.192	1.106
Labour issue evaluations				
Crime	0.874	0.825	**1.459**	1.009
NHS	1.128	0.778	0.986	1.047
Education	1.022	1.189	0.898	0.963
Economy	0.853	**1.458**	1.053	1.003
National identity (Equally Scottish and British)				
Scottish not British	**0.175**	**1.984**	0.745	1.256
More Scottish than British	**1.981**	1.367	0.748	0.781
More British than Scottish	0.814	1.652	1.068	1.211
British not Scottish	1.486	0.594	1.327	0.724
Constitutional preference (Don't know)				
Oppose referendum	1.315	1.289	1.083	**0.546**
Independence	0.484	0.505	1.132	2.174
More powers	1.336	1.596	1.898	0.828
Status quo	2.036	1.292	0.868	1.180
Abolish Scottish Parliament	2.790	1.700	1.087	0.577

Party on Scottish interests

Labour	**0.714**	**2.311**	0.912	0.848
SNP	0.766	**0.680**	1.059	**2.127**
Conservative	**2.000**	1.115	**0.522**	1.047
Lib Dem	0.888	0.943	**2.657**	**0.550**
N	1,238	1,238	1,238	1,238
Nagelkerke R^2	0.559	0.619	0.400	0.655
Original % correct	82.4	76.7	84.6	62.9
Model % correct	90.2	87.7	88.1	86.5
Improvement	7.8	11.0	3.5	23.6

Table A6.1 *Logistic regression of Labour voting by overall performance evaluations (with controls)*

	Regional vote	*Constituency vote*
Party identification (None)		
Conservative	**0.259**	**0.390**
Labour	**2.488**	**3.416**
Lib Dem	**0.083**	0.354
SNP	**0.073**	**0.249**
Other	0.715	1.198
Leader evaluations		
McConnell	**1.204**	**1.209**
Salmond	**0.879**	0.918
Goldie	**0.855**	0.974
Stephen	0.885	**0.844**
Blair	**1.307**	1.087
Brown	1.023	1.044
Cameron	0.974	0.974
Issue opinions		
Cut taxes/spending (0–10 scale)	**1.143**	1.032
Tough on criminals (0–10 scale)	0.928	0.984
Supports Iraq war	0.883	0.898
Supports Trident	0.974	0.927
Opposes council tax	1.096	0.685
Labour issue evaluations		
Crime	0.951	0.817
NHS	0.929	0.875
Education	1.158	1.092
Economy	**1.528**	**1.404**
National identity (Scottish not British)		
More Scottish than British	0.903	1.032
Equally Scottish and British	0.737	1.008
More British than Scottish	2.562	1.611
British not Scottish	0.534	0.494
Oppose independence referendum	1.342	**1.495**
Constitutional preference (Don't know)		
Independence	**0.157**	0.738
More powers	0.998	2.366
Status quo	0.983	1.953
Abolish Scottish Parliament	1.288	2.739
Labour overall evaluations		
UK level	1.088	**1.475**
Scottish level	**1.507**	**1.493**

N	1,238	1,238
Nagelkerke R^2	0.662	0.608
Original % correct	81.8	76.7
Model % correct	90.2	87.8
Improvement	8.4	11.1

Table A6.2 *Logistic regression of Labour constituency voting by overall performance evaluations (with controls): (i) Scottish Parliament responsible for 0–3 issues; (ii) Scottish Parliament responsible for 4–6 issues*

	Scottish Parliament responsible for:	
	0–3 issues	*4–6 issues*
Party identification (None)		
Conservative	0.344	**0.242**
Labour	**2.449**	**5.734**
Lib Dem	0.483	0.303
SNP	**0.146**	0.453
Other	1.029	1.338
Leader evaluations		
McConnell	**1.193**	**1.209**
Salmond	1.011	**0.833**
Goldie	0.859	1.107
Stephen	**0.787**	0.865
Blair	1.071	**1.140**
Brown	0.994	1.086
Cameron	1.038	0.927
Issue opinions		
Cut taxes/spending (0–10 scale)	1.128	0.892
Tough on criminals (0–10 scale)	0.982	1.012
Opposes Iraq war	0.913	0.829
Opposes Trident	0.998	0.866
Opposes council tax	**0.437**	0.679
Labour issue evaluations		
Crime	0.993	0.750
NHS	0.902	0.774
Education	0.769	1.322
Economy	**1.780**	0.967
National identity (Scottish not British)		
More Scottish than British	0.868	1.118
Equally Scottish and British	0.909	1.280
More British than Scottish	2.131	1.755
British not Scottish	0.337	0.768
Oppose independence referendum	1.347	1.446
Constitutional preference (Don't know)		
Independence	1.051	0.582
More powers	2.882	1.622
Status quo	2.901	1.319
Abolish Scottish Parliament	5.142	1.135

Labour overall evaluations

UK level	**2.403**	0.961
Scottish level	1.287	**2.272**
N	512	707
Nagelkerke R^2	0.639	0.638
Original % correct	73.0	79.1
Model % correct	86.3	89.0
Improvement	13.3	9.9

Table A7.1 *OLS regression analysis of post-election like–dislike ratings by campaign exposure and pre-election like–dislike ratings (unstandardised coefficients)*

	Conservative	Labour	Lib Dem	SNP
Constant	0.58	0.86	1.64	0.65
Exposure to campaigning by:				
Conservative	**0.23**	0.06	−0.13	−0.12
Labour	−0.07	**0.28**	0.14	**−0.16**
Lib Dem	0.03	−0.08	0.13	0.01
SNP	0.04	−0.08	−0.11	**0.35**
Pre-election like–dislike rating:				
Conservative	**0.83**	–	–	–
Labour	–	**0.84**	–	–
Lib Dem	–	–	**0.70**	–
SNP	–	–	–	**0.85**
N	1,407	1,420	1,401	1,405
R^2	0.75	0.76	0.56	0.74

Table A7.2 *Multiple regression analysis of constituency vote share by campaign expenditure and 2003 constituency vote share (unstandardised coefficients)*

	Conservative	Labour	Lib Dem	SNP
Constant	−0.35	4.63	3.29	7.16
Party spending as % of maximum:				
Conservative	0.02	**−0.02**	−0.02	−0.01
Labour	0.01	**0.07**	−0.03	−0.01
Lib Dem	**−0.02**	−0.02	**0.06**	0.00
SNP	0.00	−0.02	−0.01	**0.05**
Pre-election like–dislike rating:				
Conservative	**0.96**	–	–	–
Labour	–	**0.62**	–	–
Lib Dem	–	–	**0.77**	–
SNP	–	–	–	**0.73**
N	73	73	73	73
R^2	0.91	0.89	0.88	0.80

Table A7.3 *OLS regression analysis of difference between constituency and regional vote share by campaign expenditure (unstandardised coefficients)*

	Conservative	Labour	Lib Dem	SNP
Constant	1.28	−0.79	3.87	0.17
Party spending as % of maximum:				
Conservative	**0.03**	0.00	−0.01	−0.01
Labour	−0.01	**0.05**	−0.04	0.00
Lib Dem	−0.02	−0.01	**0.07**	−0.02
SNP	−0.01	−0.01	−0.02	**0.03**
N	73	73	73	73
R^2	0.43	0.54	0.52	0.34

Table A8.1 *OLS regression analysis of constituency turnout, 2007 Scottish Parliament election and 2005 UK general election (England and Wales only)*

	Scottish Parliament election 2007		UK general election 2005 (England/Wales)	
	B	Beta	B	Beta
Constant	9.7		25.9	
% owner occupiers	**0.441**	0.717	**0.225**	0.104
% aged 65+	**0.538**	0.215	**0.209**	0.215
Marginality 2003	**0.095**	0.199	–	–
Marginality 2001	–	–	**0.210**	0.479
N		73		569
R^2		0.708		0.662

Table A8.2 *Logistic regression of voting versus non-voting (social characteristics), 2007 Scottish Parliament election and 2005 UK general election (Scotland only)*

	Scottish Parliament election 2007	UK general election 2005 (Scotland)
Age (18–34)		
35–54	**2.132**	2.041
55+	**3.044**	**4.524**
Sex (Male)		
Female	**0.730**	**0.843**
Occupation (Professional/managerial)		
Other non-manual	0.934	0.784
Manual	1.132	0.595
Tenure (Owner occupiers)		
Local authority	0.729	**0.636**
Privately rented	0.826	**0.411**
Housing association	0.548	0.362
Marital status (Married/widowed)		
Partner	0.632	0.726
Separated/divorced	**0.949**	0.623
Single	1.037	0.606
Highest educational qualification (None)		
Degree	**2.825**	2.716
Professional/diploma/teaching	2.390	1.292
School certificate	1.242	**1.417**
Vocational/technical/other	1.107	1.470
Religion (None)		
Church of Scotland	2.757	1.326
Catholic	1.616	1.064
Other	1.545	0.969
N	1,355	863
Nagelkerke R^2	0.187	0.225
Original % correct	53.2	62.9
Model % correct	66.1	72.0
Improvement	12.9	7.1

Table A8.3 *Logistic regression of voting versus non-voting (composite model), 2007 Scottish Parliament and 2005 UK general election: (i) Scotland; (ii) England and Wales*

	2007 Scottish Parliament	2005 UK general election: Scotland	2005 UK general election: England and Wales
Age (18–34)			
35–54	**2.026**	1.945	**1.822**
55+	**2.327**	**3.820**	**1.812**
Sex (Male)			
Female	0.990	0.831	**1.426**
Occupation (Professional/managerial)			
Other non-manual	1.106	1.438	0.826
Manual	**1.527**	0.934	**0.594**
Tenure (Owner occupiers)			
Local authority	0.808	**0.434**	0.692
Privately rented	0.890	0.599	**0.577**
Housing association	0.588	**0.231**	0.761
Marital status (Married/widowed)			
Partner	0.695	0.809	1.237
Separated/divorced	0.952	0.677	0.694
Single	0.970	1.118	**0.637**
Highest educational qualification (None)			
Degree	**2.016**	**5.752**	**2.042**
Professional/diploma/teaching	**1.912**	1.906	1.373
School certificate	1.213	1.855	1.214
Vocational/technical/other	1.268	2.107	1.170
Religion (None)			
Church of Scotland/Anglican	**2.006**	1.166	0.700
Catholic	1.154	**0.420**	0.740
Other	1.144	0.803	1.675
Party supporter (No)			
Yes	1.212	**1.974**	**1.405**
Political interest (Great deal/quite a lot)			
Some	**0.508**	0.549	0.887
Not much/none	**0.313**	0.805	0.715
Party difference (Great deal/quite a lot)			
Some	0.948	0.558	0.902
Not much/none	1.108	0.720	0.715

Matters/cares who wins (Great deal/quite a lot)

Some	0.685	–	–
Not much/not at all	**0.355**	**0.424**	**0.308**

Voting is citizen's duty (Agree)

Neither	**0.371**	0.611	**0.281**
Disagree	**0.184**	**0.203**	**0.210**

Likely constituency result (Easy winner)

Clear winner	0.733	1.092	1.210
Close	0.778	**2.484**	1.449
Other/don't know	**0.307**	0.921	2.187

Likely overall result (Easy winner)

Clear winner	1.413	0.804	1.135
Close	**2.584**	0.893	1.287
Other/don't know	**2.721**	0.988	3.165

Canvassed (No)

Yes	**0.671**	**2.218**	**1.377**

N	1,355	437	1,550
Nagelkerke R^2	0.425	0.387	0.38
Original % correct	53.2	72.1	69.0
Model % correct	76.0	81.3	79.3
Improvement	22.8	9.2	10.3

Table A9.1 *Stepwise OLS regression analyses of percentage of ballots rejected in constituency and list contests (significant variables only)*

	Constituency		List	
	B	Beta	B	Beta
Glasgow	2.498	0.428	0.782	0.315
Lothians	2.089	0.342	0.591	0.227
Socialist Labour list share	1.718	0.298	–	–
Solidarity list share	0.355	0.225	–	–
% professional/managerial	–0.067	–0.179	–	–
% with no car	–	–	0.075	1.001
Persons per hectare	–	–	–0.035	–0.583
% agriculture	–	–	0.071	0.208
N		73		73
Adjusted R^2		0.832		0.545

Table A10.1 *Logistic regression of regional voting (versus not voting) for each party: full model*

	Con	Lab	Lib Dem	SNP
Demographics				
Age	0.990	0.987	0.998	**1.026**
Female	1.225	1.328	0.998	0.857
Lives in rural area	1.245	0.774	1.381	1.151
Live outside central belt	**2.195**	1.157	1.886	0.872
Socioeconomic				
Social class A, B	0.274	1.032	1.850	0.820
Social class C1	0.407	0.845	1.815	1.480
Social class C2, D, E	0.377	1.630	0.912	1.962
Home owner	1.266	1.710	0.699	1.444
Highest qualification (None)				
Degree level	1.816	0.678	1.866	1.074
Highers/A level	0.921	0.616	1.203	0.921
Standard/GCSE	1.755	1.149	1.002	0.923
Religion (None)				
Church of Scotland	0.593	1.057	0.479	0.680
Catholic	0.895	**2.055**	1.382	0.797
Other religion	0.596	0.901	0.663	0.444
Newspaper (Non-reader)				
Tabloid	1.531	**2.174**	0.831	0.989
Broadsheet	2.574	1.311	0.556	1.013
Party identification (None)				
Conservative	**10.457**	**0.364**	1.065	0.649
Labour	0.582	**3.013**	0.351	**0.194**
Lib Dem	0.139	**0.053**	8.491	**0.279**
SNP	1.642	**0.111**	0.283	**2.279**
Other	0.238	0.487	–	**0.110**
Leader evaluations				
McConnell	**0.844**	**1.239**	0.902	1.056
Salmond	0.940	0.928	0.921	1.010
Goldie	1.130	**0.848**	0.901	0.996
Stephen	1.042	0.910	**1.170**	1.119
Blair	0.889	**1.279**	0.911	0.959
Brown	1.019	0.999	1.072	0.987
Cameron	**1.317**	0.994	1.023	0.966
Issue opinions				
Opposes Iraq war	1.065	0.830	0.837	1.299
Opposes Trident	0.866	1.050	0.879	1.017
Opposes council tax	1.013	1.098	1.279	0.812
Cut taxes/spending	1.016	**1.172**	1.004	1.070
Tough on criminals	0.961	0.941	1.019	0.973

Issue evaluations

Labour crime	1.144	0.960	1.244	1.031
SNP crime	0.780	1.081	1.202	**1.578**
Labour health	1.801	0.905	0.908	0.920
SNP health	1.205	1.188	0.917	1.213
Labour education	0.747	1.048	0.774	0.902
SNP education	1.190	1.104	**0.648**	0.961
Labour economy	1.023	**1.528**	0.705	0.835
SNP economy	0.774	0.758	1.155	**2.012**

National identity (Equally Scottish and British)

Scottish not British	**0.291**	1.739	**0.268**	1.652
More Scottish than British	1.205	1.018	**0.382**	1.534
More British than Scottish	1.352	2.907	0.628	1.133
British not Scottish	0.656	0.611	0.750	0.760

Constitutional preference (Status quo)

Oppose referendum	**3.234**	1.395	0.669	0.432
Independence	**0.196**	**0.169**	0.993	**4.024**
More powers	0.709	0.816	**2.168**	1.610
Abolish Scottish Parliament	1.375	0.759	1.053	0.634

Party on Scottish interests

Labour	1.360	**1.657**	1.493	**0.620**
SNP	0.819	0.713	1.065	**1.891**
Conservatives	**1.741**	1.050	0.757	1.175
Lib Dems	**0.442**	0.808	**1.775**	0.799

Performance evaluations

Labour UK government	**0.699**	1.047	0.889	1.268
Labour Scottish Executive	0.942	**1.457**	1.137	0.693
Lib Dem Scottish Executive	0.696	0.874	**2.221**	0.757

Campaign exposure

Conservative	1.242	0.739	**0.605**	0.958
Labour	0.925	1.011	1.355	**0.678**
Lib Dem	0.730	1.956	0.733	1.198
SNP	0.846	0.723	0.682	1.382

Perceived campaign tone

Conservative	1.228	0.975	0.755	0.820
Labour	1.027	**1.335**	1.240	1.065
Lib Dem	1.409	0.833	**1.435**	0.732
SNP	0.835	0.802	0.789	**1.730**

N	1,236	1,236	1,236	1,236
Nagelkerke R^2	0.701	0.705	0.493	0.770
Original % correct	83.8	81.8	90.2	66.7
Model % correct	93.4	90.9	92.2	90.0
Improvement	9.6	9.1	2.0	32.3

Table A10.2 *Logistic regression of constituency voting (versus not voting) for each party: full model*

	Con	Lab	Lib Dem	SNP
Demographics				
Age	0.990	0.987	0.994	**1.017**
Female	0.884	1.380	1.395	**0.591**
Lives in rural area	**2.108**	**0.393**	1.537	1.233
Live outside central belt	1.263	**0.612**	**1.690**	1.036
Socioeconomic				
Social class A, B	0.848	1.538	0.641	0.821
Social class C1	0.965	0.810	1.219	1.028
Social class C2, D, E	1.290	1.154	0.601	1.549
Home owner	1.614	1.285	0.803	1.116
Highest qualification (None)				
Degree level	0.579	0.532	2.456	1.829
Highers/A level	0.453	1.028	1.246	1.481
Standard/GCSE	1.057	1.131	1.164	1.339
Religion (None)				
Church of Scotland	1.959	0.872	0.844	0.930
Catholic	0.842	1.232	**0.130**	1.104
Other religion	1.842	1.206	0.958	**0.505**
Newspaper (Non-reader)				
Tabloid	1.174	0.980	0.704	1.705
Broadsheet	1.652	0.962	1.065	1.348
Party identification (None)				
Conservatives	**4.806**	0.404	**0.124**	**0.353**
Labour	**0.188**	**3.602**	0.901	**0.137**
Lib Dems	**0.154**	0.355	**5.027**	**0.142**
SNP	0.608	0.320	**0.261**	1.837
Other	1.688	0.780	0.626	0.451
Leader evaluations				
McConnell	0.960	**1.199**	**0.849**	1.021
Salmond	0.999	0.977	0.933	0.989
Goldie	1.016	0.967	1.049	0.942
Stephen	0.989	**0.861**	1.057	**1.136**
Blair	0.993	1.054	0.940	0.950
Brown	1.073	1.004	1.029	0.938
Cameron	**1.178**	0.962	**1.130**	0.994
Issue opinions				
Opposes Iraq war	1.019	0.903	0.925	1.041
Opposes Trident	0.936	0.963	0.839	**1.249**
Opposes council tax	1.416	0.660	1.313	0.842
Cut taxes/spending	1.069	1.047	0.922	1.055
Tough on criminals	1.007	0.993	1.002	1.015

Issue evaluations

Labour crime	1.001	0.650	1.197	1.225
SNP crime	0.760	1.121	1.361	1.140
Labour health	1.157	0.735	0.977	1.135
SNP health	1.266	1.170	0.777	0.985
Labour education	1.061	1.111	0.807	0.919
SNP education	1.012	0.823	1.051	**1.752**
Labour economy	0.934	1.289	0.992	1.113
SNP economy	0.631	0.796	0.914	**1.707**

National identity (Equally Scottish and British)

Scottish not British	**0.113**	1.880	0.674	1.551
More Scottish than British	**2.264**	1.086	0.676	0.846
More British than Scottish	0.828	1.756	0.836	1.422
British not Scottish	1.171	0.594	1.245	0.628

Constitutional preference (Status quo)

Oppose referendum	1.428	1.213	0.833	0.729
Independence	0.287	0.626	1.265	1.164
More powers	0.676	1.618	2.146	0.518
Abolish Scottish Parliament	1.210	1.662	1.595	**0.364**

Party on Scottish interests

Labour	0.847	**2.001**	1.245	0.894
SNP	0.885	0.802	1.044	**1.456**
Conservatives	**1.808**	1.153	**0.465**	1.004
Lib Dems	0.855	0.955	**1.821**	0.796

Performance evaluations

Labour UK government	**0.509**	**1.601**	0.788	1.401
Labour Scottish Executive	1.070	1.271	1.109	**0.531**
Lib Dems Scottish Executive	0.754	1.319	**1.982**	0.691

Campaign exposure

Conservatives	1.229	1.355	0.953	0.698
Labour	1.266	**1.572**	0.780	0.800
Lib Dems	0.720	0.922	**1.655**	0.800
SNP	0.750	**0.624**	0.631	**2.444**

Perceived campaign tone

Conservatives	1.147	1.091	0.903	0.819
Labour	1.059	**1.479**	**0.721**	1.023
Lib Dems	1.287	0.716	**1.529**	**0.639**
SNP	0.963	0.998	0.798	**1.635**

N	1,236	1,236	1,236	1,236
Nagelkerke R^2	0.611	0.672	0.511	0.736
Original % correct	82.4	76.7	84.6	62.9
Model % correct	90.9	88.5	89.1	88.6
Improvement	8.5	11.8	4.5	25.7

References

Alvarez, R., T. Hall and M. Llewellyn (2008) 'Are Americans confident their ballots are counted?', *Journal of Politics*, 7, 754–66.

Anderson, C., A. Blais, S. Bowler, T. Donovan and O. Listhaug (2005) *Losers' Consent: Elections and Democratic Legitimacy*, Oxford: Oxford University Press.

Archer, J. and P. Taylor (1981) *Section and Party: A Political Geography of American Presidential Elections from Andrew Jackson to Ronald Reagan*, Chichester: Wiley.

Atkeson, L. (1999) '"Sure, I voted for the winner!" Overreport of the primary vote for the party nominee in the NES', *Political Behavior*, 21(3), 197–215.

Bartle, J. (2001) 'The measurement of party identification in Britain: where do we stand now?', *British Elections and Parties Review*, 11, 1–14.

Belli, R., M. Traugott, M. Young and K. McGonagle (1999) 'Reducing vote over-reporting in surveys', *Public Opinion Quarterly*, 63, 90–108.

Bennie, L., J. Brand and J. Mitchell (1997) *How Scotland Votes*, Manchester: Manchester University Press.

Birch, S. (2008) 'Electoral institutions and popular confidence in electoral processes: a cross-national analysis', *Electoral Studies*, 27, 305–20.

Breuilly, J. (1993) *Nationalism and the State*, Manchester: Manchester University Press.

Bromley, C., J. Curtice, D. McCrone and A. Park (eds) (2006) *Has Devolution Delivered?*, Edinburgh: Edinburgh University Press.

Brown, A., D. McCrone, L. Paterson and P. Surridge (1999) *The Scottish Electorate*, Basingstoke: Macmillan.

Burt, P. (2006) 'Proposals for "a fairer way" of local tax', press release with the publication of the Independent Review of Local Taxation, 9 November, www.scotland. gov.uk/News/Releases/2006/11/09122711.

Butler, D. and Stokes, D. (1969) *Political Change in Britain* (1st edition), Basingstoke: Macmillan.

Butt, S. (2006) 'How voters evaluate economic competence: a comparison between parties in and out of power', *Political Studies*, 54, 743–66.

Caramani, D. (2004) *The Nationalization of Politics: The Formation of National Electorates and Party Systems in Europe*, Cambridge: Cambridge University Press.

Carman, C. and R. Johns (2007) 'Attitudes to coalitions and split-ticket voting: the Scottish Parliament elections of 2007', paper presented at the Conference 'Voters, coalitions and democratic accountability', University of Exeter, 5 October.

Carman, C. and R. Johns (2008) 'Linking political disengagement and process assignments', paper presented at the ERS/University of Glasgow Conference 'Impact of electoral reform on democratic engagement in Scotland', Glasgow, 23 February.

Carman, C., J. Mitchell and R. Johns (2008) 'The unfortunate natural experiment in ballot design: the Scottish parliamentary elections of 2007', *Electoral Studies*, 27, 442–59.

Clarke, H., D. Sanders, M. Stewart and P. Whiteley (2004) *Political Choice in Britain*, Oxford: Oxford University Press.

Clarke, H., D. Sanders, M. Stewart and P. Whiteley (2009) *Performance Politics and the British Voter*, Cambridge: Cambridge University Press.

Converse, P. (1964) 'The nature of belief systems in mass publics', in D. Apter (ed.), *Ideology and Discontent*, London: Free Press of Glencoe, 206–61.

Crewe, I., T. Fox and J. Alt (1977) 'Non-voting in British general elections 1966–October 1974', in C. Crouch (ed.), *British Political Sociology Yearbook*, 3, London: Croom Helm, 38–109.

Curtice, J. (2006) 'Is Holyrood accountable and representative?', in C. Bromley, J. Curtice, D. McCrone and A. Park (eds), *Has Devolution Delivered?*, Edinburgh: Edinburgh University Press, 90–108.

Cutler, F. (2008) 'One voter, two first-order elections?', *Electoral Studies*, 27, 492–504.

Dalton, R. and M. Wattenberg (2000) *Parties Without Partisans: Political Change in Advanced Industrial Democracies*, Oxford: Oxford University Press.

Denver, D. (2003) 'A "wake up!" call to the parties? The results of the Scottish Parliament elections 2003', *Scottish Affairs*, 44, 31–53.

Denver, D. (2007a) '"A historic moment"? The results of the Scottish Parliament elections 2007', *Scottish Affairs*, 60, 61–79.

Denver, D. (2007b) *Elections and Voters in Britain* (2nd edition), Basingstoke: Palgrave Macmillan.

Denver, D. and J. Fisher (2009) 'Blair's electoral record', in T. Casey (ed.), *The Blair Legacy*, Basingstoke: Palgrave Macmillan, 23–38.

Denver, D. and G. Hands (1997) *Modern Constituency Electioneering: Local Campaigning in the 1992 General Election*, London: Frank Cass.

Denver, D. and G. Hands (2004a) 'Exploring variations in turnout: constituencies and wards in the Scottish Parliament elections of 1999 and 2003', *British Journal of Politics and International Relations*, 6, 527–42.

Denver, D. and G. Hands (2004b) 'Labour's targeted constituency campaigning: nationally directed or locally produced?', *Electoral Studies*, 23, 709–26.

Denver, D. and I. MacAllister (1999) 'The Scottish Parliament elections 1999: an analysis of the results', *Scottish Affairs*, 28, 10–31.

Denver, D., J. Mitchell, C. Pattie and H. Bochel (2000) *Scotland Decides: The Devolution Issue and the Scottish Referendum*, London: Frank Cass.

Denver, D., G. Hands and I. McAllister (2003a) 'Constituency marginality and turnout in Britain revisited', *British Elections and Parties Review*, 13, 174–94.

Denver, D., G. Hands, J. Fisher and I. MacAllister (2003b) 'Constituency campaigning in Britain 1992–2001: centralization and modernization', *Party Politics*, 9, 541–59.

Downs, A. (1957) *An Economic Theory of Democracy*, New York: Harper.

Duverger, M. (1954) *Political Parties*, London: Methuen.

Electoral Commission (2007) *Scottish Elections 2007: The Independent Review of the Scottish Parliamentary and Local Government Elections 3 May 2007*, London: Electoral Commission.

Evans, G. and R. Andersen (2005) 'The impact of party leaders: how Blair lost Labour votes', in P. Norris and C. Wlezien (eds), *Britain Votes 2005*, Oxford: Oxford University Press, 162–80.

Fieldhouse, E. and D. Cutts (2005) 'The Liberal Democrats: steady progress or failure to seize the moment?', in A. Geddes and J. Tonge (eds), *Britain Decides: The UK General Election 2005*, Basingstoke: Palgrave Macmillan, 70–88.

Fieldhouse, E. and A. Russell (2001) 'Latent Liberals? Sympathy and support for the Liberal Democrats in Britain', *Party Politics*, 7, 711–38.

Fiorina, M. (1981) *Retrospective Voting in American National Elections*, New Haven, CT: Yale University Press.

Fisher, J. and D. Denver (2008) 'From foot-slogging to call centres and direct mail: a framework for analysing the development of district-level campaigning', *European Journal of Political Research*, 47, 794–826.

Fisher, J., D. Denver and G. Hands (2006) 'The relative electoral impact of central party co-ordination and size of party membership at constituency level', *Electoral Studies*, 25, 664–76.

Flemming, G. (1995) 'Presidential coattails in open-seat elections', *Legislative Studies Quarterly*, 20, 197–211.

Foley, M. (2000) *The British Presidency*, Manchester: Manchester University Press.

Franklin, M. (1985) *The Decline of Class Voting in Britain*, Oxford: Oxford University Press.

Ghaleigh, N. (2008) 'The Scottish Parliament elections 2007 – what kind of hackery is this?', *Edinburgh Law Review*, 12, 137–44.

Gschwend, T., R. Johnston and C. Pattie (2003) 'Split-ticket patterns in mixed-member proportional election systems: estimates and analyses of their spatial variation at the German Federal Election, 1998', *British Journal of Political Science*, 33, 109–27.

Hasen, R. (2004) 'A critical guide to Bush vs. Gore scholarship', *Annual Review of Political Science*, 7, 297–313.

Heath, A. and B. Taylor (1999) 'New sources of abstention?', in G. Evans and P. Norris (eds), *Critical Elections: British Parties and Voters in Long-Term Perspective*, London: Sage, 164–80.

Heath, A., R. Jowell and J. Curtice (1991) *Understanding Political Change*, Oxford: Pergamon.

Heath, A., I. McLean, B. Taylor and J. Curtice (1999) 'Between first and second order: a comparison of voting behaviour in European and local elections in Britain', *European Journal of Political Research*, 35, 389–414.

Himmelweit, H., M. Biberian and J. Stockdale (1978) 'Memory for past vote: implications of a study of bias in recall', *British Journal of Political Science*, 8(3), 365–75.

Hough, D. and C. Jeffery (2005) 'An introduction to multi-level electoral competition', in D. Hough and C. Jeffery (eds), *Devolution and Electoral Politics*, Manchester: Manchester University Press, 2–13.

Issacharoff, S., P. Karlan and R. Pildes (2001) *When Elections Go Bad: The Law of Democracy and the Presidential Election of 2000*, New York: Foundation Press.

Jaensch, D. (1976) 'The Scottish vote 1974: a realigning party system?', *Political Studies*, 24, 306–19.

Johns, R. and C. Carman (2008) 'Coping with coalitions? Scottish voters under a proportional system', *Representation*, 44, 301–15.

Johnston, R. and C. Pattie (2003) 'Spatial variations in straight- and split-ticket voting and the role of constituency campaigning at New Zealand's first two MMP elections: individual-level tests', *Australian Journal of Political Science*, 38, 535–47.

Johnston, R. and C. Pattie (2006) *Putting Voters in Their Place: Geography and Elections in Great Britain*, Oxford: Oxford University Press.

Johnston, R. and C. Pattie (2007) 'Funding local political parties in England and Wales: donations and constituency campaigns', *British Journal of Politics and International Relations*, 9, 365–95.

Kavanagh, D. (1995) *Election Campaigning: The New Marketing of Politics*, Oxford: Blackwell.

Keating, M. (1988) *State and Regional Nationalism*, London: Harvester Wheatsheaf.

Kendrick, S. (1983) 'Social change and nationalism in modern Scotland', PhD dissertation, University of Edinburgh.

Key, V. O. (1955) 'A theory of critical elections', *Journal of Politics*, 17, 3–18.

King, A. (2001) 'Why a poor turnout points to a democracy in good health', *Daily Telegraph*, 17 May.

King, A. (ed.) (2002) *Leaders' Personalities and the Outcomes of Democratic Elections*, Oxford: Oxford University Press.

Knack, S. and M. Kropf (2003) 'Voided ballots in the 1996 presidential election: a county-level analysis', *Journal of Politics*, 65, 881–98.

Lundberg, T. (2007) *Proportional Representation and the Constituency Role in Britain*, Basingstoke: Palgrave Macmillan.

Lundberg, T. (2008) 'Scotland's ballot paper problem: a comparative and critical analysis', paper presented at the ERS/University of Glasgow Conference 'The impact of electoral reform on democratic engagement in Scotland', Glasgow, 23 February.

Malhotra, N. and J. Krosnick (2007) 'The effect of survey mode and sampling on inferences about political attitudes and behavior', *Political Analysis*, 15, 286–323.

McCrone, D. (1992) *Understanding Scotland: The Sociology of a Stateless Nation*, London: Routledge.

McLaren, J. (2007) 'Scotland's prosperity: from political to economic regeneration', in M. Keating (ed.), *Scottish Social Democracy: Progressive Ideas for Public Policy*, Brussels: Peter Lang, 169–90.

Miller, W. (1981) *The End of British Politics?*, Oxford: Clarendon Press.

Mitchell, J. (1990) *Conservatives and the Union: A Study of Conservative Party Attitudes to Scotland*, Edinburgh: Edinburgh University Press.

Mitchell, J. (1996) *Strategies for Self-Government: The Campaigns for a Scottish Parliament*, Edinburgh: Polygon.

Mitchell, J. (2009) 'The Westminster years', in G. Hassan (ed.), *The Modern SNP: From Protest to Power*, Edinburgh: Edinburgh University Press, in press.

Mitchell, J. and L. Bennie (1995) 'Thatcherism and the Scottish question', in C. Rallings, D. M. Farrell, D. Denver and D. Broughton (eds), *British Elections and Parties Yearbook 1995*, London: Frank Cass, 90–104.

Mughan, A. (2000) *Media and the Presidentialization of Parliamentary Elections*, Basingstoke: Palgrave Macmillan.

Nisbett, R. and T. Wilson (1977) 'Telling more than we can know: verbal reports on mental processes', *Psychological Review*, 84, 231–59.

Norris, P. (2000) *A Virtuous Circle: Political Communications in Postindustrial Societies*, Cambridge: Cambridge University Press.

Park, A. and McCrone, D. (2006) 'The devolution conundrum?', in C. Bromley, J. Curtice, D. McCrone and A. Park (eds), *Has Devolution Delivered?*, Edinburgh: Edinburgh University Press, 15–28.

Paterson, L. (2006) 'Sources of support for the SNP', in C. Bromley, J. Curtice, D. McCrone and A. Park (eds), *Has Devolution Delivered?*, Edinburgh: Edinburgh University Press, 46–68.

Paterson, L., A. Brown, J. Curtice, K. Hinds, D. McCrone, A. Park, K. Sproston and P. Surridge (2001) *New Scotland, New Politics?*, Edinburgh: Polygon.

Pattie, C. and R. Johnston (1998) 'Voter turnout at the British general election of 1992: rational choice, social standing or political efficacy?', *European Journal of Political Research*, 33, 263–83.

Pattie, C. and R. Johnston, R. (2003) 'Local battles in a national landslide: constituency campaigning at the 2001 British general election', *Political Geography*, 22, 381–414.

Rallings, C. and M. Thrasher (2005) 'Not all "second-order" contests are the same: turnout and party choice at the concurrent 2004 local and European Parliament elections in England', *British Journal of Politics and International Relations*, 7, 584–97.

Reif, K.-H. and H. Schmitt (1980) 'Nine second-order national elections: a conceptual framework for the analysis of European election results', *European Journal of Political Research*, 8, 3–44.

Sanders, D., J. Burton and J. Kneeshaw (2002) 'Identifying the true identifiers: a question wording experiment', *Party Politics*, 8, 193–205.

Sanders, D., H. Clarke, M. Stewart and P. Whiteley (2007) 'Does mode matter for modeling political choice? Evidence from the 2005 British Election Study', *Political Analysis*, 15, 257–85.

Särlvik, B. and I. Crewe (1983) *Decade of Dealignment: The Conservative Victory of 1979 and Electoral Trends in the 1970s*, Cambridge: Cambridge University Press.

Sartori, G. (1976) *Parties and Party Systems: A Framework for Analysis*, Cambridge: Cambridge University Press.

Schulze, H. (1994) *States, Nations and Nationalism*, Oxford: Blackwell.

Scotland Office (2006) 'E-counting to be used in 2007 elections', press release, 9 June, www.scotlandoffice.gov.uk/our-communications/release.php?id=3530.

Scottish Executive (1999) 'Donald Dewar statement to Parliament', press release accompanying First Minister's statement on Executive's first legislative programme, 16 June, www.scotland.gov.uk/News/Releases/1999/06/70443f93-0966-41eb-b085-301c81386f8e.

Seawright, D. and J. Curtice (1995) 'The decline of the Scottish Conservative and Unionist Party, 1950–92: religion, ideology or economics?', *Contemporary Record*, 9, 319–42.

Seligman, M. (1998) *Learned Optimism*, New York: Simon and Schuster.

Seyd, P. and P. Whiteley (1992) *Labour's Grassroots: The Politics of Party Membership*, Oxford: Clarendon Press.

Sinclair, D. and R. M. Alvarez (2004) 'Who overvotes, who undervotes, using punchcards? Evidence from Los Angeles County', *Political Research Quarterly*, 57, 15–25.

SPICe (2007) 'Briefing: election 2007', Edinburgh: Scottish Parliament Information Centre.

Stewart, J. (2006) 'A banana republic? The investigation into electoral fraud by the Birmingham election court', *Parliamentary Affairs*, 59, 654–67.

Stokes, D. (1963) 'Spatial models of party competition', *American Political Science Review*, 57, 368–77.

Studlar, D., I. McAllister and B. Hayes (1998) 'Explaining the gender gap in voting: a cross-national analysis', *Social Science Quarterly*, 79(44), 779–98.

Surridge, P. (2004) 'The Scottish electorate and Labour', in G. Hassan (ed.), *The Scottish Labour Party*, Edinburgh: Edinburgh University Press, 69–85.

Surridge, P. (2006) 'A better Union?', in C. Bromley, J. Curtice, D. McCrone and A. Park (eds), *Has Devolution Delivered?*, Edinburgh: Edinburgh University Press, 29–45.

Swaddle, K. and A. Heath (1989) 'Official and reported turnout in the British general election of 1987', *British Journal of Political Science*, 19, 537–51.

Trilling, R. (1975) 'Party image and electoral behavior', *American Politics Quarterly*, 3, 284–314.

van der Eijk, C., M. Franklin and M. Marsh (1996) 'What voters teach us about Europe-wide elections: what Europe-wide elections teach us about voters', *Electoral Studies*, 15, 149–66.

Vass, S. (2007) 'SNP finds friends in the press … and plenty enemies too', *Sunday Herald*, 6 May.

Weisberg, H. (ed.) (1995) *Democracy's Feast: Elections in America*, Chatham, NJ: Chatham House.

Whiteley, P. and P. Seyd (2003) 'How to win a landslide by really trying: the effects of local campaigning on voting in the 1997 British general election', *Electoral Studies*, 23, 301–24.

Whiteley, P., M. Stewart, D. Sanders and H. Clarke (2005) 'The issue agenda and voting in 2005', in P. Norris and C. Wlezien (eds), *Britain Votes 2005*, Oxford: Oxford University Press, 146–61.

Wlezien, C., M. Franklin and D. Twiggs (1997) 'Economic perceptions and vote choice: disentangling the endogeneity', *Political Behavior*, 19, 7–17.

Index